THE BIBLICAL RESOURCE SERIES

Published

Adele Berlin, *The Dynamics of Biblical Parallelism,*
Revised and Expanded Edition

Richard A. Burridge, *What Are the Gospels? A Comparison
with Graeco-Roman Biography,* Second Edition

John J. Collins, *The Apocalyptic Imagination,* Second Edition

John J. Collins, *Between Athens and Jerusalem: Jewish Identity
in the Hellenistic Diaspora,* Second Edition

Frank Moore Cross Jr. and David Noel Freedman,
Studies in Ancient Yahwistic Poetry

Roland de Vaux, *Ancient Israel: Its Life and Institutions*

S. R. Driver, *A Treatise on the Use of the Tenses in Hebrew
and Some Other Syntactical Questions*

Joseph A. Fitzmyer, S.J., *The Semitic Background of the New Testament*

Volume I: *Essays on the Semitic Background of the New Testament*

Volume II: *A Wandering Aramean: Collected Aramaic Essays*

Joseph A. Fitzmyer, S.J., *To Advance the Gospel,* Second Edition

Birger Gerhardsson, *Memory and Manuscript* and
Tradition and Transmission in Early Christianity

Hermann Gunkel, *Creation and Chaos in the Primeval Era and the Eschaton:
A Religio-Historical Study of Genesis 1 and Revelation 12*

Richard B. Hays, *The Faith of Jesus Christ: The Narrative Substructure
of Galatians 3:1–4:11,* Second Edition

Colin J. Hemer, *The Letters to the Seven Churches of Asia in Their Local Setting*

Sigmund Mowinckel, *The Psalms in Israel's Worship*

Sigmund Mowinckel, *He That Cometh: The Messiah Concept
in the Old Testament and Later Judaism*

Anthony J. Saldarini, *Pharisees, Scribes, and Sadducees in Palestinian Society*

Mark S. Smith, *The Early History of God: Yahweh and the Other Deities in Ancient
Israel,* Second Edition

Samuel Terrien, *Till the Heart Sings: A Biblical Theology of Manhood and Womanhood*

THE DYNAMICS OF BIBLICAL PARALLELISM

Adele Berlin

Revised and Expanded Edition

With the addition of
"The Range of Biblical Metaphors in *Smikhut*"
by Lida Knorina

William B. Eerdmans Publishing Company
Grand Rapids, Michigan / Cambridge, U.K.

Dove Booksellers
Dearborn, Michigan

First edition © 1985 Adele Berlin
Published 1985 by Indiana University Press, Bloomington
Revised and Expanded Edition © 2008 Adele Berlin
All rights reserved

Revised edition published jointly 2008 by
Wm. B. Eerdmans Publishing Co.
2140 Oak Industrial Drive N.E., Grand Rapids, Michigan 49505 /
P.O. Box 163, Cambridge CB3 9PU U.K.
www.eerdmans.com
and by
Dove Booksellers
13904 Michigan Avenue, Dearborn, Michigan 48126
www.dovebook.com

Printed in the United States of America

12 11 10 09 08   7 6 5 4 3 2 1

Library of Congress Cataloging-in-Publication Data

Berlin, Adele.
  The dynamics of biblical parallelism.

  English and Hebrew.
  Bibliography: p.
  Includes index.
  1. Hebrew language — Parallelism. 2. Bible. O.T.-Language, Style.
I. Title.
PJ4740.B47   1985   809'.93522   84-48250
ISBN 978-0-8028-0397-9

For
Moshe Greenberg
and
Barry L. Eichler

עשה לך רב וקנה לך חבר

And also in memory of
Tikva Frymer-Kensky
and
Michael O'Connor

CONTENTS

FOREWORD

A worthy subject in the hands of a balanced scholar is always a pleasure, and often a welcome relief, to read. Adele Berlin writes felicitously, and she is a reliable Old Testament scholar. In this newly reprinted edition of *The Dynamics of Biblical Parallelism*, Berlin probes the linguistic phenomenon of parallelism in which "two or more similar elements are combined in contiguous expression; that is, similarity is super-imposed on contiguity." Her results are valuable.

Robert Alter and James Kugel, as well as Stephen Geller and Michael O'Connor, among others, have treated the subject, but Berlin's book distinguishes itself by integrating Russian linguist Roman Jakobson's pioneering work as the theoretical foundation for offering parallelism as a pervasive feature with semantic, phonological, morphological, and lexical aspects. Most handbooks stop at "semantic."

I agree with Berlin that the features of parallelism—using words and expressions sharing the same class, deep syntactic structure, or sound and meaning—form a single effect that is both synonymous and antithetical. This simultaneous converging-diverging effect is close to Jacques Derrida's familiar concept of *differance* as set forth in *Of Grammatology* (1967), which is no surprise since Berlin builds upon the work of Jakobson, one of Derrida's precursors.

In his 1985 review of *The Dynamics of Biblical Parallelism*, Patrick D. Miller suggested that Berlin should deal with the important poetic phenomena of metaphor, redundancy, and ambiguity in more detail. Addressing this concern, Berlin's current edition includes Lida Knorina's "The Range of Biblical Metaphors in *Smikhut*," a linguistic analysis of metaphor, which adds dimension to this previously understated level of parallelism.

Teachers may want to consult an outside resource, namely, Rolf A. Jacobson's "Teaching Students to Interpret Religious Poetry (and to Expand their Avenues of Thinking)" (*Teaching Theology and Religion*, vol. 7, no. 1) for pedagogical help with integrating into the classroom the material contained in Berlin's study. Notably, even Jacobson's bibliography cites works much older than this text's original 1985 publication date, some even dating to the nineteenth century. Therefore, relying on Berlin's meticulous research and sound insights, the reader can be sure the treatise is, indeed, currently among the best works on biblical parallelism.

For anyone interested in the linguistic analysis of biblical poetry, this new edition of *The Dynamics of Biblical Parallelism*, twenty-two years after its first run, promises to contribute to the current renascence in the study of Hebrew poetry studies, just as it did during the renascence in the 1970s. Berlin has decided to preserve her discussion intact to avoid unraveling or distorting the original argument. An admirable first edition, after all, need only be reprinted, and not revised.

I am confident that the reader will readily agree with Berlin herself that the study of parallelism is, above all else, fun.

David Noel Freedman

PREFACE TO THE REVISED
AND EXPANDED EDITION

I am gratified that William B. Eerdmans Publishing Company is making *The Dynamics of Biblical Parallelism,* first published more than twenty years ago, available to a new generation of students and scholars. It did not seem to me wise to rewrite any part of the book since that invariably leads to some unravelling of the original presentation, so I have simply corrected small errors. I have also added a new and very short introduction to give a sense of the pertinent scholarly activity at the time the book was written and to provide a quick overview of the subsequent study of parallelism.

I am most pleased that this new volume also contains an unpublished paper by a Russian linguist, Lida Knorina, here made public for the first time. The paper, "The Range of Biblical Metaphors in *Smikhut,*" does not deal with parallelism, but rather with metaphor, a much neglected area of biblical poetry that has lately begun to garner the serious study it deserves. Knorina analyzes a subgroup of metaphors, those that occur in the construct state *(smikhut)*. Although written over ten years ago, and never completed, I still find it innovative and instructive to those who value the linguistic analysis of poetry. Knorina's linguistic analysis of metaphor makes a nice complement to my linguistic categorization of parallelism. Metaphor, like parallelism, is at the heart of biblical poetry and is also present, less pervasively, in prose; and linguistic approaches to them can help us better understand their workings.

This book was originally dedicated to my teacher, Moshe Greenberg, and to my colleague and friend, Barry Eichler. I would like to rededicate this book to them. They have remained for me throughout the years models of deep learning and of extraordinary human kindness and concern for the world. They are, in the very highest sense, scholars, teachers, and friends. And now, with sadness, I add a dedication in memory of two friends and colleagues, Tikva Frymer-Kensky and Michael O'Connor.

Adele Berlin
August, 2006

PREFACE TO THE FIRST EDITION

To paraphrase Amos 7:14, I am not a linguist nor a disciple of linguists, but a biblical scholar. Yet I have found in linguistics many insights that can be used to explain the biblical text. The aspect of the text which I have singled out for consideration here is parallelism — a phenomenon which is highly visible in the Bible and which has also figured prominently in studies by linguists, especially those of the late Roman Jakobson. In fact, it was from Jakobson's writings that I first glimpsed a view of parallelism alternative to the one presented by most biblicists. Jakobson's influence is obvious in the coming chapters, for, while I am well aware of the criticisms that have been levelled against him, I am convinced that his approach has more potential than any other for providing us with a comprehensive and integrated view of parallelism in all its facets. At the same time, I have not limited myself to Jakobson or to structural linguistics, but have ventured into psycholinguistics and textlinguistics. My grasp of these disciplines is admittedly incomplete, but it seemed to me enough, having found in them certain insights, to use these insights to further our understanding of biblical parallelism. The purpose of this book, then, is not to espouse or substantiate a particular linguistic theory or methodology, but to use linguistics, in its broadest sense, to explain parallelism as it occurs in the Hebrew Bible. I have attempted to get at the basics of what biblical parallelism is and how it works.

This book has taken a number of years to complete. It was begun with a study of the grammatical aspect of biblical parallelism which was supported by an NEH Summer Stipend (1978) and published in the *Hebrew Union College Annual* L (1979), 17-43. A later study, which now forms part of Chapter IV, was published as "Parallel Word Pairs: A Linguistic Explanation" in *Ugarit-Forschungen* 15 (1983), 7-16. The bulk of the work was completed in 1982-83 with the help of grants from the American Association of University Women and the General Research Board of the University of Maryland.

During these years I benefited from contacts with several colleagues and it is my pleasure to acknowledge them here. Michael O'Connor read an earlier draft of Chapter I and offered extensive and perceptive comments. Stephen Geller, Edward Greenstein, Francis Landy, and Dennis Pardee provided me with their unpublished manuscripts and exchanged views with me on a number of points. As always, my husband has been a source of support and encouragement. Finally, there are two men who, although they have had no direct influence on the study at hand, have, since my formative years, embodied for me the ideals of fine scholarship and teaching. This book is dedicated to them.

Translations of biblical passages are my own, in consultation with the major modern Bible translations. The purpose of the translation is to make clear the particular phenomenon under discussion, so I have designed the translation (sometimes accompanied by partial transliteration) to do this as efficiently as possible. This occasionally produces different renderings for the same verse if it is used to illustrate different aspects of parallelism.

The lineation of passages was also designed to highlight parallelisms and does not always correspond to lines of verse. Indeed, some of the examples are not verse at all.

The symbol // indicates "parallel to" in the traditional sense of occurring in parallel lines. Hebrew word pairs which occur in juxtaposition and English word associations are marked by - (hyphen), although these are also considered an aspect of parallelism.

INTRODUCTION

The late 1970s and early 1980s saw a growth of interest in literary aspects of the Hebrew Bible. This was the beginning of the heyday of modern literary theory—formalism and structuralism, seasoned with the New Criticism that preceded it — and biblical scholars soon saw the benefits of applying these analytic methods to the biblical text. While literary scholars of the Bible focused mainly on narrative, and continued to do so when Deconstruction and various other forms of postmodern literary theory came onto the scene, poetry was also, if to a lesser extent, the subject of literary analysis, especially the formal structures of Hebrew biblical poetry. Of course, scholarly interest in biblical poetry was not new; it dates from ancient times and resurfaces in every generation.[1] In its modern pre-Formalist stage, analysis centered on the question of meter (another ancient quest), and various metric systems were proposed. In due course, scholars moved to the analysis of the text's lexical structure, more specifically, the patterning of words in poetic lines, in configurations of AABB, ABAB, ABBA, and the like. (Many studies of chiasm, in poetry as well as in prose, appeared at this time.) At about the same time, studies of parallel word-pairs became popular. These word-pairs were then thought to have been fixed into formulaic sets used as the building blocks of orally composed poetry, an idea that derived from the Parry-Lord theory of oral composition of Homeric poetry. Parry and Lord identified formulaic phrases as the basis of oral composition, but since the Bible did not utilize formulaic phrases, biblical scholars found their functional equivalent in parallel word pairs.[2] Studies of meter, fixed word pairs, and lexical patterning are rather different from each other, but in some sense, all of these efforts may be seen as calling attention to the formal properties of poetic discourse and the techniques that enabled its composition, and thus they

---

1. James L. Kugel, *The Idea of Biblical Poetry: Parallelism and Its History* (New Haven: Yale University Press, 1981). See also my entry on "Poetry, Old Testament," in *Dictionary of Biblical Interpretation* (Nashville: Abingdon, 1999), pp. 290-296.

2. See my critique of fixed word pairs in Chapter IV. The Parry-Lord theory has subsequently fallen by the wayside.

prepared the way for a more theoretically sophisticated study of the formal properties of poetry and of parallelism.

Formalism and Structuralism, it should be remembered, were born in the discipline of linguistics, and with their advent came the linguistic study of poetry, most notably by Roman Jakobson. Although Jakobson's work dates from the 1960s, it took over a decade for it to kindle an interest among scholars of biblical poetry. *The Dynamics of Biblical Poetry* is an application of Jakobsonian principles to biblical parallelism, an important dimension of biblical poetry.

My book was not written in a vacuum. A number of linguistic studies of biblical poetry, including studies of parallelism, preceded it and influenced it. Primary among them are the works of T. Collins, A. Cooper, J. de Moor, S. Geller, E. Greenstein, P. Miller, M. O'Connor, D. Pardee, S. Parker, S. Segert, and W.G. E. Watson.[3] All of these scholars were, in one way or another, struggling to define or analyze biblical verse lines, parallelisms, or other dimensions of poetic discourse using linguistics as their main tool. Not all, however, were Jakobsonian in orientation.

At about the same time, new progress was being made in the non-linguistic study of parallelism, most famously by Robert Alter and James Kugel. They are the more direct heirs to the work of Robert Lowth, who may be called the "father of parallelism" (even though the study of parallelism predates him by centuries, as shown by Kugel).[4] As such, Alter and Kugel were in a position to overturn the Lowthian categorization of parallelism into three types (synonymous, antithetic, synthetic), replacing it by the idea that there are multiple ways in which the second line of a parallelism may go beyond the first line. The important point is that the second line does not merely repeat the idea of the first, but goes beyond it in any number of ways: modifying it, extending it, or intensifying it.[5] Both Alter and Kugel came to this understanding of parallelism independently at more or less the same moment — an idea whose time had come. In my

---

3. See the Bibliography near the end of the book.

4. For Rashi's appreciation of parallelism see now Mayer I. Gruber, *Rashi's Commentary on Psalms* (Leiden: Brill, 2004), pp. 150-54.

5. As early as 1963, Luis Alonso-Schökel wrote: "Parallelism can serve to amplify or to concentrate; it may enlarge the image or explain it . . . ; it can harmonize two things or put them in tension" (*Estudios de poética hebrea*, 230; quoted in *The Hebrew Bible in Literary Criticism*, compiled and edited by Alex Preminger and Edward L. Greenstein [New York: Unger, 1986], p. 153).

book I discussed Kugel's work, published in 1981, at some length. I should
have given more weight to Alter's work as well, since two of his articles on
parallelism were available in 1983, although his *The Art of Biblical Poetry*
was not published until 1985, the same year my book was published.[6]

My own thinking about parallelism, already partially shaped by earlier linguistic studies, also benefited from this new way of looking at it developed by
Alter and Kugel. My book, then, stands at a certain moment in the convergence of the linguistic study of poetic discourse and the non-linguistic study
of parallelism. In both the Lowthian, or, rather, anti-Lowthian, analysis of
Alter and Kugel, as in the linguistic analysis by other scholars, the semantic
and syntactic relationships between parallel lines dominate the discussion.
Those relationships were my primary focus, and I found that my linguistic
description of parallelism, following upon other contemporary descriptions
of different aspects of parallelism, provided a confirmation and an explanation of the conclusions reached through other means by Alter and Kugel. In
other words, I could describe, from a linguistic perspective, many of the ways
whereby the second line of a parallelism could go beyond the first.

Since the goal was to provide a linguistic framework for the study of
parallelism, most of the book is taken up with linguistic categories of description: the morphologic, syntactic, lexical, semantic, and phonological
categories through which parallelism can be understood. But in the last
chapter I began to explore how these various linguistic categories interact
within a text. I began to appreciate the intricacies of parallelism, its various nuances, and the seemingly infinite possibilities for its construction.
Some parallelisms have a certain playfulness, a way of engaging the reader
in unexpected equivalences and contrasts that are a hallmark of parallelism. It may be a surprising combination of words or phrases or a tension
in the syntax of the lines. Since it is always fun to look at these examples, I
provide two of them here.

Ps 79:11

תבוא לפניך אנקת אסיר
כגדל זרועך הותר בני תמותה

Let the groan of the *prisoner* come before you;
As befits your great arm, *release those about to die.*

---

6. Robert Alter, *The Art of Biblical Poetry* (New York: Basic Books, 1985).

The word *prisoner,* literally, "the bound one," has two parallel terms linked with it. The more usual associate of "bind" is *release,* and that occurs here as a verb whose subject is God. This is not grammatically parallel but is lexically parallel; it employs a common word association (see Chapter IV). The second term associated with *prisoner* is *those about to die.* These terms are semantically parallel; they both refer to the same referent, although *those about to die* extends the meaning of *prisoner.* Note, too, that *the groan of the prisoner* is the grammatical subject of its line while *those about to die* is the grammatical object in the parallel line. And *prisoner* is singular while *those about to die* is plural (morphological parallelism). These various linguistic types of parallelism that are described in detail in the book are combined in this verse.

Job 5:14

יומם יפגשו חשך
וכלילה ימששו בצהרים

By day they will meet darkness;
And as at night they will grope at noon.

The linguistic sophistication and complexity of the book of Job is on display in this parallelism. The usual word associates, *day* and *night,* are here placed in the same position in their respective lines (at the head), giving the impression that they are grammatically parallel, as in so many cases when something occurring by day is paralleled by something occurring at night. Similarly placed are *darkness* and *noon* (bright sunshine), another, less common, set of associated words. But while these pairs may be lexically parallel, they do not function that way here. The parallel to *by day* is *at noon,* and the parallel to *night* is *darkness.* This is not an antithetic parallelism contrasting day and night, to use Lowth's old term, but a synonymous parallelism wherein both lines speak about the daytime. To be sure, the second line goes beyond the first in describing the metaphoric blindness of the enlightened; they are most like blind people when the sun is brightest. Notice also the sound pair in *meet (ypgšw)* and *grope (ymššw),* helping to draw together two words that are not normally associated.

The study of parallelism, whether on a theoretical macro level or on the level of specific examples, continues to be engaging. More than ever, I appreciate the elasticity of this trope and the artistic creativity of the writers who employed it so well. The study of parallelism is fun.

The Study of Parallelism since 1985

The study of biblical parallelism reached its apogee in the mid-1980s, and waned after that as there was little new to say of a theoretic nature and as the linguistic study of poetry gave way to other approaches to poetry. However, there continued to be what I would call derivative studies, including refinements to the older categories of parallelism (e.g. janus parallelism, metathetic parallelism, and the like) and analyses of parallelism in specific biblical and other ancient texts. Below is a representative collection of studies of parallelism, by no means comprehensive, published after 1985. Arranged alphabetically according to author, the list includes research on parallelism in biblical poetry, biblical prose, and postbiblical and extrabiblical texts as well as studies addressing the importance of parallelism in exegesis and in translation.

Avishur, Yitshak. ‏החזרה והתקבולת בשירה המקראית והכנענית: התבניות הסגנוניות של‏ ‏התקבולת דפוסי והתפתחות החרוז בצלעות החזרה‏ *Ha-Hazarah veha-tikbolet ba-shirah ha-Mikra'it veha-Kena'anit: ha-tavniyot ha-signoniyot shel ha-hazarah be-tsal'ot he-haruz ve-hitpathut defuse ha-tikbolet.* Tel Aviv-Yafo: Pirsume Merkaz arkhe'ologi, 2002.

Barco del Barco, Francisco Javier del. "Syntactic Structures of Parallelism: A Case Study in Biblical Prophecy." *Journal of Northwest Semitic Languages* 29, no. 1 (2003), 37-53.

Berlin, Adele. "Azariah de' Rossi on Biblical Poetry." *Prooftexts* 12 (1992), 175-83.

———. "Rams and Lambs in Psalm 114:4 and 6: The Septuagint's Translation of X // ‏בן‏ Y Parallelisms." *Textus* (forthcoming).

Burden, Jasper Jacobus. "Reconsidering Parallelism in the Old Testament." *Old Testament Essays* 4 (1986), 141-76.

Ceresko, Anthony R. "Janus Parallelism in Amos's 'Oracles against the Nations' (Amos 1:3-2:16)." *JBL* 113, no. 3 (1994), 485-90.

Clines, David J. A. "The Parallelism of Greater Precision: Notes from Isaiah 40 for a Theory of Hebrew Poetry." In *Directions in Biblical Hebrew Poetry.* Edited by Elaine R. Follis. Sheffield: JSOT Press, 1987. Pp. 77-100.

Elwolde, John F. "Non-contiguous Parallelism as a Key to Literary Structure and Lexical Meaning in Job 28." In *Job 28: Cognition in Context.* Edited by Ellen van Wolde. Leiden: Brill, 2003. Pp. 103-18.

Gray, Patrick. "Points and Lines: Thematic Parallelism in the Letter of James and the 'Testament of Job.'" *New Testament Studies* 50, no. 3 (2004), 406-24.

Gruber, Mayer Irwin. "The Meaning of Biblical Parallelism: A Biblical Perspective." *Prooftexts* 13, no. 3 (1993), 289-93.

Harris, Robert A. *Discerning Parallelism: A Study in Northern French Medieval Jewish Biblical Exegesis.* Brown Judaic Studies 341. Providence: Brown University Press, 2004.

Irwin, William Henry. "Conflicting Parallelism in Job 5,13; Isa 30,28; Isa 32,7." *Biblica* 76, no. 1 (1995), 72-74.

Landy, Francis. "Recent Developments in Biblical Poetics." *Prooftexts* 7, no. 2 (1987), 163-78.

Levine, Nachman. "Vertical Poetics: Interlinear Phonological Parallelism in Psalms." *Journal of Northwest Semitic Languages* 29, no. 2 (2003), 65-82.

Malul, Meir. "Janus Parallelism in Biblical Hebrew: Two More Cases (Canticles 4,9.12)." *Biblische Zeitschrift* 41, no. 2 (1997), 246-49.

Martens, Elmer A. "Narrative Parallelism and Message in Jeremiah 34-38." *Early Jewish and Christian Exegesis: Studies in Memory of William Hugh Brownlee.* Edited by Craig A. Evans and William F. Stinespring. Atlanta: Scholars Press, 1987. Pp. 33-49.

Nel, Philip J. "Parallelism and Recurrence in Biblical Hebrew Poetry: A Theoretical Proposal." *Journal of Northwest Semitic Languages* 18 (1992), 135-43.

Noegel, Scott B. *Janus Parallelism in the Book of Job.* Sheffield: Sheffield Academic Press, 1996.

Pardee, Dennis. "Acrostics and Parallelism: The Parallelistic Structure of Psalm 111." *Maarav* 8 (1993), 117-38.

———. *Ugaritic and Hebrew Poetic Parallelism: A Trial Cut (" 'nt" I and Proverbs 2).* Leiden and New York: Brill, 1988.

Paul, Shalom M. "Polysensuous Polyvalency in Poetic Parallelism." In *Shaarei Talmon: Studies in the Bible, Qumran, and the Ancient Near East Presented to Shemaryahu Talmon.* Edited by Michael Fishbane and Emanuel Tov. Winona Lake, Ind.: Eisenbrauns. 1992. Pp. 147-63.

Payne, Geoffrey. "Parallelism in Biblical Hebrew Verse." *JSOT* 8, no. 1 (1994), 126-40.

Polak, Frank H. "Poetic Style and Parallelism in the Creation Account (Genesis 1.1-2.3)." In *Creation in Jewish and Christian Tradition.* Edited by Henning Graf Reventlow and Yair Hoffman. JSOT Sup. Series 319. Sheffield: Sheffield Academic Press, 2002. Pp. 2-31.

Reyburn, William D. "Poetic Parallelism: Its Structure, Meaning, and Implication for Translators." *Issues in Bible Translation* (1988), 81-112.

Reymond, Eric D. *Innovations in Hebrew Poetry: Parallelism and the Poems of Sirach.* Atlanta: SBL, 2004.

Rosengren, Allan. *Parallelism in Prose.* Ph.D. dissertation, University of Copenhagen. 1998.

Rousseau, François. *La poétique fondamentale du texte biblique: le fait littéraire d'un parallélisme élargi et omniprésent.* Montréal: Editions Bellarmin and Paris: Editions du Cerf, 1989.

Segert, Stanislav. "Parallelism in the Alphabetic Apostrophe to Zion." *Archiv Orientální* 64, no. 2 (1996), 269-77.

Tauberschmidt, Gerhard. *Secondary Parallelism: A Study of Translation Technique in LXX Proverbs.* Atlanta: SBL, 2004.

Tsumura, David Toshio. "Janus Parallelism in Hab. III 4." *VT* 54, no. 1 (2004), 124-28.

―――. "Literary Insertion, A X B Pattern, in Hebrew and Ugaritic: A Problem of Adjacency and Dependency in Poetic Parallelism." *Ugarit-Forschungen* 18 (1986), 351-61.

―――. "Vertical Grammar: The Grammar of Parallelism in Biblical Hebrew." In *Hamlet on a Hill: Semitic and Greek Studies Presented to Professor T. Muraoka on the Occasion of His Sixty-fifth Birthday.* Edited by M. F. J. Baasten and W. Th. van Peursen. Leuven and Dudley, Mass.: Peeters, 2003. Pp. 487-97.

Watson, Wilfred G.E. "Half-line Parallelism as Indicative of Verse in Hebrew Prose." In *Verse in Ancient Near Eastern Prose.* Edited by Johannes C. de Moor and Wilfred G. E. Watson. Kevelaer: Butzon & Bercker; Neukirchen-Vluyn: Neukirchener Verlag, 1993. Pp. 331-44.

―――. "Number Parallelism in Mesopotamian Texts." *Maarav* 7 [1991] (1993), 241-52.

Willis, John Thomas. "Alternating (ABA'B') Parallelism in the Old Testament Psalms and Prophetic Literature." In *Directions in Biblical Hebrew Poetry.* Edited by Elaine R. Follis. Sheffield: JSOT Press, 1987. Pp. 49-76.

My own efforts in disseminating the understanding of parallelism and of biblical poetry can be found in the following sources.

"Introduction to Hebrew Poetry." In *The New Interpreter's Bible* (Nashville: Abingdon, 1996). 4:301-15.

"Parallelism." In *Anchor Bible Dictionary.* Garden City, N.Y.: Doubleday, 1992. 5:155-62.

"Parallelism." In *The New Interpreter's Dictionary of the Bible.* Forthcoming.

"Poetry, Old Testament." In *Dictionary of Biblical Interpretation.* Nashville: Abingdon, 1999. Pp. 290-96.

"Reading Biblical Poetry." In *The Jewish Study Bible.* New York: Oxford University Press, 2004. Pp. 2097-2104.

ABBREVIATIONS

BASOR	*Bulletin of the American Schools of Oriental Research*
CBQ	*Catholic Biblical Quarterly*
Chr	Chronicles
Deut	Deuteronomy
Eccl	Ecclesiastes
Ex	Exodus
Ezek	Ezekiel
fem.	feminine
Gen	Genesis
GPRF	R. Jakobson, "Grammatical Parallelism and Its Russian Facet"
Hab	Habakkuk
Hag	Haggai
HAR	*Hebrew Annual Review*
Hos	Hosea
HUCA	*Hebrew Union College Annual*
HVS	M. O'Connor, *Hebrew Verse Structure*
IDB	*Interpreter's Dictionary of the Bible*
Idea	J. Kugel, *The Idea of Biblical Poetry*
Isa	Isaiah
JANES	*Journal of the Ancient Near Eastern Society*
JAOS	*Journal of the American Oriental Society*
JBL	*Journal of Biblical Literature*
Jer	Jeremiah
Josh	Joshua
JQR	*Jewish Quarterly Review*
JSOT	*Journal for the Study of the Old Testament*
JSS	*Journal of Semitic Studies*
Jud	Judges
Kgs	Kings
Lam	Lamentations
Lev	Leviticus
LP	R. Jakobson, "Linguistics and Poetics"
LXX	Septuagint

Mal	Malachi
masc.	masculine
Mic	Micah
MT	Massoretic Text
Nah	Nahum
Neh	Nehemiah
Num	Numbers
pl.	plural
Pr	Proverbs
Ps	Psalms
RSP	*Ras Shamra Parallels* (ed. L. Fisher). All references to *RSP* are to M. Dahood's "Ugaritic-Hebrew Parallel Pairs"
RSV	Revised Standard Version
Sam	Samuel
SBL	Society of Biblical Literature
sing.	singular
Song	Song of Songs
UF	*Ugarit-Forschungen*
VT	*Vetus Testamentum*
Zeph	Zephaniah

I
PARALLELISM
AND
POETRY

In 1753, in the third of his *Lectures on the Sacred Poetry of the Hebrews*, Robert Lowth observed "a certain conformation of the sentences" which is

> chiefly observable in those passages which frequently occur in the Hebrew poetry, in which they treat one subject in many different ways, and dwell upon the same sentiment; when they express the same thing in different words, or different things in a similar form of words; when equals refer to equals, and opposites to opposites: and since this artifice of composition seldom fails to produce even in prose an agreeable and measured cadence, we can scarcely doubt that it must have imparted to their poetry . . . an exquisite degree of beauty and grace.

The phenomenon which Lowth described here (and again in Lecture XIX) was more precisely defined in 1778 in his introduction to *Isaiah*.

> The correspondence of one Verse, or Line, with another, I call Parallelism. When a proposition is delivered, and a second is subjoined to it, or drawn under it, equivalent, or contrasted with it, in Sense; or similar to it in the form of Grammatical Construction; these I call Parallel Lines; and the words or phrases answering one to another in the corresponding Lines Parallel Terms.

Although Lowth was not the first to recognize parallelism,[1] he promoted it to a place of prominence in biblical studies. His definition became classic, and his tripartite subdivision of its types (explicated in Lecture XIX of *Lectures on the Sacred Poetry of the Hebrews* and also in *Isaiah*) remained the standard for many years—the skeletal model which subsequent scholars fleshed out in their own studies, some adding to it or modifying it, but none until recently breaking free from it completely. Lowth had identified

I

a feature which has continued to fascinate readers of the biblical text. Parallelism has both delighted us, for its effect is unmistakable, and frustrated us, for the way that it works is elusive. We have sought it by collecting and classifying its types, as Lowth began, and when the three original types could not capture its essence we added more types and subtypes; so that now we hear not only of synonymous, antithetic, and synthetic parallelism, but also of incomplete parallelism, staircase parallelism, janus parallelism, metathetic parallelism, and so on. Given the powers of discrimination that the human mind possesses, the longer we examine parallelism the more discrete types we are likely to find.

I do not come to propose new types, nor to reclassify old ones. What is sorely needed is a fresh approach to parallelism as a whole. We have been so busy dissecting the trees, branches, and leaves that we have lost sight of the forest. The forest is a dynamic microworld in which many different components function in relation to each other. It is not enough to recognize the individual components; we have not perceived the essence of the forest until we have seen that its various components belong to a multifaceted, balanced system. Parallelism, like a forest, has many aspects. Some are well known, others little studied. But more than anything, we must begin to see all these aspects—and all types and subtypes of parallelism—as parts of a total system of linguistic usage.

Parallelism is a linguistic phenomenon. It uses language—words, phonemes, grammar—in a variety of interesting ways. It is therefore fitting that we should approach it from a linguistic perspective, as well as from the perspective of biblical studies. Great advances have been made in both of these areas since Lowth's time, and there is no reason that his views of parallelism should remain canonized. But though we leave these views behind in search of more adequate ones, the fundamental insight which he provided should not be lost. Lowth may have been mistaken in some of his ideas, and he was certainly limited in his linguistic knowledge, but he was right about the essence of parallelism; it is a *correspondence of one thing with another*. Parallelism promotes the perception of a relationship between the elements of which parallelism is composed, and this relationship is one of correspondence. The nature of the correspondence varies, but in general it involves repetition or the substitution of things which are equivalent on one or more linguistic levels. The notion of *equivalence*, and its counterpart *opposition* or *contrast*, will emerge again and again in the various areas of linguistics to which we will have recourse; but the amazing thing is that it is already present in a primitive form in Lowth's observation that "equals refer to equals, and opposites to opposites." Lowth, however, did not understand this as broadly as we do, for he did not understand linguistics as we do. We are able to see many more equivalences and oppositions on many more linguistic levels. It is these linguistic equivalences that we wish to examine in greater depth, for they constitute the phenomenon called parallelism.

The definition of parallelism offered here is much broader than that found in most biblical studies, in which parallelism is usually considered to involve only semantic and/or grammatical equivalences and to operate only between two or more consecutive lines. This narrow view of parallelism would seem to be a legacy of Lowth, who spoke of the correspondence of one verse, or line, with another. Once we admit smaller segments as being parallel—e.g., words, phrases, even sounds—though the lines to which they belong are not parallel, we raise the incidence of parallelism within a text. And if we do not restrict our search for linguistic equivalences to adjacent lines or sentences, but take a global view, finding equivalences anywhere within a text, we raise the incidence of parallelism still more. This more encompassing definition of parallelism is the one developed by Roman Jakobson, and it should be borne in mind that it differs from the definition used by most biblical scholars. Jakobson's view is preferable because it enables us to unify phenomena whose relationships have not been perceived. For instance, the device known as inclusio, in which the first and last lines of a text contain the same words or phrases, is actually a form of parallelism and should be recognized as such.[2] (However, in actual practice, most of our examples of parallelism will come from adjacent lines, for that is where it is most manifest.) Furthermore, Jakobson's approach allows us to see more readily that the parallelisms touted as indicators of poetry are no different from the linguistic equivalences in prose texts. Certain linguistic usages, including a systematic exploitation of equivalences, are a mark of biblical style as a whole. They are not limited to one genre, although they may be more prominent in the one usually called poetry.

PARALLELISM AND POETRY IN BIBLICAL STUDIES

This brings us to the difficult matter of prose vs. poetry as it relates to the Bible, and especially as it relates to parallelism. Biblicists have long equated parallelism with poetry. No doubt this is another of Lowth's legacies, although a careful reading of his Lecture III will show that he recognized "this artifice of composition" in prose as well. Nevertheless, since biblical poetry lacks any easily discernable meter, or any comparable feature that marks it as verse,[3] the burden of identification came to rest on the presence of parallelism—more specifically, on the parallelism of consecutive lines. This is not to say that every line of poetry had to be paralleled, but that, by and large, where there was parallelism there was poetry. (When taken to an extreme this resulted in the "discovery" of snippets of poetry in otherwise prosaic contexts.)

The matter rested here, with little argument and much vagueness, until the recent discussion by James Kugel in *The Idea of Biblical Poetry*. Kugel not only questioned the equation of parallelism with poetry, but attacked the whole notion that one can differentiate prose from poetry in the Bible. It is the first point that is of interest to our study, but Kugel's line of argument cannot be understood without reference to his view of the prose-poetry issue.

Kugel begins by citing a number of parallelisms from Genesis and Exodus, that is, passages normally considered prose, and goes on to find parallelism[4] in the Moabite Stone, an inscription whose very literariness may be questioned. This leads him to the observation that "the same traits that seem to characterize Hebrew 'poetry' also crop up in what is clearly not poetry" (*Idea*, 63). This, of course, is true, and it applies not only to parallelism but to other rhetorical figures. The converse, that not all lines in poetry are parallelistic or symmetrical, is also shown, mainly from Ps 119 and 122. In other words, Kugel sees, as I have already suggested, that not all poetry is parallelisms and not all parallelisms are poetry. But this does not prove that there is no difference between prose and poetry, as Kugel would appear to have us believe;[5] it only proves that the distinction cannot be made solely on the basis of parallelism. Kugel falls prey to a faulty premise. He tacitly accepts the equation of parallelism with poetry (even as he rejects it—*Idea*, 70) and then, wherever he finds parallelism he is forced to call it poetry—but, since he knows it isn't poetry, he calls it "elevated style." The truth is, as linguists have shown (cf. Hiatt and Werth), that parallelism is not in and of itself a mark of poetry as opposed to prose, or even of elevated style as opposed to ordinary discourse; it is a common feature of all language. And yet, as we will soon see, in a certain sense parallelism *is* the essence of poetry.[6]

But we leave this apparent paradox for the moment and return to Kugel's argument. Kugel's struggle with terms like "prose" and "poetry" is part of a large reluctance he has about any form of labelling of the biblical text outside of the Bible's own. In the end, he will not even admit that it can be called literature: "One might well ask: what is literary about the Bible at all? Certainly it does not identify itself as literature, and often such self-definition as does occur seems clearly to place it elsewhere" (*Idea*, 303).[7] Clearly, if Kugel rejects the Bible as literature—i.e., as "artful composition"—then to distinguish literary subtypes on the basis of artfulness becomes a meaningless exercise. Thus Kugel pushes his view to an extreme that in the end threatens to defeat his purpose.

But despite what has been perceived as Kugel's nihilism, he fortunately does not heed his own advice and goes on to discuss those features which make the text literary, or in his words, elevated in style. Here he has something to contribute to the prose-poetry problem and to the role of parallelism in it.

> If one puts aside the notions of biblical poetry and prose and tries to look afresh at different parts of the Bible to see what it is about them that distinguishes one from another, it will soon be apparent that there are not two modes of utterance, but many different elements which elevate style and provide for formality and strictness of organization. Consistently binary sentences, an obvious regard for terseness, and a high degree of semantic parallelism characterize some sections; less consistent (and less consistently semantic) parallelism is found in other parts. . . . This represents a continuum of organization or formality, with parallelism of different intensity and consistency characterizing a great span of texts. [*Idea*, 85]

Kugel is saying, and I basically agree, that there is a continuum of elevated style in the Bible. Some passages are more elevated than others, but, to some extent, one can find this elevated style throughout. Elevated style is largely the product of two elements: terseness and parallelism. Where these two occur to a high degree we have what would be called (by everyone but Kugel) poetry; where they are largely (but never entirely) lacking, we have less-poetic expression, which corresponds to what we call prose.

It is not parallelism per se, but the predominance of parallelism, combined with terseness, which marks the poetic expression of the Bible. And since the difference between poetic and less-poetic sections is a matter of degree, we would not expect different *kinds* of parallelism in "prose" and "poetry," but only different perceptions of their dominance.[8] The perception of the dominance of parallelism in poetry is not only a factor of its quantity, for large amounts can be found in prose, but also a factor of the terseness which tends to produce phonetic and syntactic balance in parallel lines. As we will see shortly, parallelism appears to be the constructive principle on which a poem is built, while a prose passage might have just as much parallelism but not seem to be built on this structure.

The notion of terseness plays a central role in another description, not unlike Kugel's, of the essence of poetic expression. Speaking in reference to a translation of a Chinese poem, W. Empson says:

> Lacking rhyme, metre, and any overt device such as comparison, these lines are what we should normally call poetry only by virtue of their compactness; two statements are made as if they are connected, and the reader is forced to consider their relations for himself. The reason why these facts should have been selected for a poem is left for him to invent; he will invent a variety of reasons and order them in his own mind. This, I think, is the essential fact about the poetical use of language. [24–25]

What is left, Empson asks, if we strip away all devices and structures from a poem? Only its "compactness" and its sense of "connectedness." These correspond to what we have been calling terseness and parallelism. A poem distills and condenses its message, removing "unnecessary" words and leaving only the nucleus of the thought. At the same time, without losing its terseness, it constructs relationships between its parts such that the final product is unified.

Relevant to all of this is the paratactic style of biblical poetry. The lines are placed one after another with no connective or with the common, multivalent conjunction *waw*; rarely is a subordinate relationship indicated on the surface of the text. This has bearing both on the terseness of the poem and on its connectedness. The lines, by virtue of their contiguity, are perceived as connected, while the exact relationship between them is left unspecified. Empson understood that such contiguity creates the impression of connectedness and forces the reader to "consider their relations for himself" and to "invent a variety of reasons" to explain the relationship.[9] Here parallelism plays a significant role, for parallel lines are perceived as "more" connected. Parallelism, because it involves linguistic correspondences, increases the feeling of connectedness between its parts; in parallelism there is no doubt that "two statements are made as if they were connected," so the reader cannot avoid considering their relationship. It is parallelism more than anything else that creates the perception of "couplets" in biblical poetry. And because the lines in these couplets are terse, that is, stripped of all but their essential components, they tend to correspond in the number of components that remain, thereby appearing "balanced" in length or rhythm.[10] In this sense we can say that biblical poetry is characterized by a high incidence of terse, balanced parallelism.

PARALLELISM AND POETRY IN LINGUISTIC STUDIES

The definition of poetry and the place of parallelism in it has occupied not only biblical scholars but also linguists. At the center of this effort was Roman Jakobson, who, probably more than any other person, has influenced the linguistic study of parallelism in the many languages in which it is used (cf. Fox). For Jakobson, parallelism—and, as mentioned earlier, he used the term in a broader sense than do most biblical scholars—is the core of poetic language. His most famous pronouncement on the subject, piercingly insightful and maddeningly general, states that "the poetic function projects the principle of equivalence from the axis of selection into the axis of combination. Equivalence is promoted to the constitutive device of the sequence" (LP, 358). The same idea appears in a different form in his "Poetry of Grammar and Grammar of Poetry": "One may state that in poetry similarity is superimposed on contiguity and hence 'equivalence is promoted to the constitutive device of the sequence'" (602).

There are a number of terms that require explanation, and, to the extent feasible, I will present them in Jakobson's own words. "Selection" and "combination" [this also corresponds to "similarity" and "contiguity," "paradigmatic" and "syntagmatic"] are "the two basic modes of arrangement used in verbal behavior." One selects from a group of similar or paradigmatic elements, and one then arranges the selected item, along with items selected from other groups, into a contiguous or syntagmatic chain. As Jakobson puts it:

> If "child" is the topic of the message, the speaker selects one among the extant, more or less similar, nouns like child, kid, youngster, tot, all of them equivalent in a certain respect, and then, to comment on this topic, he may select one of the semantically cognate verbs—sleeps, dozes, nods, naps. Both chosen words combine in the speech chain. The selection is produced on the base of equivalences, similarity and dissimilarity, synonymity and antonymity, while the combination, the build up of the sequence, is based on contiguity. [LP, 358]

We can illustrate using Jakobson's own example. If we take a sentence like

    1.   The child sleeps.

and apply to it Jakobson's principle in which equivalent elements (those in the same paradigmatic class) are arranged in a contiguous sequence, it yields sentences like

    2.   The child sleeps; the youngster dozes.

    3.   The child, the little tot, gently dozes and sleeps.

    4.   The child dozed off, and, as they talked, the youngster slept.

It is clear from sentences 2 and 3 that the type of parallelism found in the Bible is at least one realization of Jakobson's principle. Actually, sentence 4 could be considered a parallelism, too; in fact, "the principle of equivalence appears to be equated with parallelism" (Werth, 24).

The parallelisms in these examples involve semantic classes (words for "child" and "sleep") and grammatical classes (nouns and verbs). But this does not exhaust the linguistic classes that come into play in parallelism, for in Jakobson's words, "pervasive parallelism inevitably activates all the levels of language" (GPRF, 423); so phonetic and phonologic equivalences, as well as lexical and grammatical ones, will be activated in parallelism. Jakobson thus subsumes rhythm, rhyme, and meter under his definition of parallelism. Parallelism alone, in this broad sense, comes to be equated with "the poetic function": "Or, to quote another master and theoretician of poetic language, G. M. Hopkins, the artifice of poetry 'reduces itself to the principle of parallelism': equivalent entities confront one another by appearing in equivalent positions" (GPRF, 423). This is not far from Kugel's statement, arrived at from a different direction, that "it would be incorrect to call parallelism a rhetorical figure or trope. . . . It was more like *the* trope, the one shape of elevated speech" (*Idea*, 86).

Kugel's "elevated speech" includes prose and poetry but presumably excludes ordinary discourse. Jakobson's "poetic function" is a more abstract concept. It is used most often in connection with poetry or poetic language, but actually it is broader than "poetry" and "elevated speech," for it may occur in all speech.

Jakobson outlines six functions of language which may be present in a message in any combination (LP, 353–57). The *referential* function orients the message toward the referent or context—the person or object being discussed. The *emotive* function focuses on the addresser, expressing his attitude about the message. The *conative* function orients toward the addressee, often employing vocatives and imperatives. The *phatic* function sets up and maintains contact between the addresser and addressee, and often consists of ritualized or stereotyped exchanges like "How are you?" In the *metalingual* function, language is used to explain itself; words define or gloss other words or messages, as in "What do you mean?" The *poetic* function is "the set (*Einstellung*) toward the MESSAGE as such, focus on the message for its own sake" (LP, 356). The poetic function is, of course, present in poetry, but it is not limited to poetry; nor is the poetic function the only function found in poetry. "Any attempt to reduce the sphere of poetic function to poetry or to confine poetry to poetic function would be a delusive oversimplification. Poetic function is not the sole function of verbal art but only its dominant, determining function, whereas in all other verbal activities it acts as a subsidiary, accessory constituent" (LP, 356). Indeed, parallelism, which is the way in which the poetic function manifests itself, is illustrated by Jakobson in ordinary speech: *Joan and Margery*, with the shorter term before the longer, sounds better than *Margery and Joan*; a speaker prefers *horrible Harry*, because of its alliteration, to *dreadful Harry*. Once again, but from a linguist instead of a biblicist, we see that the same device which marks poetry as poetic also occurs in nonpoetic verbal art and even in ordinary speech.

It is, then, not the mere presence, even in large amounts, of the poetic function that distinguishes poetry, but its "dominance." In poetry, the poetic function overrides the other functions. This cannot be shown by a quantitative measure; the dominance of the poetic function cannot be calculated solely by the number of parallelisms in a text. True, as Jakobson has shown in his many analyses of Russian, English, French, and even biblical poems, there is plenty to be found in these. But when parallelisms were sought in prose, linguists discovered that there was also much recurrence of sound, words, and grammar in such things as newspaper articles, modern fiction, and scholarly treatises. In fact, one can hardly surpass the telephone directory for its repetitive patterns of phonological, lexical, and morphological items (Werth, 54), and the same can be said of the Bible's genealogical lists.[11] A computer study of parallelism[12] on the sentence level from a cross-section of standard English prose published in the United States in 1961 shows that of a sample of 7315 sentences, 46% contained at least one parallelism (Hiatt). Nonpoetic texts not only have parallelism— they have a lot of it!

The question is not how much parallelism a text has, but how much of it is effective and meaningful in terms of focusing the message on itself (the poetic function). There is bound to be a certain amount of random repetition of equivalent linguistic categories in any kind of writing; since a language has a limited number of phonemes and morphemes, they will, sooner or later, be used again within a text. And when it comes to lexical-semantic items, which are less limited than phonemic and grammatical ones—if one continues to discuss a particular subject, one is bound to use the same or similar terms to refer to it (cf. Werth, 60). It is really a question of the "poetic effect" of these parallelisms—their "psychological validity" or "perceptibility," or how striking they are (Werth, 61).[13] The poetic effect is the result of an interaction between verbal form and meaning (Werth, 63). One cannot simply list formal equivalences without taking into account their semantic impact, for one does not know a priori which equivalences or oppositions are perceptible or meaningful to the reader. Werth, whose critique of Jakobson is reflected in the foregoing remarks, suggests that

> the impact of the repetition varies according to the type of repetition . . . and the type of linguistic unit. . . . For example, simple phonological repetition is usually euphonious [has no relevance to meaning], though it can be used to give emphasis to a higher level repetition. . . . Simple lexical repetition almost always carries emphasis rather than being purely euphonious. . . . Much the same is true for simple syntactic repetition. Lexical category repetition would tend to lack impact, though syntactic category repetition . . . would almost always be emphatic . . . , as in antithesis. . . . Semantic repetition (i.e., complete or partial synonymy), of course, occurs only at the lexical and syntactic levels. [68]

Werth here distinguishes three types of effects: semantic effects, emphatic effects, and euphonious effects. The effect varies according to the type of parallelism, with semantic parallelism having the greatest effect and phonological repetition having the least. (We shall see in the following chapters that biblical parallelism in "poetry" has a great deal of semantic and syntactic parallelism—precisely the kinds that Werth finds poetically meaningful.) But Werth also notes that the notion of effect is essentially subjective and still beyond the capabilities of linguistics to identify and describe formally (cf. also Erlich, 26).

Some of the same ideas that Werth expressed in 1976 as an attack on Jakobson appear in L. Waugh's 1980 clarification in support of Jakobson's views. I cite those that explain, once again, the relationship between parallelism and poetry, and that correlate with the ideas presented so far.

Waugh, like the others, notes that there are parallelisms in prose, but she emphasizes that despite their presence, they are not systematically

used there—they do not constitute *the constructive device* of the text as they
do in poetry.

> This is not to say that in prose there are no parallelisms or repetitions or any
> other of the devices particularly associated with poetry; but rather to say
> that such symmetries are not the constructive device of prose and are not as
> systematically used. . . . Such parallelisms as may occur in prose are subor-
> dinated to the referential (or other) function. And they are used . . . only
> when their use would not contradict or combat the main referential thrust of
> the discourse. . . . Similarly, equivalence relations of various sorts . . . may
> be important for relations within prose, but again it should be repeated that
> equivalence does not thereby become the constitutive device of the se-
> quence. [64–65]

"Constitutive device" means the formal device upon which the poem is
constructed; this is apparently what Jakobson meant by "equivalence is
promoted to the constitutive device of the sequence" (LP, 358), and it is a
crucial part of his definition of the poetic function.

The matter of the perceptibility of parallelism is touched on by Waugh's
next comment.

> Of course, the other side of equivalence is difference and the other side of
> similarity is dissimilarity. By projecting equivalence (and perforce differ-
> ence) into the axis of combination, the *contrast* between or within paral-
> lelistic elements comes to the fore and indeed contrast, as much as equiv-
> alence, becomes an important part of the structuration of the poem. . . . [as
> E. Holenstein indicates] "In addition to the projection of the principle of
> equivalence from the axis of selection into the axis of combination, there is
> also in poetry a projection of the principle of contrast for the significative,
> selective, and combinatorial operations into the level of a patent 'palpable,'
> and 'perceptible' form. . . ." In the referential use of language, contrast
> very often resides not in elements linked by various equivalence relations
> but rather in elements which are in simple contiguity with each other. The
> poetic function is different from the strictly referential function by the
> strong *linkage of contrast with equivalence*. [65]

It is the idea of *contrast*, perceptible opposition, that is important in the
poetic function. For it is not only that parallelism involves equivalence,
but that within that equivalence there is an opposition. For example, one
can parallel any adjective with any other adjective and create a morphological parallelism, but the combination of *the weak boy // the strong boy* is,
under normal circumstances, a more effective parallelism than *the weak
boy // the blond boy* because within the equivalent terms *weak* and *strong*
there is an inherent contrast, whereas this contrast does not exist between

weak and *blond*. (But in a text with pervasive parallelism, which sets up
the expectation of effective parallelism in the mind of the reader, there will
be a tendency to equate or contrast *weak* and *blond*.) Thus the perception
of contrast (and that includes positive or negative contrast) within a set of
equivalences makes a parallelism effective. The contrast may exist as a semantic fact (as in synonyms, antonyms, etc.) or may be a product of the
formal structure of the text. In a text where the generation of such contrasts is the constructive principle, we have poetry.

To illustrate this let us compare one small section from the prose and
poetic accounts concerning what Sisera was given to drink.

Jud 4:19   ויאמר אליה השקיני נא מעט מים כי צמתי
                            ותפתח את נאוד החלב ותשקהו ותכסהו

He said to her, "Please give me a little drink of water,
for I am thirsty. And she opened the milk container
and gave him a drink, and covered him.

Jud 5:25   מים שאל
                            חלב נתנה
                            בספל אדירים הקריבה חמאה

Water he asked,
Milk she gave;
In a princely bowl she offered curds.

The prose account contains parallelism. Jud 4:19 repeats the same root,
השקה, and uses *water* and *milk*, both potable liquids (a semantic equivalence) and both nouns used as direct objects (a grammatical equivalence).
But not much is made, on a structural level, of the correspondence between *water* and *milk*. There is a subtle semantic dissonance between Sisera's request and Yael's compliance, but because the clauses expressing
them are syntactically different (i.e., not equivalent), the contrast between
them is not brought sharply into focus. In Jud 5:25, however, the contrast
between *water* and *milk* is unmistakable because the clauses in which they
occur are exactly parallel syntactically (even in the order of the components), and there is an inherent semantic contrast in *asked* and *gave* and a
morphological contrast in the gender of *he asked // she gave*. This forces
the contrast between *water* and *milk* into the mind of the reader; not only
are the two nouns parallel in the sense that they come from the same morphological class, but they take on a *semantic* contrast as well. That is, they
involve semantic effects, as Werth calls them. These effects are enhanced
by the addition of בספל אדירים הקריבה חמאה, which is not to be misun-

derstood as yet a third action, but as a repeated expression (a semantic equivalent) of the action of חלב נתנה. The semantic equivalence of
חלב נתנה with בספל אדירים הקריבה חמאה underlines the semantic contrast
with מים שאל. (חלב נתנה and בספל אדירים הקריבה חמאה have their own
contrasts within their equivalences: the second clause upgrades the first,
making a noble-religious [הקריבה־אדירים] gesture out of a common, every-
day one.) As Waugh has indicated, in the poetic function there is a strong
linkage of contrast with equivalence. Such contrast as there is in prose is
mainly a product of the *contiguity* of elements rather than a product of
equivalences. If there is a perceptible contrast between *water* and *milk* in
Jud 4:19, it is because the two occur contiguously, but there is no structural reinforcement for this contrast.

Waugh goes on to point out that

> this projection of both equivalence and contrast is not only a way of giving
> an internal, autonomous structure to the poem, but is also a way of *tran-*
> *scending the linearity* proper to any linguistic text. Through parallelisms the
> text is no longer a linear string but is subdivided in various ways. . . .
> Again, the more strictly linear character of prose is separated from the more
> non-linear character of poetry. [65]

Jud 4:19 contains linear actions; the story moves from one thing to the
next: he asked for water, she opened the milk container, she gave him
drink, she covered him. Jud 5:25 breaks the linearity first of all by expressing what looks like three actions but what really represents two. Thus
each clause does not have a unique temporal slot in a sequence as it does in
the prose version. The synonymity or simultaneity of the last two phrases
can then be read back into the first, so that the asking and giving are not
sequential but simultaneous—two parts of one picture. The poetic version
is more nonlinear.[14]

This can be seen even more clearly in the description of Sisera's murder.
The prose account, which I have set out clause by clause for the sake of
clarity, is found in Jud 4:21; the poetic account, following the massoretic
arrangement, is in Jud 5:26–27.

Jud 4:21	ותקח יעל אשת חבר את יתד האהל
	ותשם את המקבת בידה
	ותבוא אליו בלאט
	ותתקע את היתד ברקתו
	ותצנח בארץ
	והוא נרדם ויעף
	וימת

And Yael, Heber's wife, took the tent peg,
And she placed the mallet in her hand,
And she approached him stealthily,
And she drove the peg into his skull,
And it sank down to the ground—
[he was asleep, having been exhausted]—
And he died.

Jud 5:26–27

ידה ליתד תשלחנה
וימינה להלמות עמלים
והלמה סיסרא מחקה ראשו
ומחצה וחלפה רקתו
בין רגליה כרע נפל שכב
בין רגליה כרע נפל
באשר כרע שם נפל שדוד

Her hand to the peg she stretched,
And her right hand to the workmen's hammer,
And she hammered Sisera, crushed his head,
And split and pierced his skull.
At her feet he crumpled, fell, lay,
At her feet he crumpled, fell,
Where he crumpled there he lay, destroyed.

The clauses in the prose account are parallel in that they all begin with
verbs, and two of them (ותתקע את היתד ברקתו and ותשם את המקבת בידה)
have the same syntax and a number of other equivalences. But the over-
whelming impression is one of linearity; we are shown step by step what
Yael did and then what Sisera did. Now the same sequence is present in the
poetic account: the taking of the murder weapons, the piercing through of
Sisera's skull, the collapse and expiration of Sisera—but the stringlike
quality is gone. The parallel structure subdivides the action into a *continuous but yet overlapping sequence.* As she took the peg she also grasped the
hammer; with it she hammered Sisera, crushing his head; she crushed it as
she pierced through his skull. Sisera's expiration is described by a series of
repeating verbs: he crumpled, fell, lay, crumpled, fell, crumpled, fell dead.
Does this represent one action or many? The "synonymous" parallelism
here may not be a repeated expression of one action, but an expression of
several similar and repeated actions—the writhing of the dying Sisera. The
careful temporal structure laid out in the prose—1) Sisera had been ex-
hausted (ויעף), 2) he had fallen asleep (נרדם), 3) and now died (וימת)—is
refashioned into a nontemporal picture of a man dying, dead, dying, dead
at Yael's feet.

The tension between prosaic linearity and poetic contiguity is perhaps best illustrated in the scholarly discussion of Jud 5:26a, especially in regard to the word pair יד // ימין ("hand // right hand"). A "prosaic" reading of this verse specifies that it refers to two separate actions (either sequential or simultaneous), as found also in Jud 4:21. These two actions presumably involved the use of two different hands, since the alternative would be to have Yael juggling both the peg and the hammer in one hand—a patently ridiculous, if not impossible, feat. But the parallelism has equated the two actions, partially by its syntax (notice that the syntax is not parallel in Jud 4:21), and partially by the use of the pair יד and ימין. In other words, the verse may enumerate two physical actions but it has fused them together into a unity representing Yael's preparations to murder Sisera.[15]

This unity is undermined by scholars who insist, wrongly in my opinion, that יד means "left hand" when it is paired with ימין.[16] To do so suggests that the verse wishes to contrast what the right hand and the left hand were holding; but if this had been intended the pair ימין // שמאל ("right // left") would have been used (cf. Jud 7:20). If there is a contrast to be made in our passage it is between Yael's hand and Sisera's head (and then Yael's feet). יד // ימין are not coordinates, but rather a term // subordinate; that is, יד is the more general term and ימין is a subcategory of it (see below, chapter 4). A look at other verses containing this pair will prove the point.

Ps 138:7b

תשלח ידך
ותושיעני ימינך

You extend your hand;
Your right hand saves me.

Isa 48:13

אף ידי יסדה ארץ
וימיני טפחה שמים

My own hand founded the earth;
My right hand spread out the sky.

Ps 89:26

ושמתי בים ידו
ובנהרות ימינו

I will set upon the sea his hand;
And upon the rivers his right hand.

In these verses it is even doubtful that reference is being made to two distinct actions; certainly it is not a question of two separate hands. God does not extend one hand and save with the other, nor did he use one to form the earth and the other to form the sky. Even a distributional reading, yielding something like "My right and left hands made the earth and sky" for Isa 48 : 13, will not help, for here again ימין // שמאל would have been used, as in

Pr 3 : 16

ארך ימים בימינה
בשמאלה עשר וכבוד

Length of days is in her right hand;
In her left hand are wealth and honor. [Cf. also Isa 9 : 19]

In all of these verses, whether they involve one actual action or two, the separateness of the parts is suppressed and homogenized. The parallelism forges oneness out of twoness. The point in Jud 5 : 26, and in the other verses employing יד // ימין, is not which hand did what, but that the actions were performed, as we say in English, handily.

Finally, the idea of terseness, which we found in Kugel and in Empson, is also present in more technical language in Waugh.

> In any linguistic discourse, there is a constant interplay of two major dichotomies: *explicitness* vs. *ellipsis* on the one hand and *redundancy* vs. *ambiguity* on the other hand. Moreover, these two dichotomies share the common property of posing the problem of the amount of information conveyed by the given discourse. . . . Redundant signs are those signs which inform about other signs in the text and thus cannot be said to provide independent information. . . . Ambiguous signs are those which, even when in context of other signs, provide more than one interpretation. . . . Elliptical structures are those in which certain signs have been left out, but are assumed to be known to the addressee, while explicit structures are those fully replete with signs. . . . Now, the poem, which is focussed upon itself and upon the sign as sign, plays with both of these dichotomies, and while on the one hand poetic expression may be elliptic, on the other hand it extracts from the reduced expressions a multiplicity of meaning (ambiguity). [73]

In a later chapter we will explore in greater detail the role of parallelism vis à vis redundancy and ambiguity. For now we can conclude that terseness and parallelism seem to be the characteristics of poetic language whether one examines it from the point of view of a linguist, literary critic, or biblical scholar. Poetry uses parallelism as its constitutive or constructive device, while nonpoetry, though it contains parallelism, does not structure its message on a systematic use of parallelism.

In biblical poetry, as elsewhere, the structuring of the poem involves parallelism on many levels of language at once. Syntactic and semantic parallelism are the most obvious, but there are others as well. The combined effect of these parallelisms makes parallelism, the poetic function, operative as the dominant function of the poem.

The subject of my discourse is biblical parallelism, not biblical poetry, but because the two are closely allied, it was important to separate them as well as to show their interconnection. There are several benefits to be derived from the study of biblical parallelism. One is to increase our understanding of biblical Hebrew, its elasticity, the possibilities for its expressive permutations. Parallelism activates all levels of language, and what better way is there to observe these levels than to see them at work in parallelism. Second, through the study of parallelism we come to a better understanding of poetic texts. If, indeed, parallelism is the constructive device of poetry, then we cannot comprehend a poem's structure, its unity, until we have discovered which things it equates and which it contrasts. And related to the unity of a poem is its message, its meaning. The poetic function—the "focus on the message for its own sake"—is achieved through parallelism; and so parallelism becomes our entrée into the message. Through the relationships which parallelism creates we are shown the poem's meaning.

II

THE
LINGUISTIC
STUDY OF
BIBLICAL
PARALLELISM

It is not surprising, in view of the nexus between poetry and parallelism, that few biblical studies start out focused on parallelism. They begin, rather, as studies of biblical poetry which, because of its nature, sooner or later include or become studies of parallelism. Thus for the history of the study of biblical parallelism one must survey the history of the study of biblical poetry. Fortunately, a large part of this research is now available: Kugel traces the "idea of biblical poetry" from postbiblical times until Lowth, and post-Lowthian studies are summarized in O'Connor, *HVS*. So it remains only to give a brief account of the most recent studies, with respect to their stance on the linguistic analysis of parallelism.[1]

Most contemporary scholars have abandoned the models of Lowth and his successors and are seeking new models for a reassessment of biblical poetry. Almost all of them (e.g., Collins, Cooper, Geller, Greenstein, O'Connor, Pardee—and Kugel is the exception here) have looked to linguistics for a model. In this they are not unlike scholars of other poetic traditions, for, despite some valid criticism of its methodology, linguistics is fast becoming the prism through which poetry is viewed. This prism may in time be replaced by another, but for now it is showing us a spectrum of features that was never visible before.

Perhaps the most obvious linguistic feature that recent studies have called to our attention is syntax. Almost all current studies of biblical poetry center on syntactic analyses; the analysis may be on the level of surface structure, major syntactic components or constituents, or the deep structure—but in one way or another, a description and/or comparison of the syntax of adjacent lines is involved. When a certain degree of matching or correlation of the syntax of adjacent lines is recognized, the scholar begins to speak of parallelism, and, indeed, may define parallelism in terms of this syntactic matching. What is confusing, albeit interesting from the point of view of the history of this scholarship, is that each scholar, because he is looking at a different structural level, has a different threshold at which point two lines are deemed parallel.

Terence Collins, for instance, whose 1978 study is one of the earliest of this new wave, examines the constituents of a sentence (subject, object, verb, modifier of the verb) and finds that these occur in four basic patterns which yield four Basic Sentences.[2] Since the order of the constituents is not significant, and the constituent may consist of one of a number of form classes (e.g., subject may be pronoun, noun, noun phrase, noun clause) it is clear that Collins is not operating on the outermost surface structure of the text. But neither is he reaching the deep structure, for he considers אני ידעתי אפרים, "I knew Ephraim," and וישראל לא נכחד ממני, "And Israel was not hidden from me" (Hos 5 : 3) to be two different basic sentences (NP¹—V—NP² and NP¹—V—M). (A generative linguist would see that this verse involves both active-passive and positive-negative transformations and could be considered two realizations of one basic sentence, if one works on the level of deep structure.) Collins then examines poetic lines from the prophetic corpus and finds that there are four general Line-Types:

I   The line contains only one Basic Sentence.

II   The line contains two Basic Sentences of the same kind, such that all of the same constituents appear in both sentences.

III The line contains two Basic Sentences of the same kind, but some of the constituents do not appear in both (i.e., there is ellipsis).

IV The line contains two different Basic Sentences.

Collins goes on to document occurrences of each Line-Type in all its permutations, called Line-Forms, and makes a number of significant observations about the frequency and patterning of these Line-Forms in various prophetic books. My interest in his study, however, is not in what he has to say about prophecy or poetry, but in what he has to say about parallelism. Because Collins sticks with the old notion that parallelism is a semantic phenomenon, he fails to realize that he had in his hands an important tool

for analyzing parallelism in its grammatical aspect. In reality, at least three
of his Line-Types—II, III, and IV (and Type I, too, if taken together with
an adjacent line)—potentially contain parallelism. But it is only in Type II
that he sees the connection with parallelism, and to a lesser extent in Type
III. Nevertheless, despite this severe limitation, Collins does perceive that
there is a certain tension between his system of categorization and the common system of semantic classification of parallel lines. And it is here that
he finds the weakness of the latter—its inappropriateness for describing
poetic lines.

> In most treatments of the subject, this kind of line [Line-Type II] is taken to
> be *the typical* line of Hebrew poetry, but it is questionable whether this sta-
> tus of pre-eminence is really warranted. One suspects that the emphasis
> placed on such lines is due chiefly to the fact that they provide the best illus-
> trations of semantic parallelism. If this latter is regarded as the hall-mark of
> Hebrew poetry, then it is natural that these lines should be elevated to the
> position of some kind of "pure ideal" of *the* Hebrew line and approached
> with quasi-metaphysical awe. An analysis based on grammatical structure
> makes it clear that such an attitude is quite unfounded. Type II accounts for
> scarcely a quarter of the lines in the prophets. . . .
>   It is true that semantic parallelism appears at its best in these lines, but
> when we try to use it as a criterion for classification we immediately meet
> with difficulties . . . in classifying lines according to semantic content we
> are often led to ignore the more basic structural patterns a poet is using.
> Two lines may have the same constituents repeated according to a specific
> pattern, and yet semantically they could go very different ways . . . it is the
> structural [i.e., grammatical] classification of lines that is the basic one.
> [92–93]

In an important advance over earlier studies, Collins puts grammar ahead
of semantics as the key to the description of Hebrew poetic patterning,
although, to be sure, he recognizes that the two interconnect (cf. 229). He
fails only to realize that grammatical structuring may be involved in parallelism no less than semantic structuring. This failure, common though it is
in studies from the last two centuries, is all the more unfortunate because
its antidote was already present in Lowth's definition of parallelism. Lowth
identified as parallel two propositions equivalent in sense *or* "similar . . .
in the form of Grammatical Construction." His successors concentrated on
the first definition (i.e., similar in sense) and ignored the second. It has
only been with the rise of modern linguistics, especially generative grammar, that biblical scholars have begun seriously to analyze the grammatical
structure of poetry (as Collins does) and to realize that from this analysis
may emerge a new way to define parallelism (as Collins does not).

The grammatical approach is espoused in a study by Stephen Geller, prepared independently of Collins's work at about the same time. Like Collins, Geller analyzes the grammatical constituents, but he is able to move to a deeper grammatical level than Collins because he introduces the idea of the "reconstructed sentence." By reconstructing the one basic sentence underlying the two parallel lines, Geller is able to fill in ellipsed terms and to equate on a deeper level constituents that are "incongruent" on the surface level. So, for example, Geller (*Parallelism*, 17) shows that in

2 Sam 22:14   ירעם מן שמים ה'
                                  ועליון יתן קולו

YHWH thundered from heaven;
Elyon sent forth his voice.

the terms ירעם, "thundered" and יתן קולו, "sent forth his voice," although grammatically incongruent, are nevertheless grammatically "compatible" because they serve the same function in the reconstructed sentence, which Geller diagrams as

ה'	מן שמים	ירעם
עליון		יתן קולו
YHWH	from heaven	thundered
Elyon		sent forth his voice

["From heaven" belongs to both lines but is ellipsed in the second.]

Geller considers both clauses as different realizations of the same underlying sentence, while Collins would consider this verse as Line-Type IV, a line containing two different Basic Sentences. Geller's analysis is therefore on a deeper linguistic level than Collins's; it penetrates deeper into the underlying grammatical structure of the lines.

Geller's study is also superior to Collins's from the point of view of the study of parallelism, for, as the title of his book (*Parallelism in Early Biblical Poetry*) shows, he is interested specifically in the phenomenon of parallelism; he is not dealing with it incidentally in the context of a study of poetry. This book was inspired by the work of Roman Jakobson, and its purpose was to establish a "method for the analysis of major aspects of parallelism, with emphasis on grammatical and semantic parallelism" (4).[3] Thus grammatical parallelism, which Collins let slip through his fingers, is the major focus of Geller's work, although he is always aware of semantic parallelism as well.

Grammatical parallelism reaches its ultimate prominence in Edward

Greenstein's "How Does Parallelism Mean?" Cognizant of the work of Collins, Geller, and others, Greenstein goes farther and makes grammatical parallelism serve as the definition for all parallelism. Parallelism for Greenstein is the repetition of a syntactic pattern, regardless of the semantic content; in other words, parallelism is grammatical parallelism. Now, to be sure, grammatical parallelism has long been *part* of the definition of parallelism—from Lowth's dictum and Casanowicz's definition which Greenstein cites,[4] to the recent studies that I have been discussing; but Greenstein is the first biblicist to *limit* parallelism to grammatical parallelism alone. This would mean, theoretically at least, that the same semantic content expressed in syntactically different clauses would not be considered parallel; and that two syntactically similar clauses, no matter how different their contents, would automatically be parallel. (I am speaking of adjacent or juxtaposed clauses.) Now such extremes are rare, because grammatical and semantic parallelisms generally co-occur; but our theoretical constructions do exist. A verse like

Ps 106:35   ויתערבו בגוים
                             וילמדו מעשיהם

            They intermingled with the nations;
            They learned their ways.

is semantically parallel but not syntactically parallel (even on the level of deep structure—see below); while a verse like

Ps 111:5   טרף נתן ליראיו
                             יזכר לעולם בריתו

            Food he gives to his fearers;
            He remembers his covenant forever.

is syntactically parallel on the surface structure (although one line has an indirect object and the other has an adverb), but the semantic relationship between the lines is not immediately apparent (cf. also Ps 111:4a and 5a). To be sure, these verses are somewhat out of the ordinary. As Greenstein explains, grammatical and semantic parallelisms tend to co-occur because there is a psychological nexus between structure and meaning.

> Most significantly parallelism contributes to the meaning of Biblical verse by structuring the ways in which we perceive its content. The presentation of lines in parallelism has the effect of reinforcing the semantic association between them. It has long been observed that when discrete materials appear to us in similar form, we are led to seek, and find, some meaningful correlation between them. This, for example, is the underpinning principle

of rhyme: rhyme creates or tightens an association between two or more words or phrases. Repetition of syntactic structure, which is what I have explained as parallelism, can perform the same function. The psychological nexus between semantic sense and syntactic structure has been demonstrated experimentally. When subjects were presented with a sentence of a particular grammatical form and were then asked to produce another sentence having the same form, subjects tended to formulate a sentence that not only mirrored the structure of the model but also echoed something of its semantics. For example, the test sentence *The lazy student failed the exam* elicited such responses as: *The smart girl passed the test. The industrious pupil passed the course. The brilliant boy studied the paper.* [64]

This statement has important implications for understanding parallelism, some of which will be further explained in subsequent chapters, but for now I will comment on its relevance to Greenstein's insistence that parallelism is exclusively a matter of grammar. It is true that a similarity in structure leads to a perception of some correlation in meaning. We can see this at work in Ps 111 : 5: we tend to seek, and find, a semantic relationship between the two lines even though there are no word pairs or overall semantic equivalence. We equate "giving food" with "remembering the covenant"; "his fearers" are those with whom he has made "his covenant." Or we look for a historical nexus: the covenant at Sinai co-occurred with the providing of food in the wilderness. But just because similarity in structure promotes a semantic relationship does not mean that difference in structure prevents it. As our other example, Ps 106 : 35, shows, there can be semantic correlations even in the absence of structural repetition. Should we not consider Ps 106 : 35 to be a semantic parallelism? The psycholinguistic results that Greenstein cites likewise do not prove that semantic similarity cannot occur in lines differently structured. They simply underscore the tendency for grammatical and semantic parallelisms to co-occur, because both are part of the same associative process (see chapter 4). In short, I cannot agree with Greenstein that syntactic repetition lies at the base of parallelism and that semantic parallelism is a result of this repetition. In many cases it may be the other way around: the desire to repeat a thought may have produced a syntactic repetition along with it. There is no reason to give syntax priority over semantics (or vice versa); both are important aspects of parallelism, along with some other aspects to be mentioned later.

But let us return to a fuller explanation of Greenstein's thesis. What Greenstein means by syntactic repetition is syntactic repetition at the level of the deep structure; syntactically similar sentences have the same deep structure no matter what their surface structure may be. (If the surface structure is identical, then they are also parallel even if the deep structure is not—cf. Greenstein's note 20.) By a method similar to but linguistically more rigorous than Geller's reconstructed sentence, Greenstein shows through a series of tree diagrams that parallel sentences have the same deep structure.[5] Thus, for example, two clauses as apparently disparate as

Ps 105:17   שלח לפניהם איש
                            לעבד נמכר יוסף

He sent before them a man
As a slave was Joseph sold.

are diagrammed (Greenstein, p. 48, after removing the passivization from the second clause) as:

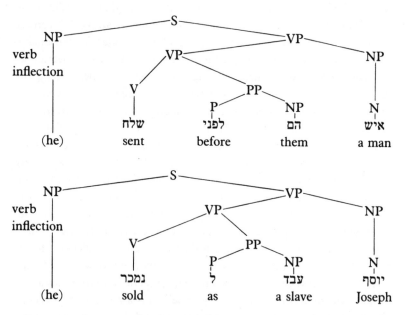

The diagram should be read as follows. S is a sentence which consists of a subject (or topic) represented by a noun-phrase (NP) and a predicate (or comment) represented by a verb-phrase (VP). The NP is manifested in this case through the pronominal inflection of the verb ("he"). The VP comprises a VP and an object in the form of a NP. The VP itself comprises a verb (V) and an adverbial modifier in the form of a prepositional phrase (PP), consisting of a preposition (P) and a noun-phrase. The NP which is the direct object of the verb is represented by a noun (N).

Greenstein's work has the merit of attempting to put the analysis of parallelism on a firm linguistic (*viz.* grammatical) basis. His concern, like Geller's and mine, was specifically with parallelism, not with poetry. Greenstein took grammar about as far as it could go in terms of parallelism by making it the criterion for the identification of parallelism.

M. O'Connor's concern in *Hebrew Verse Structure*, on the other hand, was with poetry, not with parallelism per se, and he took grammar as far as it could go as the basis for describing biblical poetry.[6]

Collins and Geller accepted the convention in modern scholarship of what constitutes a poetic line and did not attempt to define it; they were concerned with describing the various grammatical patterns that occur within or between lines of poetry. O'Connor's quest was to define the poetic line, and this he did solely in terms of grammar: a line consists of a series of syntactic constraints—limits on the number of units, constituents, and clauses that it may contain. O'Connor's use of grammar to define the line is analogous to Greenstein's use of grammar to define parallelism.

In doing this, O'Connor gives primacy to the line over the couplet as the basic poetic entity, whereas the others, because they are dealing with syntactic relationships often involving more than one line, tend to give more prominence to the couplet. Since the line is of primary concern to O'Connor, the relationship between lines, which in many cases involves parallelism, becomes secondary. O'Connor's study, then, like Collins's, is a study of the grammatical structure of poetry rather than a study of parallelism per se. It does, however, have much to contribute to the study of parallelism. I will summarize it in part here and will have recourse to many of its details in subsequent chapters.

O'Connor disarms and probably antagonizes biblical scholars by calling parallelism "a congeries of phenomena" (*HVS*, 5). But in saying this he does not mean that parallelism does not exist or that it is not important, only that it is composed of many different phenomena, some of them syntactic and others not, some of them admitting to precise description and others not. O'Connor feels that the reason that former scholars have had so much trouble defining parallelism is that they confused these different phenomena. They failed to perceive what I call the multiaspect and multilevel nature of parallelism; that is, parallelism may involve semantics, grammar, and/or other linguistic features, and it may occur on the level of the word, line, couplet, or over a greater textual span.

The parts of parallelism that O'Connor deals with most extensively (i.e., those that are most amenable to his linguistic approach) are those that have received the most attention in recent biblical studies: word pairs and grammatical parallelism on the line level. Since it is the latter that we have been tracking, we will present O'Connor's contribution to it here and leave his discussion of word pairs for a later chapter.

The name that O'Connor gives to grammatical parallelism on the level of the line is "matching." Lines match "if their syntactic structures are identical" (*HVS*, 119), or, as O'Connor's modification goes: "two lines match if they are identical in constituent structure except for gapping" (*HVS*, 128). As in the previously cited studies, word order and gapping do not affect the syntactic structure. It is tempting to equate O'Connor's matching with Greenstein's grammatical parallelism (and in fact Greenstein seems to do so in his note 14), but it is actually closer to Collins's Type II and Type III sentences. O'Connor considers matching to be a correspondence on the surface structure, because "constituent structure" is determined on the basis of the surface structure of the clause (cf. *HVS*, 314). Therefore, O'Connor's matching accounts for only part of the lines that Greenstein would consider parallel. In fact, O'Connor himself finds that only about one-third of his corpus contains matching and declares that "matching does not involve all lines which could be regarded as 'parallelistic'" (*HVS*, 119).[7]

Although O'Connor's notion of line-level grammatical parallelism is more limited than Greenstein's, his notion of what can be considered parallelistic is much broader, for matching, while it is "the phenomenon most widely referred to as parallelism" (*HVS*, 119), is only one of several phenomena that create parallelism. My own view of parallelism agrees most closely with O'Connor's (although I feel that for grammatical parallelism one must go to the deep structure as Greenstein has done). Like all the aforementioned scholars, I find linguistics to be helpful in analyzing parallelism. But linguistics, it must be remembered, is more than grammar; and parallelism is more than grammar, too. Linguistics includes phonology, morphology, syntax, and semantics, and all of these play a role in parallelism.[8] As Roman Jakobson said, and his statement has inspired more than one study of biblical parallelism, "Pervasive parallelism inevitably activates all the levels of language—the distinctive features, inherent and prosodic, the morphological and syntactic categories and forms, the lexical units and their semantic classes in both their convergences and divergences acquire an autonomous poetic value" (*GPRF*, 423). Indeed, as O'Connor would agree, parallelism activates all the levels of language, not just the syntactic; and as Jakobson would have approved, we should examine as many of these levels as possible. In order to avoid confusion, I will use the term *aspect* to refer to the area of linguistics activated (phonology, morphology, etc.) and the term *level* to specify how much of the textual structure is involved—in most cases either the word or the line or clause. The aspects which are most evident in biblical parallelism are the semantic and grammatical aspects. These have received the most attention on the level of the line, but treatments of them have by no means been exhaustive. Analysis of the lexical aspect on the word level—word pairs—has been going on for some time but has missed the mark, linguistically speaking. Analysis of the phonological aspect has barely begun.

I will deal with each aspect separately, but it is the intertwining of aspects and levels that contributes to the feeling of pervasiveness in biblical poetic parallelism. If we accept that the poetic function (i.e. parallelism) makes contiguous those things which are similar ("projects . . . from the axis of selection into the axis of combination" [*LP*, 358]), then pervasive parallelism (or canonical—Jakobson's terms for the kind of parallelism in the Bible and elsewhere) does so in many ways, projecting from many axes of selection into many axes of combination. Parallelism, as discussed in chapter 1, is a matter of equivalences (or correspondences) and contrasts, or perhaps better, contrasts within equivalences. And the more equivalences and/or contrasts that can be brought into play, the stronger the feeling of parallelism will be. A small example will illustrate.

Lam 5:2   נחלתנו נהפכה לזרים
                בתינו לנכרים

> Our land was turned over to strangers;
> Our houses to foreigners.

On the line level it is easy to see that the syntax is the same in both lines (with a gapped verb in the second line). There is syntactic equivalence even without looking below the surface structure. The semantics of the two lines is likewise very close. Some would call it synonymous, stressing the equivalence. Kugel, who insists that B goes beyond A, stresses the contrast. One could make a case for Kugel's view in that losing houses is even more severe than losing a land holding. And while זר and נכרי occur elsewhere as a word pair (Isa 28:21; 61:5; Pr 27:2; Job 19:15), they are not totally synonymous. זר is used for one who is not a member of the "in-group," be he a member of the household (1 Kgs 3:18), relative (Deut 25:5), member of the priesthood (Num 1:51 and passim), or member of one's society as a whole (Job 15:19); נכרי is used only of a non-Israelite (cf. Gen 17:12; Ex 12:43; Neh 9:2). So the first line of Lam 5:2 taken alone could signify the loss of one's ancestral land to a nonrelative, but the second line redefines this with forceful clarity by speaking of the loss of one's living place to a non-Israelite.

On the word level there are grammatical equivalences and also contrasts: נחלתנו and בתינו are both from the same word class (nouns with possessive suffixes) and serve the same syntactic function (subject). But the first is feminine and singular and the second is masculine and plural. There is complete grammatical identity between לזרים and לנכרים.

In addition to these grammatical and semantic aspects, phonology comes into play. There are three phonologic equivalences in these two lines:

נחלתנו נהפכה ל // לנכרים

nḥl . . . nh . . . l // lnk . . .

נחלתנו // בתינו

-ataynu // -ataynu

לזרים // לנכרים

-rim // -rim

The phonologic equivalences underline the semantic and grammatical ones. In the last two phonologic pairings, *-ataynu // -ataynu* and *-rim // -rim*, words which are grammatically and semantically similar also contain similar sounds. The first, *nḥl // lnk*, is more striking (but not uncommon, as I will show in chapter 5), because it equates by sound words which are not otherwise linguistically equivalent. This pairing thereby binds the two lines even more closely, forming a frame of sounds around this verse.

All of these equivalences are present in a relatively small and simple parallelism, containing only five words approximately evenly distributed in two lines with the same surface structure. It stands to reason that in longer, more complex parallelisms the possibilities for various types of equivalences and contrasts increase. Since I cannot present all of them, I have elected to isolate several and will devote separate chapters to them. I will also point out, occasionally, the tension that may exist among these equivalences—i.e., among the different aspects of parallelism. The aspects to be discussed are 1) the grammatical, 2) the lexical, 3) semantic, and 4) the phonological. These will be analyzed on the levels of the word and the line or clause. The following chart provides an overview of these aspects and how they manifest themselves on the two levels.

Level	Aspect		
	Grammatical	Lexical-Semantic	Phonological
Word	morphological equivalence and/or contrast	word pairs	sound pairs
Line or clause	syntactic equivalence and/or contrast	semantic relationship between lines	phonological equivalence of lines

As the chart shows, the goal of this book is to present an overarching, integrated, and linguistically based description of biblical parallelism.

In most cases I will be dealing with lines that are parallel, but, when it comes to the level of the word or other single constituent of a line, one must include, as Dahood has done (cf. *RSP* I, 80–81, 87), words and phrases that are in juxtaposition or in collocation when these show the same kinds of linguistic correspondences.[9] (Juxtaposition is the occurrence of both parts of the pair within one phrase;[10] collocation is an unspecified relationship at an unspecified distance within the same passage.) The same word pair or sound pair may appear in parallel lines, or in combination within the same line or at a greater distance from one another, no matter if the passage is prose or poetry. They are thus to be regarded as part of the same phenomenon of parallelism. The principle behind the pairing is the same, regardless of the context in which it occurs. Parallelism, juxtaposition, and collocation are all part of the same phenomenon of combining elements which are in some way linguistically equivalent. This is what I mean by parallelism.

That the pairing in juxtaposition and collocation is in essence the same as the pairing in parallel lines can be demonstrated by the fact that the same pair of words may occur in all three arrangements. One example is אהל, "tent," and משכן, "tabernacle, dwelling place." This pair is found in parallel lines in

Num 24:5   מה טבו אהליך יעקב
                               משכנתיך ישראל

How good are your tents [ʾhl], O Jacob;
Your dwelling places [mškn], O Israel. [cf. also Isa 54:2; Jer 30:18;
Ps 78:60]

This pair is found in what I would call a prose parallelism, but what Dahood calls juxtaposition, in

2 Sam 7:6   ואהיה מתהלך באהל ובמשכן

      I have moved about in Tent and Tabernacle [*bʾhl wbmškn*].

The pair is in juxtaposition in

Job 21:28   ואיה אהל משכנות רשעים

      Where is the dwelling-tent of the wicked [*ʾhl mšknwt*].

The juxtaposition is reversed in Ps 78:55 and Ps 120:5. And, finally, the pair is in collocation in

Ps 15:1   מי יגור באהלך
                מי ישכן בהר קדשך

      Who can sojourn in your tent [*ʾhl*];
      Who can dwell [*yškn*] on your holy mountain.

The last verse is particularly instructive because it not only shows that parallelism, juxtaposition, and collocation belong to the same phenomenon, but also that equivalence in one linguistic aspect need not imply equivalence in all linguistic aspects.

I have adopted Dahood's designation of "collocation" for the word pair in Ps 15:1 even though the verse consists of parallel lines. What makes the pairing of our words here different from their pairing in Num 24:5 is that in Num 24:5 ʾhl and mškn are both lexical and semantic equivalents while in Ps 15:1 ʾhl and yškn are lexical equivalents but not semantic equivalents (the semantic pairs are הר קדשך // אהלך, "your tent // your holy mountain," and יגור // ישכן, "sojourn // dwell"). If we bring grammar into the discussion we see that the pair is also grammatically equivalent in Num 24:5; in Ps 15:1 there is no direct grammatical relationship between אהלך and ישכן.[11] Thus the types of equivalences manifest in parallelism can be quite different. We have here two parallelisms in which the same lexical pair behaves very differently. Thus we see, once again, that to base an analysis of parallelism solely on semantics or grammar is to miss some of the subtle play that may be present. Parallelism gets its effectiveness from the interplay of equivalences in the various linguistic aspects. But before we can appreciate this interplay we must investigate these aspects individually. This is the task to which the next three chapters are devoted.

III

THE GRAMMATICAL ASPECT

The grammatical aspect of parallelism—grammatical equivalence and/
or contrast—is one of the fundamental aspects of biblical parallelism.
There is almost always some degree of grammatical correspondence between parallel lines, and in many cases it is the basic structuring device of
the parallelism—the feature that creates the perception of parallelism. In
this chapter I will examine this grammatical aspect more extensively in order to see exactly which grammatical equivalences are present and how
they manifest themselves.[1] Since the study of grammar is usually sub-
divided into morphology and syntax, I will subdivide grammatical parallelism into these two categories. Syntactic parallelism is the syntactic
equivalence of one line with another line. (Most studies of grammatical
parallelism have dealt only with a comparison of the syntax of the lines as a
whole.) Morphologic parallelism involves the morphologic equivalence or
contrast of individual constituents of the lines. Many lines contain more
than one type of grammatical parallelism; and sometimes the boundary between morphologic and syntactic parallelism is indistinct.

Those who have studied the grammar of parallel lines are well aware that
the surface structure of the lines is identical in only a small percentage of
cases. One such case is

Ps 103:10   לא כחטאינו עשה לנו
                          ולא כעונתינו גמל עלינו

    Not according to our sins did he deal with us;
    And not according to our transgressions did he requite us.

The surface structure of the two lines is the same, both in respect to syntax
and morphology. Every component of the first line is mirrored in the sec-

ond. The syntax of both lines is Negative—Prepositional Phrase—Verb—
Indirect Object. The corresponding terms are morphologically identical:

לא // לֹא
"not // not"
negative particle

כחטאינו // כעונתינו
"according to our sins // according to our transgressions"
preposition + noun (masc. pl.) + possessive suffix (1st person pl.)

עשה // גמל
"he dealt // he requited"
verb (*qal*, 3rd person, masc., sing., perfect)

לנו // עלינו
"to us // on us"
preposition + 1st person pl. suffix

This is actually an example of grammatical identity or repetition. While
there is not lexical repetition (the same words are not used in both lines),
there is the repetition of the same grammatical structure. This verse is the
exception, for more often we find grammatical equivalence: the second
line substitutes something grammatically different, but equivalent, for a
grammatical feature in the first line. The substitution may involve only one
element, e.g., a pronoun in place of a noun, in which case we have morphologic parallelism; or it may involve a transformation in the syntax of
the entire line, e.g., from indicative to interrogative, and then we would
speak of syntactic parallelism. The important thing to remember is that
although there is a difference in the two grammatical structures, they are
in some way equivalent to one another. In nonparallelistic discourse only
one would occur, and either one could substitute for the other (semantics
permitting); but in parallelistic discourse they are *both* present. Thus
grammar has been projected from the axis of selection to the axis of
combination.

MORPHOLOGIC PARALLELISM

In this section I will present examples of morphologic pairings from different word classes, and pairings from the same word class with different
morphologic elements.

A. Morphologic Pairs from Different Word Classes

This type of parallelism involves words from different parts of speech. The following kinds of pairing may occur.

1. Noun // Pronoun

Ps 33:2   הודו לה' בכנור
                                          בנבל עשור זמרו לו

> Praise *YHWH* with the lyre;
> With the ten-stringed harp sing to *him*.

Ps 33:8   יראו מה' כל הארץ
                                        ממנו יגורו כל ישבי תבל

> Let all the earth fear *YHWH*;
> Let all the world's inhabitants dread *him*.

2. Noun/Pronoun // Relative Clause[2]

Ps 105:26[3]   שלח משה עבדו
                                          אהרן אשר בחר בו

> *He sent Moses his servant*;
> Aaron *whom he had chosen*.

Lam 5:1   זכר ה' מה היה לנו
                                         הביט וראה את חרפתנו

> Attend, YHWH, *what has happened to us*;
> Look and see *our disgrace*.

Song 3:1   על משכבי בלילות בקשתי את שאהבה נפשי
                                          בקשתיו ולא מצאתיו

> On my couch at night I sought *the one I love*;
> I sought *him* but did not find him.

3. Prepositional Phrase // Adverb

Ps 34:2   אברכה את ה' בכל עת
                                          תמיד תהלתו בפי

> I bless YHWH *at all times*;
> *Always* praise of him is in my mouth.

Ps 42:9   יומם יצוה ה' חסדו
                                          ובלילה שירה עמי

By day may YHWH commission his faithful care;
And *in the night* may a song to him be with me.[4]
[cf. also Ps 121:6.]

Job 5:14   יומם יפגשו חשך
                                   וכלילה ימששו בצהרים

By day they encounter darkness;
And they grope as in the night *at noon*.

Isa 52:3   חנם נמכרתם
                                   ולא בכסף תגאלו

You have been sold *without a price*;
And not *for money* will you be redeemed.

4. Substantive (noun, adjective, participle) // Verb

This category will be treated in greater detail in the section on syntactic
parallelism, since it often involves a nominal clause parallel to a verbal
clause. I cite several examples here, first those which employ the same root
in both word classes, then those which utilize different roots.

Ps 145:18   קרוב ה' לכל קראיו
                                 לכל אשר יקראהו באמת

YHWH is near to all *his callers*;
To all *those who call him* in truth.

Ps 97:9   כי אתה ה' עליון על כל הארץ
                               מאד נעלית על כל אלהים

For you, YHWH, *are highest* over all the world;
You *have been heightened* greatly over all gods.

Ps 34:19   קרוב ה' לנשברי לב
                                 ואת דכאי רוח יושיע

YHWH *is near* to the heartbroken;
And the dispirited he *will save*.

Mic 6:2   כי ריב לה' עם עמו
                               ועם ישראל יתוכח

For YHWH *has a quarrel* with his people;
And with Israel *will he dispute*.

There is really nothing unusual about such pairings, for the members of
each category are normally used as substitutes for each other in biblical

Hebrew: pronouns take the place of nouns, prepositional phrases and adverbs often serve the same syntactic function and are not always distin-
guishable, and a relative clause may serve as a subject or object—the same
syntactic slot also filled by nouns and pronouns. The evidence seems to
indicate that any word classes that serve the same syntactic function can be
paired in morphologic parallelism.

B. Morphologic Pairs from the Same Word Class

It is perhaps more usual to find that word pairs are from the same word
class—i.e., nouns // nouns, verbs // verbs—but even here the words need
not be morphologically identical. Singulars can parallel plurals, perfects
can parallel imperfects, as in the following examples.

1. Contrast in Tense

The paralleling of *qtl* and *yqtl* verbs is a well-known and amply docu-
mented phenomenon.[5] It occurs with verbs from the same root, as in

Ps 29:10   ה' למבול יָשָׁב
                                וַיֵּשֶׁב ה' מלך לעולם

        YHWH sat enthroned at the Flood;
        YHWH sits enthroned, king forever.

Isa 14:25   וְסָר מעליהם עלו
                             וסבלו מעל שכמו יָסוּר

        And his yoke shall drop from on them;
        And his burden shall drop from his shoulder.[6]

Isa 60:16   וְיָנַקְתְּ חלב גוים
                             ושד מלכים תִּינָקִי

        You shall suck the milk of nations;
        And the breasts of royalty you shall suck.

The same phenomenon is found in prose:

Gen 1:5   וַיִּקְרָא אלהים לאור יום
                            ולחשך קָרָא לילה

        And God called the light Day;
        and the darkness he called Night.

Ex 4:11   מי שָׂם פה לאדם
                             . . . או מי יָשׂוּם אלם

Who makes speech for man;
or who makes a mute . . .

Lev 25:10   וְשַׁבְתֶּם אִישׁ אֶל אֲחֻזָּתוֹ
                                    וְאִישׁ אֶל מִשְׁפַּחְתּוֹ תָּשֻׁבוּ

You will return each man to his land holding;
and each man to his family you will return.

Verbs from different roots appear in *qtl-yqtl* parallelism in

Ps 26:4   לֹא יָשַׁבְתִּי עִם מְתֵי שָׁוְא
                                    וְעִם נַעֲלָמִים לֹא אָבוֹא

I do not consort with scoundrels;
And with hypocrites I do not associate.

Job 6:15   אַחַי בָּגְדוּ כְמוֹ נַחַל
                                    כַּאֲפִיק נְחָלִים יַעֲבֹרוּ

My brothers are as treacherous as a wadi;
Like a wadi-stream they run dry.

It is important to emphasize that the *qtl-yqtl* shift, of which we have given only a few examples, occurs not for semantic reasons (it does not indicate a real temporal sequence) but for what have been considered stylistic reasons.[7] But it is not just something vaguely "stylistic"; we can now recognize it for what it is—a kind of grammatical parallelism.

2. Contrast in Conjugation

Verbs from the same root but in different conjugations may be paired,[8] such as

Ps 24:7   שְׂאוּ שְׁעָרִים רָאשֵׁיכֶם   *qal*
                וְהִנָּשְׂאוּ פִּתְחֵי עוֹלָם   *niphʿal*

Lift up, O gates, your head;
And be lifted up, O eternal doors.

Ps 38:3   כִּי חִצֶּיךָ נִחֲתוּ בִי   *niphʿal*(!)
                וַתִּנְחַת עָלַי יָדֶךָ   *qal*

For your arrows have struck me;
Your hand has come down upon me.

This phenomenon was called the active-passive sequence by U. Cassuto,[9] and the factitive-passive sequence by M. Held (*JBL* 84, 272–82). However, the shift is not limited to specific conjugations or grammatical voice, as can be seen from the following verses listed by M. Dahood: Ps 64:5 (*qal-hiph⁽il*); Ps 77:12 (*Ketiv*) (*hiph⁽il-qal*); Ps 139:21 (*pi⁽el-qal*).[10] In addition to the verses cited by the aforementioned scholars,[11] the following verses contain the pairing of the same verbal root in different conjugations.

| Gen 6:12 | וירא אלהים את הארץ והנה נִשְׁחָתָה | *niph⁽al* |
| | כי הִשְׁחִית כל בשר את דרכו על הארץ | *hiph⁽il* |

God saw the earth: it looked corrupt—
for all flesh had corrupted its ways on earth.

| Gen 17:17 | הלבן מאה שנה יִוָּלֵד | *niph⁽al* |
| | ואם שרה הבת תשעים שנה תֵּלֵד | *qal* |

Can a child be born to a hundred-year-old man;
Can Sarah, a ninety-year-old woman, give birth.[12]

| I Sam 1:28 | וגם אנכי הִשְׁאִלְתִּהוּ לה' | *hiph⁽il* |
| | כל הימים אשר היה הוא שָׁאוּל לה' | *qal* |

And I, in turn, lend him to YHWH;
for as long as he lives he is lent to YHWH.

| Isa 1:19–20 | . . . טוב הארץ תֹאכֵלוּ | *qal* |
| | . . . חרב תְּאֻכְּלוּ | *pu⁽al* |

. . . the good of the earth you will eat;
. . . you will be devoured by the sword.

This is a play on words made possible because the root *ʾkl* occurs in different conjugations with different meanings: the *qal* means "to eat" and the *pu⁽al* is used in the sense of "to be consumed."

Isa 33:1	הוי שׁוֹדֵד ואתה לא שָׁדוּד
	וּבוֹגֵד ולא בָגְדוּ בך
	כהתמך שׁוֹדֵד תּוּשַׁד
	כנלתך לִבְגֹד יִבְגְּדוּ בך

Ho, Plunderer and you are not plundered;
And Betrayer and they did not betray you.
When you have done being a plunderer, you will be plundered;
When you have finished betraying, they will betray you.

The root *šdd* occurs here in the *qal* and *huph⁽al* forms; the root *bgd* only in different forms of the *qal*. Not only does *šdd* show variation in conjugation, but repetition of the same pattern for both verbs is avoided by using *šdd* in passive constructions and *bgd* in active (impersonal) constructions.

Isa 66:13   כְּאִישׁ אֲשֶׁר אִמּוֹ תְּנַחֲמֶנּוּ   *pi'el*
                   כֵּן אָנֹכִי אֲנַחֶמְכֶם   *pi'el*
                   וּבִירוּשָׁלַ͏ִם תְּנֻחָמוּ   *pu'al*

Like a man whose mother comforts him;
So will I comfort you;
And in Jerusalem you will be comforted.

Jer 20:14   אָרוּר הַיּוֹם אֲשֶׁר יֻלַּדְתִּי בּוֹ   *pu'al*
          יוֹם אֲשֶׁר יְלָדַתְנִי אִמִּי אַל יְהִי בָרוּךְ   *qal*

Cursed be the day on which I was born;
The day on which my mother bore me, let it not be blessed.

Jer 23:19   הִנֵּה סַעֲרַת ה' חֵמָה יָצְאָה
                   וְסַעַר מִתְחוֹלֵל   *hitpa'el*
                   עַל רֹאשׁ רְשָׁעִים יָחוּל   *qal*

Look, the storm of YHWH goes forth in fury;
And [it is] a whirling storm;
Upon the heads of the wicked it will whirl.
                                   [cf. Jer 30:23]

Hos 12:13–14   . . . וּבְאִשָּׁה שָׁמָר   *qal*
                   . . . וּבְנָבִיא נִשְׁמָר   *niph'al*

. . . And for a wife he guarded [the sheep];
. . . And by a prophet it [Israel] was guarded.

Mic 6:14b   וְתַסֵּג וְלֹא תַפְלִיט   *hiph'il*
                   וַאֲשֶׁר תְּפַלֵּט לַחֶרֶב אֶתֵּן   *pi'el*

You will conceive/labor but will not bring forth;
And what you bring forth I will deliver to the sword.

Job 22:30   יְמַלֵּט אִי נָקִי   *pi'el*
                   וְנִמְלַט בְּבֹר כַּפֶּיךָ   *niph'al*

He will deliver the unclean;
And he will be delivered through the purity of your hands.

Furthermore, just as word pairs may be found in juxtaposition and collocation, in addition to parallel lines, so, too, the pairing of verbs of different conjugations occurs in these arrangements.

Gen 7:23   וַיִּמָּחוּ מִן הָאָרֶץ . . . וַיִּמַח אֶת כָּל הַיְקוּם   *qal . . . niph'al*

And he blotted out all existence . . . they were blotted out from the earth.

Gen 25:21   וַיֵּעָתֶר לוֹ ה' . . . וַיֶּעְתַּר יִצְחָק לה'   *qal . . . niph'al*

Isaac entreated YHWH . . . and YHWH was entreated by him
[i.e., responded to his plea].

Lev 13:19–20   . . . וְנִרְאָה אֶל הכהן. וְרָאָה הכהן . . .   *niphᶜal . . . qal*

. . . and it shall be seen by the priest. And the priest saw. . . .

Josh 6:1   . . . ויריחו סגרת וּמְסֻגֶּרֶת   *qal piᶜel*

Jericho was closed and shut tight. . . .

Isa 45:1   לרד לפניו גוים

ומתני מלכים אֲפַתֵּחַ   *piᶜel*

לִפְתֹּחַ לפניו דלתים   *qal*

ושערים לא יסגרו

Treading down nations before him;
And the loins of kings I will loosen.
Loosening [opening] doors before him;
And not letting gates be closed.

Isa 57:20   והרשעים כים נִגְרָשׁ כי השקט לא יוכל   *niphᶜal*

וַיִּגְרְשׁוּ מימיו רפש וטיט   *qal*

And the wicked are like a tossing sea that cannot be calm;
And its waters toss up mire and mud.

Ezek 14:6   שׁוּבוּ וְהָשִׁיבוּ   *qal hiphᶜil*

return and let return

Zeph 2:1   הִתְקוֹשְׁשׁוּ וָקוֹשּׁוּ   *hitpaᶜel qal*

gather yourselves and gather

Mal 2:10–11   מדוע נבְגַּד איש . . . בָּגְדָה יהודה . . .   *niphᶜal . . . qal*

why is a man betrayed . . . Judah betrayed. . . .

Ps 92:13–14   . . . צדיק כתמר יִפְרָח   *qal*

. . . בחצרות אלהינו יַפְרִיחוּ   *hiphᶜil*

The righteous will bloom like a palm. . . .
. . . in the courts of our God they will be allowed to bloom.

Both a shift in tense and a shift in conjugation are found in

Hos 5:5   וישראל ואפרים יִכָּשְׁלוּ בעונם   *niphᶜal, yqtl*

כָּשַׁל גם יהודה עמם   *qal, qtl*

And Israel and Ephraim will be tripped by their sin;
Judah also tripped with them.

M. Held's explanation for the shift in conjugation is that "the device is stylistic and would seem to aim at stressing and emphasizing the effect or result of the action referred to in the first stichos" (*JBL* 84, 274). He also suggests (*JBL* 84, 275) that there were fewer available parallel pairs for verbs than for nouns, and so rather than repeat the same verb in the same form, it was modified slightly. This is doubtful, for, as we will see in chapter 4, every word has a potential pair, so there are as many possibilities for pairing verbs as for pairing nouns. Lists of word pairs contain more nouns than verbs because it is often the verb that is gapped, or omitted, in biblical poetry (cf. O'Connor, *HVS*, 122–27). However, Held's observation on the effect of this type of parallelism appears to be correct. Using the same root in a different conjugation (and also in a different tense) is, at times, more effective than using totally different roots because it produces the assonance and the play on words which is so much a part of biblical rhetoric. In this respect, verses containing the same verbal root in different conjugations are part of the same phenomenon as verses containing the same root in any part of speech (e.g., Job 11:18; Ruth 2:12—and see below, pp. 45, 55, 71).

3. Contrast in Person

Shifts in person in parallel lines have been noted by many commentators. My contribution to their discussion is that these shifts should be viewed not as isolated "poetic" devices, but as examples of morphologic parallelism similar to those already presented (cf. also Kugel, *Idea*, 22).

Ps 104:13   משקה הרים מעליותיו
                               מפרי מעשיך תשבע הארץ

         [*He*] waters the mountains from *his* upper chambers;
         From the fruits of *your* work the earth is sated.

Song 1:2   ישקני מנשיקות פיהו
                               כי טובים דדיך מיין

         Let *him* kiss me with the kisses of *his* mouth;
         For *your* love is sweeter than wine.

Lev 23:42   בסכת תשבו שבעת ימים
                         כל האזרח בישראל ישבו בסכת

         You shall live in booths for seven days;
         every citizen in Israel [*they*] will live in booths.

Ps 20:8 contains third and first person contrast. Eccl 5:1 has second and third person contrast, along with other grammatical contrasts to be discussed below.

4. Contrast in Gender

There may be incidental morphologic parallelism when a masculine noun is paired with a feminine noun, as in the common pair גבעות // הרים, "mountains (masc.) // hills (fem.)." The real contrast, however, comes when the same noun (or same root) appears in two different genders. Cassuto pointed out that there are Ugaritic and biblical examples which show that often a masculine word is used in reference to a male or masculine term, and a feminine synonym is applied to a female or feminine term.[13] He cited

Jer 48:46

אוי לך מואב
אבד עם כמוש
כי לקחו בניך בשבי
ובנתיך בשביה

> Woe to you, Moab;
> Lost is the people of Chemosh,
> For your sons are taken into captivity;
> And your daughters into captivity.
> [cf. also Deut 21:10–11]

Nah 2:13b

וימלא טרף חריו
ומענתיו טרפה

> And he filled his lairs with prey;
> And his dens with prey.

Isa 3:1   כי הנה האדון ה' צבאות מסיר מירושלם ומיהודה משען ומשענה

> For lo, the Lord YHWH of Hosts removes from Jerusalem and Judah
> support and support.

In Isa 3:1, Cassuto explains, the word משען, "support (masc.)" harks back to Judah (here grammatically masculine, cf. Isa 3:8), and משענה, "support (fem.)" to the feminine Jerusalem. This pattern is chiastic.

These three verses contain three sets of nearly identical word pairs: שבי // שביה, טרף // טרפה, and משען // משענה. Cassuto suggested that these sets, or at least the second term in each, were chosen in order to match the gender of another word in their respective lines. That is, the choice of these words was based on morphologic considerations.

But there is a slightly different way to view the phenomenon in these three verses. Surely there were other word pairs which were of the required gender (for example, compare Jer 48:46 with Num 21:29). One must ask why such similar terms were chosen in these verses. The use of such closely related parallel terms is so striking as to indicate an intent to emphasize their morphology. These pairs suggest to me not so much that they were selected to match the gender of other words in their lines, but that they were intended to parallel each other morphologically, much like the pairs composed of the same root in different conjugations. There are other sets of nearly identical terms—one masculine and one feminine—although they do not correlate with the gender of the surrounding words.

Jer 23:19   הנה סערת ה' חמה יצאה וסער מתחולל

Lo, the storm [s⁣ʿrt] of YHWH goes forth furiously, and [it is] a whirling storm. [sʿr] [cf. Jer 30:23]

Isa 52:2

התנערי מעפר קומי שבי ירושלם
התפתחי [התפתחו, *Ketiv*] מוסרי צוארך שביה בת ציון

Arise, get up from the dust, captive [šby] Jerusalem;
Loosen the bonds from your neck, captive [šbyh] Maiden Zion. [cf. RSV and Jer 48:46]

Other verses employ both masculine and feminine forms of the same root, although they may not be exactly synonymous or parallel:

Ezek 25:13

. . . ונתתיה חרבה
מתימן ודדנה בחרב יפלו

. . . I will lay it in ruins [ḥrbh];
From Tema to Dedan they shall fall by the sword [ḥrb].

Ezek 25:15   . . . יען עשות פלשתים בנקמה
. . . וינקמו נקם

. . . because the Philistines acted in their vengeance [nqmh]
and they avenged with vengeance [nqm] . . .
[This verse is part of a larger play on the root nqm.]

The use of the same adjective in different genders, although this is determined by the modified nouns, may also be considered morphologic parallelism since it often serves to stress or contrast the adjectives.

Gen 11:6 הן עם אחד ושפה אחת לכלם

They are *one* [masc.] people and they all have *one* [fem.] language.

Isa 66:8 היוחל ארץ ביום אחד
אם יולד גוי פעם אחת

Can a land travail in *one* [masc.] day;
Can a nation be born at *one* [fem.] stroke.

Ps 51:19 זבחי אלהים רוח נשברה
לב נשבר ונדכה אלהים לא תבזה

[True] sacrifices to God are a *contrite* [fem.] spirit;
A *contrite* [masc.] and crushed heart, God, you will not disdain.

This last verse is especially interesting, because the word רוח may be either gender, and, indeed, the pair לב and רוח appears in Ps 51:12 where both are masculine. Perhaps רוח has been used in verse 19 as a feminine form in order to produce the feminine-masculine pairing which stands out in נשבר // נשברה.

Is there any evidence for this type of morphologic parallelism involving different roots? There are verses in which there is agreement in gender within a line and contrast of gender from one line to the next.

Ps 144:12 אשר בנינו כנטעים . . .
בנתינו כזוית

For our sons are like saplings . . .
And our daughters are like cornerstones. . . .

Ps 126:2 אז ימלא שחוק פינו
ולשוננו רנה

Our mouths will be filled with laughter;
Our tongues with joy.

Pr 1:8 שמע בני מוסר אביך
ואל תטש תורת אמך

My son, heed the discipline of your father;
And do not forsake the teaching of your mother.

The arrangement of the genders in these verses may be accidental, but the result is a morphologic parallelism. The question remains: is this juxtaposition of genders effective (in the sense discussed in chapter 1; cf. p. 24)—

in other words, is it meaningful in focusing the message on itself? To put it more plainly, does the morphologic parallelism in these verses belong to the poetic function, or is it a random happening of no poetic significance. The case for poetic significance cannot be proved, for the following reason: most parallel terms are not chosen for grammatical reasons, but because they are lexically associated (this will be discussed at length in chapter 4). Since all nouns in Hebrew are either masculine or feminine, there are inevitably many combinations containing one term in each gender, e.g., גבעות // הרים, שמחה // ששון. Even pairs which appear to be morphologically based, such as בנות // בנים, אם // אב are better explained through the process of word association. Therefore, I would hesitate to consider the last three cited verses, and others like them, as examples of morphological contrast.

However, there is a verse which does seem to contain an effective morphological contrast.

Isa 3:8a   כי כשלה ירושלם
                                                      ויהודה נפל

For Jerusalem has stumbled [fem.];
And Judah has fallen [masc.].

The word יהודה may be grammatically feminine, as in Ps 114:2; Lam 1:3, or masculine, as in Hos 5:5. By choosing to construe it as masculine here (and also in Isa 3:1), Isaiah has created a morphologic parallelism. In Isa 3:8 the two genders appear to balance each other, and may even create a merismus.[14] The presence of this alternation in gender heightens the effect of the parallelism.

5. Contrast in Number

Here, too, one must take into account that some word pairs will contain one singular and one plural for lexical reasons. Most of these fall into one of the following categories:

a. Some words, such as שמים, מים, חיים are grammatically plural although they have a singular meaning. They will most likely be paired with a singular term.

b. Some words usually occur in the dual or plural, e.g., עיניים, שפתיים, but often have a singular parallel mate.

c. Some words, although grammatically singular, have a collective meaning, e.g., גוי, and will often parallel a plural.

d. One of the principles by which words are paired is subordinate //
superordinate (a part and its whole). Some of these pairs contain one singular and one plural, e.g., ירושלם // ערי יהודה (Ps 144:10), דוד // מלכים
(Jer 7:17), בנות יהודה // ציון (Ps 48:12).

e. There are what we can call for now traditional, logical, or natural
pairs, such as ירח // כוכבים, "moon // stars" (Job 25:5); בניה // בעלה
"her husband // her sons" (Pr 31:28); אב // זקנים, "father // elders"
(Deut 32:7);[15] אחד // שנים, "one // two" (Deut 32:30).[16]

Thus, there are many verses in which, for lexical-semantic reasons, a
singular term will parallel a plural one. But, in addition to these, there are
numerous verses which contain this type of parallelism for nonlexical reasons. These verses contain a singular term paralleled by a plural (or a compound, which generates a plural predicate) for no apparent reason other
than to create a morphologic parallelism.[17] This is most striking when the
same root appears in both lines in different numbers.

Song 1:3

לריח שמניך טובים
שמן תורק שמך

Your *oils* give sweet fragrance;
. . . *oil* is your name.

Ps 80:6

האכלתם לחם דמעה
ותשקמו בדמעות שליש

You have fed them *tear*-bread;
You have made them drink *tears* in measure.

Pr 14:12 = 16:25

יש דרך ישר לפני איש
ואחריתה דרכי מות

There is a [seemingly] right *path* before man;
But its end is *paths* of death.

Jud 5:28

מדוע בשש רכבו לבוא
מדוע אחרו פעמי מרכבותיו

Why does his *chariot* tarry in coming;
Why have the poundings of his *chariots* delayed.

Job 6:15

אחי בגדו כמו נחל
כאפיק נחלים יעברו

My brothers are as treacherous as a *wadi*;
Like a wadi-stream [lit.: a stream of *wadis*] they run dry.

Equally effective is the pairing of demonstrative pronouns of different number.

Isa 66:8

מי שמע כזאת
מי ראה כאלה

Who has heard *such a thing*;
Who has seen *such things*.

Jer 5:9

'העל אלה לוא אפקד נאם ה
ואם בגוי אשר כזה לא תתנקם נפשי

Shall I not call *such* (*deeds*) to account, says YHWH;
Shall I not avenge myself on *such a nation*.

Job 10:13

ואלה צפנת בלבבך
ידעתי כי זאת עמך

These things you hid in your heart;
I know that *this* is in your mind.

Job 12:9

מי לא ידע בכל אלה
כי יד ה' עשתה זאת

Who among all *these* does not know;
That the hand of YHWH has done *this*.

Job 18:21

אך אלה משכנות עול
וזה מקום לא ידע אל

These are the abodes of the perverse;
And *this* is the place of him who ignored God.

Lam 5:17

על זה היה דוה לבנו
על אלה חשכו עינינו

Because of *this* was our heart faint;
Because of *these* our eyes dimmed.

It is also striking to find two parallel verbs in different numbers.

Hos 5:5b

וישראל ואפרים יכשלו בעונם
כשל גם יהודה עמם

And Israel and Ephraim *stumble* in their sin;
Judah also *stumbles* with them.

Isa 2:4

לא ישא גוי אל גוי חרב
ולא ילמדו עוד מלחמה

Nation will not *raise* [sing.] a sword to nation;
They will no longer *learn* [pl.] war. [But cf. Mic 4:3]

Deut 32:7

זכר ימות עולם
בינו שנות דר ודר

Remember [sing.] the days of old;
Consider [pl.] the years of ages past.

Although many scholars prefer to read בין or בינה instead of בינו, there is no evidence to support such a reading. The parallelism is clearly singular // plural. This pattern is continued in the following lines of the verse

שאל אביך ויגדך
זקניך ויאמרו לך

Ask your *father* and *he* will tell you;
Your *elders* and *they* will say to you.

so that even though the pair זקנים // אב may not be primarily a morphologic pair, it reinforces the morphologic parallelism which precedes it.

The four-part parallelism in Deut 32:7 is only one of several that have a morphological pattern based on number. Other examples are

Isa 40:4

כל גיא ינשא
וכל הר וגבעה ישפלו
והיה העקב למישור
והרכסים לבקעה

Every valley will be raised;
And every mountain and hill will be lowered;
And the depression will become level;
And the ridges a plain.
[singular // plural; singular // plural]

Ps 92:13–14

צדיק כתמר יפרח
כארז בלבנון ישגה
שתולים בבית ה'
בחצרות אלהינו יפריחו

The righteous will bloom like the palm;
Like the cedar in Lebanon he will flourish;
Planted in the house of YHWH;
In the courts of our God they will bloom.
[singular // singular; plural // plural]

Ps 126:5–6

הזרעים בדמעה
ברנה יקצרו
הלוך ילך ובכה נשא משך הזרע
בא יבוא ברנה נשא אלמתיו

Those who sow in tears;
In joy will they reap;
He who indeed goes crying, carrying the seed-bag;
Will indeed come joyfully, carrying his sheaves.
[plural // plural; singular // singular]

As in the case of gender, the use of the same or similar adjectives in different number emphasizes the adjective and yields a morphologic parallelism.

Gen 11:1

ויהי כל הארץ שפה אחת ודברים אחדים

The whole earth was the same language and the same words.[18]

Isa 54:7

ברגע קטן עזבתיך
וברחמים גדלים אקבצך

For a small [sing.] moment I abandoned you;
But with great [pl.] mercy I will gather you up.[19]

As we can see from Ps 126:5–6, either a singular or a plural can be used generically in Hebrew. Moreover, we often find that a verse or passage uses both—thereby producing a morphologic parallelism.

Pr 14:33

בלב נבון תנוח חכמה
ובקרב כסילים תודע

In the heart of *a wise man* Wisdom rests;
But in the midst of *fools* it makes itself known.

Pr 18:15

לב נבון יקנה דעת
ואזן חכמים תבקש דעת

The heart of *an intelligent man* acquires knowledge;
And the ear of *wise men* seeks knowledge.

Pr 29:27

תועבת צדיקים איש עול
ותועבת רשע ישר דרך

The abomination of *righteous men* is a perverse man;
And the abomination of *a wicked man* is one whose way is straight.

Job 4:7

זכר נא מי הוא נקי אבד
ואיפה ישרים נכחדו

> Think now, what *innocent man* ever perished;
> Where *have the upright* been destroyed.

Compare also Ps 1:1–3, which speaks of the righteous in the singular, and the parallel section in verses 4 and 5, which describes the wicked in the plural.

Singular-plural alternation apparently varies freely. I have chosen at random one term, ישרי לב, "upright ones," which always occurs in the plural, and have noted that it is paralleled by צדיק, "righteous one," in Ps 64:11; 97:11; and probably 94:15, and paralleled by צדיקים, "righteous ones," in Ps 32:11 and by יודעיך, "those devoted to you," in Ps 36:11.

Finally, there is the striking juxtaposition in Lam 3:38 of הרעות והטוב, literally "the evils and the good," and the use of what is generally interpreted as a dual // plural (along with a plural // singular) in

Ps 75:11   וכל קרני רשעים אגדע
                               תרוממנה קרנות צדיק

> All *the* [*pairs of*] *horns* of the wicked [pl.] I will cut;
> But *the horns* of the righteous [sing.] shall be held high.

Before leaving this section a few comments are in order about the importance of the recognition of singular-plural parallelism on the evaluation of the correctness of the Massoretic Text. The MT contains several cases of singular-plural parallelism which are not reflected in the Versions.

Gen 12:3a   ואברכה מברכיך
                             ומקללך אאר

> I will bless *those* who bless you;
> and *he* who curses you I will curse.[20]
> [Versions: those who curse you]

Isa 44:26   מקים דבר עבדו
                             ועצת מלאכיו ישלים

> He confirms the word of his *servant*;
> And the counsel of his *messengers* he fulfills.
> [Versions: his servants]

Ps 114:2   היתה יהודה לקדשו
                             ישראל ממשלותיו

> Judah became his *holy one*;
> Israel his *dominions*.
> [Versions: his dominion]

Deut 26:13   ‫. . . ככל מצותך אשר צויתני לא עברתי ממצותיך‬

. . . according to *your entire commandment* which you commanded me; I have
not transgressed *your commandments*. [Versions: all your commandments]

We should not conclude from these examples that the MT is corrupt, or
that the Versions had a different text, but rather that the Versions were simply not sensitive to this type of parallelism or could not render it idio-
matically (as we often cannot in English) into the languages of their
translations.[21]

6. Contrast in Definiteness

A noun is considered definite in Hebrew if 1) the definite article precedes it, 2) it has a possessive suffix, 3) it is in the construct state. We find
cases in which one type of definite noun parallels another, thereby producing equivalence.

Ps 33:17   ‫שקר הסוס לתשועה‬
                                  ‫וברב חילו לא ימלט‬

The horse is a false savior;
And with *his many troops* he will not escape.

Ps 126:6   ‫. . . נשא משך הזרע‬
                               ‫. . . נשא אלמתיו‬

. . . carrying *the seed-bag*;
. . . carrying *his sheaves*.

Ps 25:9   ‫ידרך ענוים במשפט‬
                                  ‫וילמד ענוים דרכו‬

He guides the lowly in *the judgment*;
He teaches the lowly *his way*.

Eccl 7:1   ‫טוב שם משמן טוב‬
                                  ‫ויום המות מיום הולדו‬

A name is better than good oil;
And the death-day than his birth-day.

The second part of this verse contains two different (but equivalent) types
of definite terms; they contrast morphologically with the two indefinite
terms of the first part. There are a number of verses in which a definite
noun is paired with an indefinite one, yielding a contrast. (This is all the

more striking in light of the observation that the definite article tends to be
omitted in poetry.[22])

Ps 50:17   ואתה שנאת מוסר
                 ותשלך דברי אחריך

                 You hated *discipline*;
                 And you threw *my words* behind you.

Ps 108:3   עורה הנבל וכנור

                 Awake, *the harp* and *a lyre*.

Ps 114:6   ההרים תרקדו כאילים
                 גבעות כבני צאן

                 The mountains danced like rams;
                 Hills like sheep.

Pr 10:1   בן חכם ישמח אב
                 ובן כסיל תוגת אמו

                 A wise son makes *a father* glad;
                 But a foolish son is the despair of *his mother*.

Job 3:3   יאבד יום אולד בו
                 והלילה אמר הרה גבר

                 Perish *a day* on which I was to be born;
                 And *the night* which intended that a male be conceived.[23]

Lam 3:47   פחד ופחת היה לנו
                 השאת והשבר

                 Panic and *pitfall* were ours;
                 The desolation and *the destruction*.

7. Contrast in Case

There are no longer case endings in biblical Hebrew, but a noun in the
nominative (i.e., the subject) in one line may be paralleled by a noun in the
accusative (direct object) in the second line. For example,

Hos 5:3   אני ידעתי אפרים
                 וישראל לא נכחד ממני

                 I have known Ephraim;
                 And Israel has not escaped my attention.

Since this type of parallelism involves the syntax of the lines, it will be discussed below as a form of syntactic parallelism (subject // object).

8. Miscellaneous Contrast

I have illustrated what I find to be the major morphological features that can be used as equivalences in parallelism. There remains, of course, the possibility that others, too, are so used. In fact, any morphologic category that has two or more members, and any form that has two or more realizations, is a potential candidate for morphologic parallelism. One such example is

Pr 16:16   קנה חכמה מה טוב מחרוץ
                      וקנות בינה נבחר מכסף

> *Acquiring* wisdom—how much better than gold;
> And *to acquire* understanding is preferable to silver.

To conclude this section on morphologic parallelism I offer a verse in which *every* parallel term shows some kind of morphologic parallelism.

Jer 9:10   ונתתי את ירושלם לגלים מעון תנים
                      ואת ערי יהודה אתן שממה מבלי יושב

> I will turn Jerusalem into rubble, a jackals' den;
> And I will make the cities of Judah a desolation, without an inhabitant.

The same verbal root is used in the *qtl* and *yqtl* forms. None of the paired nouns match in respect to number: *Jerusalem* (sing.) // *cities of Judah* (pl.); *rubble* (masc. pl.) // *desolation* (fem. sing.); and even *jackals* and *inhabitant*, although they are not strictly speaking parallel,[24] contrast in respect to number.

I have isolated and systematized a number of morphologic parallelisms. Many of them involve words that are semantically parallel, although some do not. Those that do not, like Job 12:9, may at first elicit the reaction "but those are not parallel." But this is just the point. Parallelism is more than semantic parallelism. A morphologic parallelism is just as parallel as a semantic one, although it is of a different nature. As for morphologic pairs that are also semantic or lexical pairs—while I have stressed the grammatical nature of these pairings, I want to make clear that this does not preclude other aspects of pairing that they may manifest. In fact, morphologic pairing can be viewed as just one subprinciple of the process of linguistic association whereby all pairings of individual terms can be explained. This is the subject of chapter 4.

In summary, I have shown, first of all, that members of different word classes can be paired, and, furthermore, within a word class, all of the major morphological features can be contrasted: one tense with another, one gender with another, and so on. So far, Jakobson's dictum that "pervasive parallelism inevitably activates all the levels of language . . . the morphologic and syntactic categories and forms . . . in both their convergences and divergences" has been exemplified in respect to morphology. I will now exemplify it in respect to syntax.

SYNTACTIC PARALLELISM

Once again, my assumption is that parallel lines are equivalent in some way. In syntactic parallelism, the syntax of the lines is equivalent. In linguistic terms, this would mean that their deep structures are the same (cf. Greenstein).[25] I am not interested in discovering, through tree diagrams or other technical notation, what the deep structure is, but rather in showing, as simply as possible, what kinds of transformations occur in parallel lines.

Let me illustrate first by a series of English sentences.

1. John eats the bread.

2. John does not eat the bread.

3. Does John eat the bread?

4. The bread is eaten by John.

Sentence 1 is the basic indicative sentence. Sentence 2 transforms it into the negative, sentence 3 into the interrogative, and sentence 4 into the passive. Every language has its own rules for how these transformations are made, but most have the same or similar transformations.

In syntactic parallelism, in addition to lines with the same syntactic surface structure—i.e., no transformation—one also finds the pairing of lines in which a transformation has occurred. One should be aware, however, that it is not the original sentence that has been transformed, but rather another, unrealized sentence that is parallel to it. This will become clearer from the examples and will be explained further after all the types of transformations have been presented. The transformations that I have found to

be involved in biblical parallelism are: A.) nominal-verbal, B.) positive-
negative, C.) subject-object, D.) contrast in grammatical mood. (The
verses cited may contain ellipsis and/or the addition of terms, and also rearrangements of their components, but this does not affect their syntax.)

A. Nominal-Verbal

There are two basic sentence types in Hebrew: those without a finite
verb (nominal) and those with a finite verb (verbal). The two are paired in
the following verses.

Mic 6:2b   כי ריב לה' עם עמו
                             ועם ישראל יתוכח

For YHWH has a quarrel with his people;
And with Israel will he dispute.

Ps 34:2   אברכה את ה' בכל עת
                             תמיד תהלתו בפי

I bless YHWH at all times;
Always praise of him is in my mouth.

Ps 49:4   פי ידבר חכמות
                             והגות לבי תבונות

My mouth speaks [words of] wisdom;
And my heart's murmurings are [thoughts of] understanding.

Lam 5:19   אתה ה' לעולם תשב
                             כסאך לדור ודור

You, YHWH, will sit forever;
Your throne is for eternity.

Although they do not involve entire clauses, nominal and verbal forms are
paired in

Deut 32:1   האזינו השמים ואדברה
                             ותשמע הארץ אמרי פי

Give ear, O Heavens, so *I may speak*;
And let the earth hear *the words of my mouth*.

More striking are those in which the same root appears in both a nominal
and verbal form.

Ps 73:11   ואמרו איכה ידע אל
                                ויש דעה בעליון

They say, "How could God know?
Is there knowledge with the Most High?"

Ps 97:9   כי אתה ה' עליון על כל הארץ
                                מאד נעלית על כל אלהים

For you, YHWH, are the highest over all the world;
You have been heightened greatly over all gods.

Ruth 2:12   ישלם ה' פעלך
                                ותהי משכרתך שלמה מעם ה'

May YHWH repay your deeds;
May your recompense be paid in full from YHWH.[26]

Nominal and verbal forms of the same root also occur in passages not generally considered parallelistic.

Ex 12:10   ולא תותירו ממנו עד בקר
                                והנתר ממנו עד בקר באש תשרפו

You shall not leave any of it over until morning,
and whatever is left over of it until the morning you shall burn with fire.

Lev 13:12–13   . . . מראה הכהן. וראה הכהן . . .

. . . the sight of the priest. If the priest sees . . .

Lev 13:17   . . . וטהר הכהן את הנגע טהור הוא

. . . the priest shall declare clean the affected person; he is clean. [cf. Lev
13:34]

Lev 13:46   . . . בדד ישב מחוץ למחנה מושבו

. . . he shall dwell apart; his dwelling is outside the camp.

These are only a few of the many verses in which a nominal and verbal
clause are paired. This is sometimes accomplished through the use of the
verb "to be" which, like other verbs, is a finite verb in the perfect and
imperfect, but which, unlike other verbs, ordinarily has no participle form
and is therefore totally absent ot unrealized in what we would translate as
the present tense. Below are verses which contain a finite form of "to be"
in one line and a nominal clause of being in the other.

Gen 42:31   כנים אנחנו לא היינו מרגלים

We are honest; we are [Heb.: were] not spies.

1 Sam 3:1   ודבר ה' היה יקר בימים ההם
                       אין חזון נפרץ

The word of YHWH was rare in those days;
a vision was not [Heb.: is not] common.

Job 29:15   עינים הייתי לעור
                       ורגלים לפסח אני

Eyes I was to the blind;
And feet to the lame was [Heb.: am] I.

Here, as in the *qtl-yqtl* parallelism, there is no intent to convey a real difference in time, and so even though there appears to be a "present tense" and
a "past tense," the tense of both parallel lines should be translated the
same way. (Nominal clauses are extratemporal—cf. Blau, *Grammar*, 84.)

B. Positive-Negative

In this type of parallelism a statement phrased in the positive is paired
with one phrased in the negative. (This is not to be confused with Lowth's
"antithetic parallelism," which need not involve a negative transformation.) It is not simply a matter of transforming "John eats the bread" into
"John does not eat the bread," for the pairing of two such sentences would
make no sense. Rather, the negative transformation is performed on a parallel (i.e., equivalent) sentence, yielding possibilities like:

1. John eats the bread; John does not leave the bread uneaten.

2. John eats the bread; John does not drink the milk.

3. John eats the bread; Mary does not eat the bread.

These and others like them can be considered positive-negative parallelism.

Pr 6:20   נצר בני מצות אביך
                       ואל תטש תורת אמך

Guard, my son, the commandment of your father;
And do not forsake the teaching of your mother.

Pr 3:1   בני תורתי אל תשכח
                       ומצותי יצר לבך

My son, do not forget my teaching;
And let your heart guard my commandments.

Hab 3:17   כחש מעשה זית
                                      ושדמות לא עשה אכל
                                      גזר ממכלה צאן
                                      ואין בקר ברפתים

The olive crop has failed;
And the fields do not produce food.
The sheep have vanished from the fold;
And there is no cattle in the pens.

Compare also 1 Sam 3:1 and Gen 42:31 quoted in the previous section.
The same device is often found in prosaic passages:

Gen 37:24b   והבור רק אין בו מים

The pit was empty; there was no water in it.

Deut 9:7   זכר אל תשכח

Remember, do not forget.

1 Sam 3:2b   ועינו החלו כהות לא יוכל לראות

His eyes began to dim; he was not able to see.

1 Kgs 3:18b   ואנחנו יחדו אין זר אתנו בבית

We were alone; no stranger was with us in the house.

C. Subject-Object

Many parallel lines are structured so that the terms which are semantically parallel serve different syntactic functions in their respective lines.
It is common for one of the terms to serve as the subject and its mate to
serve as the object (direct or indirect). This structure is related to the
transformation of passivization: "John eats the bread; the bread is eaten by
John," but, since here, as in the case of positive-negative parallelism, more
is going on than the transformation of the original sentence, I prefer to call
this subject-object parallelism.

Gen 27:29   הוה גביר לאחיך
                                      וישתחוו לך בני אמך

Be a lord over your brothers;
Let the sons of your mother bow before you.

Gen 37:33   חיה רעה אכלתהו
                                  טרף טרף יוסף

A wild animal has eaten him;
Joseph is surely devoured.

Jer 1:5   . . . בטרם אצורך בבטן
                          . . . ובטרם תצא מרחם

Before I formed you in the belly . . .
Before you came out of the womb . . .

Jer 20:14   ארור היום אשר ילדתי בו
                    יום אשר ילדתני אמי אל יהי ברוך

Cursed be the day on which I was born;
The day on which my mother bore me, let it not be blessed.

Hos 5:3   אני ידעתי אפרים
                               וישראל לא נכחד ממני

I have known Ephraim;
And Israel has not escaped my attention.

Ps 2:7   בני אתה
                               אני היום ילדתיך

You are my son;
I, today, have fathered you.

Ruth 1:21   אני מלאה הלכתי
                               וריקם השיבני ה'

I went forth full;
and YHWH brought me back empty.

Lam 5:4   מימינו בכסף שתינו
                             עצינו במחיר יבאו

Our water for money we drink;
Our wood comes for a price.

Some of the verses manifesting a contrast in conjugation also involve subject-object parallelism. For example, Jer 20:14 contains a contrast in conjugation, subject-object, and positive-negative parallelism. It is not unusual for a verse to contain several different types of grammatical parallelism.

D. Contrast in Grammatical Mood

Another set of transformations involves changing a sentence from one grammatical mood into another. If we take the indicative mood as the base, then "John eats the bread" becomes in the interrogative "Does John eat the bread?"; in the jussive, "Let/may John eat the bread," and so on. It should not surprise the reader at this point to find that in parallelism a line in one grammatical mood may be paired with a line in another mood.

Ps 6:6   כי אין במות זכרך
                  בשאול מי יודה לך

For in Death there is no mention of you;
In Sheol who can acclaim you?
[indicative // interrogative]

Ps 73:25   מי לי בשמים
                  ועמך לא חפצתי בארץ

Who [else] is there for me in heaven?
And having you I lack no one/nothing on earth.
[interrogative // indicative]

Isa 44:8   היש אלוה מבלעדי
                  ואין צור בל ידעתי

Is there any god besides Me?
There is no other rock, I know none.
[interrogative // indicative]

Ps 19:13   שגיאות מי יבין
                  מנסתרות נקני

Who can discern errors?
Cleanse me from hidden [guilt].
[interrogative // imperative]

It is interesting to note that in Ps 6:6, Ps 73:25, and Isa 44:8 the interrogative implies a negative answer, and the parallel indicative supplies the negative.[27] In Ps 19:13 the answer to the question is "You, God" and this is presented indirectly (as the implied subject) in the parallel line. Thus we have here rhetorical questions which provide their own answers (cf. also Isa 41:26 and Ps 24:8, 10).

There are many cases of imperative // jussive or jussive // imperative parallelism. Some involve second person jussive and imperative (by definition, second person). Verses of this type in Psalms have been listed by M. Dahood (*Psalms* III, 423–24). There are also verses containing an imperative and a third person jussive.[28]

Deut 32:1

האזינו השמים . . .
ותשמע הארץ . . .

Give ear, O heavens . . .
And let the earth hear. . . .

Mic 6:1

קום ריב את ההרים
ותשמענה הגבעות קולך

Rise, dispute before the mountains,
And let the hills hear your voice.

Pr 3:1

בני תורתי אל תשכח
ומצותי יצר לבך

My son, do not forget my teaching;
And let your heart guard my commandments.

Eccl 5:1

אל תבהל על פיך
ולבך אל ימהר

Do not be rash with your mouth;
And let not your heart be hasty.

All categories of syntactic parallelism that I have listed involve transformations, but, as I have already mentioned, it is not the original sentence that is transformed, but rather another sentence that is syntactically parallel to it. One can analyze the operations involved as a multistage process.[29] I will do this for three verses.

1. The original sentence: "A wild animal ate him." [Gen 37:33]

2. The construction of a syntactically identical parallel: *"A wild animal surely devoured Joseph."

3. A transformation performed on the parallel line, in this case a passivization: "Joseph was/is surely devoured [by a wild animal]."

Some parallelisms involve more stages.

1. The original sentence: "I went forth full." [Ruth 1:21]

2. A syntactically identical parallel: *"I came back empty."

3. A transformation of the parallel, in this case passivization (because the verb is intransitive there is an element of causation introduced): *"I was made to come [= I was brought] back empty."

4. A further transformation—here a reactivization of the passivization, specifying the causative agent: "YHWH brought me back empty."

A slightly different set of transformations obtains in Hos 5:3.

1. The original sentence: "I have known Ephraim."

2. A syntactically identical parallel: *"I have known Israel."

3. A passivization: *"Israel was known to me."

4. A negativization of the passivization: "Israel was not hidden from me."

A parallelism may consist of lines at any stage in this process. Thus some parallel lines will be exactly the same syntactically (on the surface structure) and others will undergo one or more transformations. The same is true by analogy for morphologic parallelism. The same morphologic element may be repeated, or any equivalent on any level may be substituted. Let us take interrogative particles as a final example.

On the morphological aspect, we have the same element in both lines in

Isa 66:8   מי שמע כזאת
                       מי ראה כאלה

                 Who has heard such a thing?
                 Who has seen such things?

and different but equivalent elements (all interrogative particles) in

Isa 40:18   ואל מי תדמיון אל
                       ומה דמות תערכו לו

               To *whom* can you liken God?
               And *what* likeness can you compare to him?

Job 5:1   היש עונך . . .
                       ואל מי מקדשים תפנה

            . . . *is there* one who answers you?
            And *to whom* of the Holy Ones will you turn?

Isa 10:3   . . . ומה תעשו
                      . . . על מי תנוסו
                      . . . ואנה תעזבו

> What will you do . . .
> And to *whom* will you flee . . .
> And *where* will you leave. . . .

And we have already seen that an interrogative sentence may be paired
with one that lacks an interrogative particle or, indeed, the interrogative
mood altogether (e.g., Ps 6:6; Ps 73:25).

The purpose of this chapter was to examine the role of grammar in parallelism. At the risk of getting lost in taxonomy, I have taken pains to cite
examples of many different grammatical pairings. The weight of this evidence indicates that grammar as a whole—morphology and syntax—is
used not only to construct grammatically acceptable sentences, but is also
used to construct parallelisms. In other words, parallelism uses grammar
for a supergrammatical purpose; it makes grammar serve in the poetic function—as part of the parallelism. Perhaps this is clearest when lines are not
truly grammatically parallel but are made to look as if they were. There are a
few lines whose surface structure is the same but whose deep structure is not
(Greenstein also considers these to be grammatically parallel). The illusion
of syntactic repetition adds to the perception of parallelism.

Ps 105:6   זרע אברהם עבדו
                               בני יעקב בחיריו

> The seed of Abraham his servant;
> The sons of Jacob his chosen (pl.).

Both lines contain noun in construct—personal name—appositional noun
with 3rd singular possessive suffix: the syntax looks the same. This sameness is reinforced by the fact that every word has its semantic mate and
they occur in the same order: *seed // sons, Abraham // Jacob, servant //
chosen* (cf. note 3 for this pair). But in reality the syntax of the two lines is
not quite identical, for *his servant* is in apposition to *Abraham* while *his
chosen* is in apposition to *sons*. A "syntactic" translation would be

> The seed of his servant Abraham;
> The chosen sons of Jacob.

Another example, this one with a tension between the syntax and the
word pairs, is

Ps 49:5   אטה למשל אזני
                               אפתח בכנור חידתי

> I will incline to a proverb my ear;
> I will open with a lyre my riddle.
> [Cf. Ps 78:2]

Again the syntax is identical: verb—preposition + noun—noun + suffix.
The syntax is even identical at a higher level: verb—indirect object—direct object. But if one then equates the words with their grammatical functions, one emerges with preposterous equations: *to a proverb // with a lyre*;
my ear // my riddle. The syntax pulls the verse in one direction, toward one set of equivalences, while the word pair *proverb // riddle* pulls in another.

P. Kiparsky has said that "the linguistic sames which are potentially relevant in poetry are just those which are potentially relevant in grammar" (*Daedalus*, 1973, 235). I think that this chapter has given ample proof of the correctness of this statement, perhaps in ways that linguists did not anticipate. But my purpose is not to prove linguistic theories; it is to show how they may help biblicists toward better readings of the text. Biblicists must understand that grammar is important not only because it permits the parsing of lines, but because it helps to make poetry poetic. Parallelism activates grammatical equivalences just as it activates semantic and lexical equivalences. Therefore, before a scholar corrects a grammatical inconsistency, or dismisses it as poetic license, he must first consider its relevance to the poetic function. Above all, he must realize that, no matter whether grammatical parallelism was intentional or accidental, it is potentially important in the structure of a poem and ultimately to its meaning.

IV

THE
LEXICAL AND
SEMANTIC
ASPECTS

If the grammatical aspect provides the skeleton of the parallelism then the lexical and semantic aspects are its flesh and blood. It is, after all, the words and what they signify that give meaning to a verse or phrase. Since these aspects are most obvious, it is not surprising that they have historically received the most attention. At first it was the semantic aspect alone—that is, the sense of one line and its relationship to the sense of the parallel line—that was described. Lowth's contribution in this area, both conceptually and terminologically, has been difficult to supercede; most discussions of parallelism still speak of synonymous, antithetic, and synthetic parallelism. To be sure, Lowth deserves praise for his insights, but in some ways his model for describing the semantic relationship between parallel lines inhibited the development of this subject for a long time. Although many over the years expressed dissatisfaction with it, added to it, or modified it, only recently has biblical scholarship been able to free itself totally of Lowth's tripartite semantic division.

Most of the credit goes to Kugel, who offered the longest, most anti-Lowthian description of parallelism (cf. *Idea*, 12–15). Kugel sees the semantic relationship between *all* parallel lines as being basically always "A, what's more, B"—that is, the second line goes beyond (in any one of a number of ways) the meaning of the first (cf. especially *Idea*, 51–54). "Biblical parallelism is of one sort, 'A, and what's more, B,' or a hundred sorts; but it is not three" (*Idea*, 58). Thus Kugel destroys the notion of a tidy number of discrete semantic categories and replaces it with a general overarching semantic concept which may be realized in so many different

64

ways that they defy all but the most superficial description. I will return to consider the semantic relationship between lines later, but first I will discuss the lexical aspect of parallelism.

The lexical aspect has to do with the specific words or word groups that are paired in parallel lines. This is, of course, not totally separable from the semantic aspect, since words affect meaning (although later I will suggest that the two can and should be separated to a certain extent). But as I have done in the previous chapter, I will distinguish, for purposes of presentation, the word-level phenomenon, which I will call the lexical aspect, from the line-level phenomenon, which will be called the semantic aspect. This is especially appropriate here, because historically the study of biblical parallelism has also made this distinction. Again it was Lowth who provided the model for distinguishing "parallel lines" from "parallel terms": "When a proposition is delivered, and a second is subjoined to it . . . equivalent, or contrasted with it, in Sense . . . these I call Parallel Lines; and the words or phrases answering one to another in the corresponding Lines Parallel Terms" (*Isaiah*, viii). Lowth himself did not investigate parallel terms, but this aspect of parallelism, it turns out, benefited from much more fruitful study in later years than did the semantic aspect.

THE LEXICAL ASPECT: WORD PAIRS

The discovery of Ugaritic poems at Ras Shamra beginning in 1929 had a major effect on the study of biblical poetry. Not only did Ugaritic and Hebrew prove to be closely related languages, but the two poetic traditions had so much in common that some considered them part of one Canaanite tradition. The most obvious similarity was that both Ugaritic and Hebrew poetry used parallelism extensively and, upon closer examination, it was found that the two even used the very same parallel terms in many cases. This observation led to the monumental effort of collecting what came to be known as fixed word pairs—parallel terms that occur frequently in the Bible and in Ugaritic texts. Begun a half century ago, it continues still, and it is one of the major achievements of modern biblical research.[1]

But collecting data is one thing and interpreting it is another. What was one to make of the fact that there were a large number of parallel pairs that recurred? The conclusion reached was that there existed a stock of fixed word pairs which belonged to the literary tradition of Israel and Canaan, and that poets, specially trained in their craft, drew on this stock to aid in the oral composition of parallel lines. If, for example, a poet generated a line containing the word *ksp*, "silver," his next line would be formed around its fixed pair, *ḥrṣ*, "gold."

There are actually two separate issues involved here. One is the issue of oral composition, which remains a hypothesis for biblical poetry. The other is the issue of the existence of fixed pairs as opposed to nonfixed pairs. The connection made between theories of oral composition and word pairs is an accident of intellectual history. The discovery of Ugaritic word pairs and their similarity to Hebrew word pairs came at the same time that the Parry-Lord theory was in ascendence. Scholars simply linked newly emerging evidence with newly emerging theories. Since it proved impossible to find in Hebrew poetry the same kinds of metrical formulae that were present in Greek poetry, biblical scholars substituted what they had in abundance—parallel word pairs—and declared them to be the functional equivalents of formulae.[2] Word pairs existed, according to this line of thought, to enable a poet to compose orally.

But this leaves much unaccounted for. For one thing, it does not explain how the rest of the line, besides the word pairs, was composed. For another, the same word pairs occur in poetry that was almost certainly not composed orally.[3] For these reasons, as well as because of recent doubts about the Parry-Lord theory, the time has come, as others have already suggested, to remove the issue of oral composition from the discussion of word pairs.

That leaves us with the notion of a stock of fixed pairs—the poet's dictionary, as it has been called. This was presumably a poetic substratum of biblical Hebrew and Ugaritic, the privileged knowledge of trained poets. But this stock of pairs, once numbering a few dozen, is now over a thousand and still growing.[4] Moreover, the same pairs that occur in poetic parallelism also occur in prose—in juxtaposition, collocation, and even in construct with one another.[5] If these pairs were indeed reserved for poets, then they threaten to leave the ordinary speaker without a vocabulary. It seems obvious that we cannot separate them from the total lexicon of Hebrew. Having said that, it becomes clear that there is no qualitative difference between the so-called fixed pairs and pairs that have not been so labelled. The only difference is that fixed pairs are attested more often than nonfixed pairs.[6] This is a quantitative distinction which is of some interest in regard to specific pairs and to ancient Israelite language behavior in general; but it does not alter the fact that the process whereby words are paired is the same in all instances.

If the phenomenon of word pairs cannot be explained as a part of a literary substratum or as a necessity for oral composition, then how is it to be explained? Here, again, linguistics offers a solution, a way of understanding word pairs in a broad sense and a way of comprehending their function in parallelism. However, this time it is not structural linguistics which provides the insight, but psycholinguistics—specifically the area of psycholinguistics that concerns itself with the process of word association. For word pairs, I will shortly attempt to demonstrate, are nothing more or less than the products of normal word associations that are made by all competent speakers.[7] Biblical scholarship has been inching slowly towards this view, but since most biblical scholars lacked any knowledge of the linguistic theory of word associations they were not able to make this connection. Before I present the theory and relate it to Hebrew word pairs, let us see how close others have come to it, and yet, like Tasman, who circumnavigated Australia without ever discovering it, they were unable to perceive what lay just below their horizon.

W. Watters, whose book, though flawed, succeeds in its critique of certain assumptions about fixed word pairs, explains that "many recurring pairs may be ascribed . . . to borrowing, coincidence, or idiom" (73), and "pairs which are deemed 'rare associations' by modern scholarship, were but common associations to the poet and the public" (75). The implicit assumption here, although it is developed no further, is that both common and rare pairings (i.e., fixed and nonfixed pairs) derive from commonly held associations between words.[8] Kugel echoes this when he says that "Hebrew and Ugaritic, like most languages, had their stock of conventionally associated terms, of synonyms and near-synonyms, and of antonyms and near-antonyms" (*Idea*, 33). Kugel, too, seems to feel that there is nothing extraordinary about Hebrew word pairs—they are just conventionally associated terms. (But several of Kugel's own terms are unfortunate: "stock" brings to mind the old notion of fixed pairs, or a given body of words that could be used for pairing; and "synonyms" and "antonyms" are inaccurate, as we will see below.)

P. C. Craigie approaches the issue of word pairs from a different direction. In the context of questioning the Ugaritic origins of Psalm 29, which he feels is a *Hebrew* (not a Canaanite) psalm with a Canaanite theme, Craigie notes that some of the same word pairs occur in many different, even unrelated languages.[9] His conclusion is that "a basic parallel word pair . . . can carry no particular significance with respect to the literary interrelationship between Ugaritic and Hebrew poetry." (*UF* 11, 137). In other words, Craigie argues that the similarity between Hebrew and Ugaritic pairs cannot be used to support the view that the two poetic traditions are interrelated. Actually, though, his observation poses an even more fundamental question: is the use of word pairs a distinctive Ugaritic-Hebrew poetic device? Craigie answers in the negative: "Any poetry, in which thought parallelism is employed, will inevitably employ similar or common parallel word pairs."[10] However, Craigie does not pursue the matter; he offers no thoughts on what word pairs are or where they come from.

O'Connor, who has the most to offer on this subject, goes further by stating that "the psychotherapeutic exercise of free association reveals, if it is not obvious, that any single word in a language can be paired with any other" (*HVS*, 96). In other words, every word has a potential word pair that can be generated by every competent speaker. There is no stock of word pairs except in the sense of those pairs which occur frequently—i.e., those associations which are realized more often. Although O'Connor makes an important point here, he does not investigate the general process of word association, but restricts his study to certain specific kinds of association, and the linguistic rules whereby associated terms are ordered (that is, why A words precede B words). I want to go back to the process of association itself; I am not so much interested in the rules which govern the *order* of the terms as in the rules which explain how the terms were generated in the first place. I want to answer the question: Where do word pairs come from? In order to do this I will have recourse to the area of psycholinguistics that investigates the process of word association through word association games. The particular studies to which I will refer are H. Clark, "Word Associations and Linguistic Theory" and J. E. Deese, *The Structure of Associations in Language and Thought*. These studies are based on English word associations, but when we apply their observations and results to the lists of Hebrew word pairs we find remarkable similarities. The general rules that pertain to English word associations also pertain to Hebrew word pairs. Thus the two begin to appear as results of the same process. In this way Hebrew word pairs—all Hebrew word pairs—can be understood as the product of normal linguistic association.[11]

Before summarizing the specific rules whereby word associations are generated, there are several general observations that will clarify points that have always created confusion in biblical research.

Psycholinguists vary the time limits for responses in their word association experiments, and this leads to different results, which have been classified into three groups. When the player in a word association game is given a great deal of time, he responds with unusual associations, rich in images, and reflecting personal or idiosyncratic choices. When asked to respond more quickly, the player produces more "superficial" and more common associations. These tend to be the same ones produced by most other players, and are therefore predictable to a large extent. Finally, when pressed even faster, the player gives "clang responses," words that sound like or rhyme with the stimulus (Clark, 272–73). It is the second group of associations, those elicited most often by most players, that usually interests psycholinguists. And it is this same group that biblicists call "fixed word pairs." They are simply the most common, easily produced, word associations. There are, of course, less common pairs in the Bible, and these could be considered members of the first group—the products of more careful thought. Of course, one would not expect "clang responses" in a context where meaning is essential.

The second observation from the psycholinguistic approach is that a word may elicit itself as an association. This rarely occurs in free-association experiments because it is in the nature of the instructions of these experiments to discourage a response that is identical to its stimulus. Nevertheless, it has become a psycholinguistic assumption that "a word serving as a stimulus in free association not only yields the overtly given associate *but also yields itself as a response*" (Deese, 47). Now this corresponds to the repetition of the same word in parallel lines, which occurs so often that Dahood began to list examples in his word pair lists. Although he didn't quite know how to explain this type of pairing, he sensed that it was in some way related to the use of word pairs. Indeed, he was right. The use of a repeated word in parallel lines is part of the same phenomenon as the use of an associated word. (This applies to any word, not just the specific ones listed by Dahood.)

More dramatic proof that a repeated word and a parallel word are part of the same phenomenon can be found when we are fortunate enough to have two versions of the same parallelism. It is well known, for instance, that 2 Sam 22 and Ps 18 are the same psalm in slightly different forms. It is not a question of which is correct, but a matter of comparing alternate forms which were equally acceptable to the ancient poet.[12] In the case of word pairs, we find that in the following verses one version repeats a word while the other substitutes a parallel word.

2 Sam 22:1   מכף כל איביו ומכף שאול

From the *palm* of all his enemies and from the *palm* of Saul.

Ps 18:1   מכף כל איביו ומיד שאול

From the *palm* of all his enemies and from the *hand* of Saul.

2 Sam 22:7   בצר לי אקרא ה'
                                  ואל אלהי אקרא

When I am in distress I *call* to YHWH;
And to my God I *call.*

Ps 18:7   בצר לי אקרא ה'
                                  ואל אלהי אשוע

When I am in distress I *call* to YHWH;
And to my God I *cry out.*

2 Sam 22:32   כי מי אל מבלעדי ה'
                                  ומי צור מבלעדי אלהינו

For who is a god *except* YHWH?
And who is a rock *except* our God?

Ps 18:32   כי מי אלוה מבלעדי ה'
                                  ומי צור זולתי אלהינו

For who is a god *except* YHWH?
And who is a rock *besides* our God?

The same sort of replacement occurs in repeated phrases in the prophetic
books.

Isa 16:7   לכן ייליל מואב
                                  למואב כלה ייליל

Therefore let Moab *howl*;
As for all Moab, let it *howl.*

Jer 48:31   על כן על מואב איליל
                                  ולמואב כלה אזעק

Therefore I will *howl* about Moab;
For all Moab I will *cry out.*

Jer 23:19   הנה סערת ה' חמה יצאה וסער מתחולל
                                  על ראש רשעים יחול

Lo, the storm of YHWH goes forth in fury, a *whirling* storm;
Upon the head of the wicked it will *whirl.*

Jer 30:23   הנה סערת ה' חמה יצאה סער מתגורר
                                  על ראש רשעים יחול

Lo, the storm of YHWH goes forth in fury, a *raging* storm;
Upon the head of the wicked it will *whirl.*

These verses confirm that a word may be paralleled by itself or by a parallel word—i.e., a word that is in some sense equivalent. This shows that in parallelism absolute identity is acceptable on the lexical plane just as it is acceptable on the grammatical plane (when the grammar of the two lines is identical).

Closely related to the identical repetition of a word in parallel lines is the repetition of the same root in a different form. Chapter 3 contains many examples of the same root with some grammatical change: masculine // feminine, singular // plural, qtl // yqtl, and so forth. Related also is the phenomenon in which a single word is paralleled by a phrase containing that word. Y. Avishur (*Beth Mikra* 59, 520–21) designates this as x // x + y, as in Song 1 : 10–11, where תורים, "wreaths," parallels תורי זהב, "wreaths of gold" (cf. also Song 1 : 3, שמן תורק // שמניך). I would include other combinations that are not strictly x // x + y, such as Job 6 : 15 אפיק נחלים // נחל and Jud 5 : 28 פעמי מרכבותיו // רכבו (see below). Such pairings are analogous to English associates like *affirm-confirm, amongst-among, berry-strawberry*. In all of these cases the paired words share the same lexical base, but their forms have been differentiated by the addition of other linguistic features.

A third observation is that a word may elicit a number of different associations.[13] Linguists usually rank them statistically, from the most common to the least. For example, *man* will usually elicit *woman*, but it will elicit *boy* in a smaller number of cases (Clark, 276). For our purposes it is enough to realize, as Dahood's lists show, that a word may be paired with several others. For instance, *ʾrṣ* may be paired with itself (*RSP* I, #62), with *ym* (*RSP* I, #64), *ʿpr* (*RSP* I, #67), *šmm* (*RSP* I, #71), and so on. What determines which association is made in a given verse in the Bible? To some extent it may be the strength of the association; that is, in the general population what the most common response to *ʾrṣ* would have been. Another factor is the particular connotation which the word conjures up to the person making the association. This affects the choice of associate even in free-association games, and how much more so when the word is part of a larger semantic context, as in a line or a poem. If *ʾrṣ* is understood to mean "country" it will elicit a different term than if it is understood to mean "earth" or "dry land." So at work in any specific pairing are the normal strength and frequency of a particular association—how conventional or stereotyped it has become—and the semantic requirements of a particular context or the playfulness of a particular poet.

A final observation has to do with the reciprocity of associated words. In some cases X will elicit Y and Y will elicit X—for example, in English *soft* elicits *hard* and *hard* elicits *soft*. This is analogous to situations in which the order of the paired words may be reversed. For example, *ʾrṣ* elicits *šmm* and *šmm* elicits *ʾrṣ*; *ʾrṣ* may serve as either the A or the B word.[14] (Compare, for example, Isa 45:12 and Ps 96:11.) However, in other cases X elicits Y, but Y does not elicit X. In English *frigid* elicits *cold*, but *cold* does not elicit *frigid* (Deese, 53). (*Cold* usually elicits *hot*, for reasons discussed below.) In Hebrew *ʾkl* elicits *šth*, but *šth* rarely if ever seems to elicit *ʾkl* (but cf. Num 6:3 and Amos 9:14). This would explain the word pairs in which there is always a fixed order: always A and then B; never B and then A.

The general rules governing the formation of word associations can be divided into paradigmatic rules and syntagmatic rules (Clark). Sets of elements which can be substituted one for another in a given context are paradigmatic. In English this usually involves words of the same part of speech, e.g., *tree-flower*, *cold-hot*, *run-jump*. Syntagmatic elements are those which combine to form a larger unit, e.g., *green-grass*, *sit-down*. A word may generate both a paradigmatic and a syntagmatic associate, for instance, *stop* generates both *go* and *sign*; but the response correlates to some extent with the part of speech of the stimulus. Thus grammar is at work also, even though it might appear that word association is purely a lexical procedure. The following observations have been made for English: nouns tend to be paradigmatic, adverbs are syntagmatic, and verbs and adjectives fall in between, with about 50 percent of the associates of each being syntagmatic (Deese, 105). An interesting aside: children tend to give more syntagmatic responses than adults. For instance, when presented with the word *good*, most adults will give *bad*, but children will give *boy* (Deese, 53, Clark, 275).

A. The Paradigmatic Rules

1. The Minimal Contrast Rule

If a word has a common "opposite" it will elicit that opposite more than anything else. This is most evident in adjectives: *good-bad*, *long-short*. But many nouns also work this way: *man-woman*, as do prepositions: *up-down*, *above-below*, and also verbs: *give-take*, *go-come*. Biblical examples are the pairing of אם־אב, על־תחת (*RSP* I, #589), and עלה־ירד (*RSP* I, #421). This creates the impression that many word pairs are antonyms.

Other single-feature contrasts involve grammatical contrasts of the type discussed in chapter 3. In verbs we find ± plural (*is-are*, *has-have*), ± past tense in strong verbs (*are-were*, *take-took*). This would explain the *qtl-yqtl* pairing of the same root. (The pairing of *qtl-yqtl* forms of different roots involves a double-feature contrast.) In pronouns there may be a ± nominative contrast: *he-him* (cf. Ps 2:7 אתה // ד"), and in deictic words a ± proximal contrast: *here-there*, *this-that*.

The rules for minimal contrast are actually more complex than this. They are hierarchic; there are rules for which feature is chosen for contrast and in what order features tend to be chosen. This explains, for example, why *man* elicits *woman* more often than it elicits *boy*. We must remember, however, that these rules are not meant for predicting the associate of a particular word at any given time. They merely explain and categorize a great many word associations by a large group of people.

2. The Marking Rule

This is a particularization of the minimal contrast rule. It states that there is a greater tendency to change a feature from, rather than to, its marked value. Marking can be illustrated in nouns by *dogs*, the marked form, and *dog*, the unmarked (or zero-marked) form. The marking rule means that *dogs* elicits *dog* more than *dog* elicits *dogs*. The same is true for pairs such as *brought-bring*, *better-good*, *useless-useful*. If this holds true for Hebrew, and there is no assurance that it does, then one would expect more cases of *yqtl* // *qtl* than the reverse, more cases of plural // singular of the same word, and feminine // masculine of the same word. I have no idea if the actual occurrences of such pairs bear this out.

Clark notes, however, that there are many cases which seem to contradict the marking rule. For instance, *man*, the unmarked form, elicits *woman* more than *woman* elicits *man*; *he*, the unmarked form, elicits *him* more than the reverse. Clark therefore cautions against using the marking rule as a general rule (278). In biblical parallelism the presence of the semantic context may limit the use of the marking rule even more severely. But it would appear that some form of marking is at work when singulars and plurals of the same root are paired, masculines and feminines of the same root, and so forth (see chapter 3, p. 35).

3. The Feature Deletion and Addition Rule

The features of a word are listed hierarchically by linguists; for example, *father* = noun, singular, animate, human, male, parent. If a feature is deleted, and it is usually done from the end of the list, it generally produces a superordinate, as in *father-man*, *apple-fruit*, etc. This is, in other words, a part and its whole, or a specific member of a class and the entire class. (The tendency towards expansion of the members of a class in this kind of association may also be at work in the many cases where כל is added to the second term, cf. Kugel, *Idea*, 47–48.) A Hebrew example is ירושלם // ערי יהודה (Isa 44:26—cf. ציון // ערי יהודה in Lam 5:11). The addition of כל appears in Jer 34:7, where ירושלם parallels כל ערי יהודה. Isa 40:9 has taken the pair ציון and ירושלם, and added to it ערי יהודה.

The addition of a feature (instead of its deletion) yields a subordinate, as in *fruit-apple*, *animal-dog*. The same Hebrew pair, ירושלם // יהודה is put in this order in Jer 4:3–5. Another example is ארז // עץ (which is also used in reverse, cf. *RSP* I, #442). The device known as particularizing, common in Hebrew and other ancient near eastern parallelism, can be considered a form of feature addition.[15]

It is the feature deletion and addition rules that account, in a number of complex ways, for the large number of synonyms and near-synonyms produced on word association experiments. In general, this involves the selection of another word with the same or a similar list of features. For example, *dog* and *cat* share the following features: noun, singular, animate, mammal, small, domesticated, etc. Combinations like *dog-cat*, *apple-orange* are coordinates; in Hebrew one finds coordinates like *heart // liver* (*RSP* I, #323), *water // oil* (*RSP* I, #354).

Many associates share the same properties or appear in the same context. They can usually be explained by the deletion or addition of one or two features. In verbs one finds ± cause, yielding *kill* = *die*, *teach* = *learn*. The Hebrew counterpart would be the pairing of *qal* and *hiphᶜil* verbs.[16] In nouns the changed features may be ± abstract: *knowledge-school*, ± animate: *pill-doctor*. Hebrew pairings like ים // תנינים (Ps 74:13), *kings // throne* (Pr 16:12), those listed in Dahood, *Psalms* III, 411 as abstract // concrete, and many others can be explained by the feature deletion and addition rule.

4. The Category Preservation Rule

This rule states that the higher a feature is on the list, the less likely it is to be changed. This accounts, first of all, for the tendency toward paradigmatic responses, since part of speech is high on the list. It also explains why certain contrasts or deletions (e.g., singular-plural) occur less often than others. In general, the rule for paradigmatic responses is to "perform the least change on the lowest feature, with the restriction that the result must correspond to an English word" (Clark, 280). The least change would be changing the sign of a feature, the plus or minus, which yields a minimal contrast. Deletion of features is preferred to addition of features, and single deletions or additions are preferred to multiple ones.

In general, the paradigmatic rules of association account for a large number of Hebrew word pairs, especially the more frequently occurring ones. They also explain why so many can be called synonyms or antonyms, and, at the same time, why so many others do not fit these labels.

B. The Syntagmatic Rules

The syntagmatic rules are, according to Clark, more difficult to characterize than the paradigmatic rules. He finds that there are two which account for the bulk of syntagmatic responses.

1. The Selection Feature Realization Rule

A word often contains selectional features that limit the context in which that word may occur. To illustrate, let us take the word *young*. It has selectional restrictions on what it can modify; one can say *young boy* but not *young book*. In other words, *young* can modify animate nouns but not inanimate nouns. The syntagmatic response to *young* is one realization of the possible nouns that *young* can modify—e.g., *boy*, *woman*, etc. To simplify the procedure further: the respondent thinks, "What can this word be used with?" and gives that word as a response.[17] Other examples of syntagmatic responses are *bend-over*, *pencil-write*, *pickle-sour*.

2. The Idiom Completion Rule

This is related to the selectional feature realization rule. The idiom completion rule seeks a selectional feature that has only one realization. Clark states the rule as: "Find an idiom of which the stimulus is a part and produce the next main word" (282). Examples are *cottage-cheese*, *apple-pie*, *Oxford-University*. There are also a number of apparently paradigmatic responses which Clark feels are better understood as idiom completions. He lists *ham-eggs*, *bread-butter*, and *needle-thread*. The importance of the ambiguity of such combinations will become clearer in my discussion of Hebrew syntagmatic pairs. Clark also stresses that syntagmatic responses "are not merely continuous fragments of speech . . . , but rather responses that bear only an abstract relationship to normal speech" (283). For one thing, they do not include functional words such as *and*, *the*, but only the lexical items.

C. Syntagmatic Pairing in Hebrew

There are several different types of syntagmatic pairings in Hebrew. I will consider them under the headings of 1) conventionalized coordinates, 2) binomination, and 3) normal syntagmatic combinations.[18]

1. Conventionalized Coordinates

The idiom completion rule explains the association of two or more terms that belong to an idiom or conventional expression. For instance, the word *free* elicits *easy* because the two are part of the common expression "free and easy." The Hebrew counterparts of such associates are what E. Z. Melamed has called the breakup of stereotype phrases.[19] These consist of word pairs, in most cases coordinates, which derive from expressions which have achieved the status of idioms, such as סוס־רכב ("horse-driver") and חסד־אמת ("loyalty-truth"). The breakup of such a phrase or idiom constitutes a syntagmatic pairing, even if the pair itself appears para-digmatic, as we saw from Clark's discussion of sets like *bread-butter* and *ham-eggs*. The objections to Melamed's thesis brought by C. Whitley actu-ally center around the problem of whether pairs like סוס // רכב really de-rive from idioms or are simply paradigmatic associations. To the extent that we can prove idiom status—and this may sometimes be done on the basis of the frequency of the continuous phrase (i.e., in juxtaposition, not in parallel lines)—we can speak of the breakup of idioms. It is hard enough to decide this for certain English coordinates, like *coffee-tea*; how much more would we expect disagreement for certain Hebrew coordinates. It would seem, though, that the principle of the syntagmatic pairing of conventionalized coordinates is firmly established in Hebrew. This would include the use as parallel word pairs of words normally forming hendiadys (e.g., חסד // אמת, "loyalty // truth"), merismus (שמים // ארץ, "sky // earth"), and conventional coordinates like שור // חמור, "ox // ass" and אלמנה // יתום, "orphan // widow." The origin of such idioms, however, is a separate question; they may have arisen from paradigmatic association. (It bears repeating that such coordinates, regardless of how close in mean-ing they appear, are not synonyms.)[20]

2. Binomination

Although there may be some question concerning the status as syntag-matic constituents of certain coordinates, there is no doubt about the ele-ments of binomination. This is a term used by O'Connor (*HVS*, 112–13,

371–77) for the splitting up of the components of one personal or geographic name. Both elements clearly refer to one individual (whereas coordinates refer to two), and form one two-part name.[21] Examples are

Jud 5:12	ברק // בן אבינעם	[cf. *HVS*, 374–75]
Num 23:7	בלק // מלך מואב	[cf. *HVS*, 374–75]
Ruth 4:11	אפרתה // בית לחם	[cf. Melamed, *Scripta* VIII, 122–23][22]

3. Normal Syntagmatic Combinations

The previous two categories would fit under Clark's Idiom Completion Rule. The last category, which, for lack of a better term, I call normal syntagmatic combinations, is a manifestation of The Selectional Feature Realization Rule. It pairs words in parallel lines that are not necessarily idioms but that would normally be combined in ordinary discourse. Here, as in English, the clearest examples are those in which the part of speech of the paired words is different. For example, we find כסא, "chair, throne," paired with ישב, "sit" in Isa 16:5 and Lam 5:19.

Isa 16:5

והוכן בחסד כסא
וישב עליו באמת באהל דוד . . .

And a throne shall be established in kindness;
And he shall sit on it in faithfulness. . . .

Lam 5:19

אתה ה' לעולם תשב
כסאך לדור ודור

You, YHWH, will sit forever;
Your throne is for eternity.

Another case is the pairing of כתב, "write," and ספר, "book" in Job 19:23

מי יתן אפו ויכתבון מלי
מי יתן בספר ויחקו

There is a double parallel in this verse. First, the phrase ויכתבון בספר has been split, so that there is a syntagmatic pairing in parallel lines of these two elements. Second, the entire phrase ויכתבון בספר then parallels ויחקו. The verse should not be translated distributively either as "O that my words be written and inscribed in a book" or as "O that my words be written down, O that they be inscribed in a book." Job intends a poetic pro-

gression in 19:23–24 which should not be levelled by trying to decide
what kind of material he had in mind for his inscription. He moves from
the softest and least permanent to the hardest and most permanent: from
parchment to stone; and does so with three verbs for writing: to write, to
inscribe, to engrave.

> O that my words be written down,
> O that they be in a book, firmly inscribed,
> With a pen of iron and lead (a chisel),
> Forever engraved in rock.

It is easy to recognize syntagmatic pairs involving a verb and a noun (although these do not seem to occur frequently); somewhat more problem-
atic is the splitting of a noun and a noun-adjective-participle combination.
Difficulties arise because, while one can differentiate *morphologically* between nouns, adjectives, and participles, *syntactically* they all function the
same way and therefore may all be considered the same part of speech. If
we recall our definition that paradigmatic words substitute for one another
and that syntagmatic words combine with one another to form a larger
unit, we see that pairings of nouns, adjectives, and participles are ambiguous. Let us look at a simple demonstration. Deut 22:22 speaks of האש
השכב, "the man who lies"; Lev 14:47 reads והשכב בבית, "the one who
lies in the house." In Hebrew a participle (in this case שכב) or an adjective
can replace a noun or can be used together with it. Thus the pairing of an
adjective or participle with a noun in parallel lines is both syntagmatic and
paradigmatic. It becomes a matter of judgment as to how we perceive them
in a given case.[23] The same is true for nouns in construct, both of which
may be used independently. Without going further into the matter, I offer
the following as possible syntagmatic pairs. They occur as parallel terms,
but I have translated them as continuous expressions in order to point out
their syntagmatic nature.

Ps 3:2   צרי // קמים עלי

"The enemies who attack me"

Ps 19:13   שגיאות // נסתרות

"Hidden errors"

Job 3:20   עמל // מרי נפש

"Embittered toilers"[24]

These are not, as far as I know, idioms or conventionalized expressions, but seem to be elements of phrases that would normally occur in combination.

It is not my purpose to explain all biblical word pairs by one or another of the rules which have been presented here. It is enough to see that the linguistic rules underlying word associations also seem to fit when applied to word pairs, and in many cases provide better explanations for certain pairs than were heretofore available. Moreover, the theory of word associations is a "unified theory." It provides one explanation for a large variety of related phenomena. This theory shows that the pairing of *yqtl-qtl* forms and the breakup of idioms are of the same nature as the pairing of apparent synonyms and antonyms. It shows that the pairing of words in parallel lines is no different from the pairing in juxtaposition, collocation, and construct, and even over greater distances.[25] And it shows that the poetic pairings are the same as those in prose. All of these associations belong to the same linguistic phenomenon. Much of this was already sensed by biblicists but there was no model around which to structure the discussion. The linguistic theory of word association provides that model.

This approach to word pairs leads to the conclusion that they were not specially invented to enable the composition of parallel lines. Word pairs exist, at least potentially, in all languages, whether or not they use parallelism;[26] and in those that do use parallelism, the word pairs are not restricted to parallel lines but may occur in nonparallelistic writing as well. *It is not word pairs that create parallelism. It is parallelism that activates word pairs.* Since parallelism is essentially a form of projecting equivalences, it produces equivalents on all linguistic levels. On the lexical level these take the form of the realization of two or more words which are normally (or sometimes not so frequently) associated by speakers of the language. The lists of pairs that scholars have collected are not part of a poetic or even literary tradition. They are much more: they are a window into what psycholinguists would call the language behavior, and ultimately the whole conceptual world, of speakers of biblical Hebrew and Ugaritic.[27] They evince mundane connections like *ox* and *ass* and ethnic stereotypes like *Philistine* and *uncircumcised*.[28] Not only should we continue to collect them, but we should document their frequencies and patterns to the extent that textual remains permit. This is the linguistic task. The literary task is to see how a given author or verse uses a specific pair for his own purpose—to create his own emphasis or meaning. Does he use an unexpected

or rare association to shock his readers? Does he originate a new association of words much as he does in a simile or metaphor? Or does he give
new life to a common association? Poets, after all, use the same language
and the same linguistic rules as their audience, but it is the way in which
they use these that makes them poets.

THE RELATION BETWEEN THE LEXICAL AND THE
SEMANTIC ASPECTS

The theory of word association explains the relationship between paired
words in psycholinguistic terms rather than in semantic terms. That is,
words are paired not on the basis of a particular semantic principle (e.g.,
sameness of meaning), but as a result of a complex psycholinguistic process. This is not to say, however, that word pairing does not have a semantic component. For one thing, the pairs can be considered semantically
equivalent "insofar as they overlap in cutting up the general 'thought-
mass'" (Levin, *Linguistic Structure in Poetry*, 25); in other words, they are
part of the same semantic field. For another, it is possible to categorize the
semantic relationships between word pairs: Geller has done so in one manner[29] and even the linguistic terms that I have used—coordinate, subordinate, etc.—have overtones of semantic categorization. And, most important of all, the choice of word pairs affects the meaning of the parallelism.

How it affects the meaning is difficult to describe except by example,
for, while the process by which word pairs are matched may seem almost
automatic or instinctive, I do not think that we can dismiss their use so
easily. What we have explained so far is the process of pairing in and of
itself, divorced from the context in which it occurs. But the specific pairs
that are chosen, and how they are ordered, are both dependent on that context and contribute to it. One illustration will have to suffice.

| Lam 5:11 | נשים בציון ענו |
| | בתלת בערי יהודה |

Women in Zion they ravished;
Virgins in the cities of Judah.

This verse is composed entirely of word pairs plus a verb that is gapped in
the second line. The relationship between *women* and *virgins* is either
superordinate / / subordinate (women in the sense of all adult females)

or two coordinates (married women as opposed to virgins). In either case, the second term is more restrictive or specific than the first, since even if the terms are coordinates, married women are the more numerous, hence the more common element, while *virgins* represents a special category within society. So the way in which this word pair is ordered has the effect of restricting the meaning of the parallelism. But the other word pair, *Zion // cities of Judah*, moves in the opposite direction. Here clearly there is a subordinate // superordinate; Zion refers to one city among the cities of Judah. The effect of the second word pair is to expand the meaning of the parallelism. It might seem, then, that the two pairs are working at cross purposes, but this is not so. On the contrary, their effect is to make the sense of the verse more intense and dramatic: the action described becomes more atrocious and more widespread. Raping virgins is more offensive than raping married women,[30] and it was not confined to the capital but occurred throughout the country. So we see that the lexical and semantic aspects are intertwined.

But in another sense the lexical aspect is to be distinguished from the semantic aspect.[31] To be sure, lexical pairs are often semantic pairs (and grammatical pairs as well), but there are a number of verses in which the lexical pairs function independently of the other aspects—they are neither semantic nor grammatical equivalents. The following verses are presented in order to show that word pairs have a life of their own,[32] and that the lexical aspect is a distinct aspect of biblical parallelism.

Ps 15:1   מי יגור באהלך
                                            מי ישכן בהר קדשך

        Who will live in your *tent*?
        Who will *dwell* on your holy mountain?

The lexical pair *ʾhl // (m)škn* (*RSP* I, #15) does not function as a semantic pair. The semantic and grammatical equivalents are *ygwr // yškn* and *ʾhlk // hr qdšk*.

Ps 111:6   כח מעשיו הגיד לעמו
                                 לתת להם נחלת גוים

        The power of his deeds he told to his *people*
        In giving to them the inheritance of *nations*.

These lines are not syntactically parallel and the terms *ʿm* and *gwy*, a known pair (compare, for example, Isa 1:4), are not semantic equivalents here.

Ps 11:6   ימטר על רשעים פחים אש וגפרית
                                 ורוח זלעפות מנת כוסם

He will *rain* upon the wicked blazing coals and sulphur;
A scorching *wind* will be their portion.

Semantically, רוח זלעפות parallels פחים אש וגפרית but the verse also contains the lexical pair רוח // מטר (*RSP* I, #520).

Job 31:18   כי מנעורי גדלני כאב
                                 ומבטן אמי אנחנה

For from my youth he [the orphan] grew up with me as with a *father*;
And from my *mother*'s womb I guided her [the widow].

The semantic pair is מנעורי and מבטן אמי, but the common lexical pair
אם // אב is also present.

Pr 4:1   שמעו בנים מוסר אב
                                 והקשיבו לדעת בינה

Heed, sons, a father's discipline;
And listen in order to know *understanding*.

הקשיבו and שמעו are both a lexical and a semantic pair, but there is an
additional lexical pair: שמע // בין (*RSP* I, #567). Pr 4:1 contains a three-
way play among lexical associates. This happens in a different manner in

Isa 54:2   הרחיבי מקום אהלך
                                 ויריעות משכנותיך יטו . . .

Enlarge the place of your *tent*;
Let the *curtains* of your *dwellings* be extended. . . .

Both אהל // משכן and יריעה // אהל appear as parallel word pairs; here instead of choosing one the prophet used both. Isa 54:2 is an example in
which a term with one component parallels a term with more than one:
tent parallels *curtains of dwellings*. The terms of the double component are
both lexical associates of the first term. A similar phenomenon is found in
the following examples except that here the double component consists of
a repeated term and an associate.

Job 6:15   אחי בגדו כמו נחל
                                 כאפיק נחלים יעברו

My brothers are as treacherous as a *wadi*;
Like a *wadi-stream* they run dry.

Jud 5:28   מדוע בשש רכבו לבוא
                           מדוע אחרו פעמי מרכבותיו

Why does his *chariot* tarry in coming;
Why have the *poundings of his chariots* delayed.

Finally, a verse which sets up a false relationship based on a word pair—
a play on a word pair (not unlike the play on grammar that I discussed at
the end of chapter 3).

Job 5:14   יומם יפגשו חשך
                           וכלילה ימששו בצהרים

By day they encounter darkness;
And as in the night they grope at noon.

The familiar associates *day* and *night* are a lexical pair. They may at first
seem to be a semantic pair as well since they often occur as such and because here each occupies the same position in its respective line.[33] But actually the semantic pairs are *by day // at noon* and *darkness // night*.

All of the verses cited in this section, whether they contain word pairs or
variations on the same root, show that lexical parallelism is to be distinguished from semantic and grammatical parallelism. Words may be
lexically associated but need not be used as semantic or grammatic equivalents. Or, one might say that it is the lexical associations that promote the
perception of parallelism when grammatic or semantic equivalences are
absent, and reinforce it when they are present.

LEXICAL, GRAMMATICAL, AND SEMANTIC PATTERNING

Further proof that these three aspects can be analyzed separately comes
from verses in which there are two (or more) sets of lexical, grammatical,
or semantic elements occurring in a pattern. If we limit ourselves to two
pairs, there are three possible patterns: *aabb*, *abab*, *abba*. Biblicists are
most familiar with lexical patterning of the *abba* type (chiastic[34]), but all
three aspects can be found in all three patterns, and furthermore, they may
be found in different patterns within the same parallelism.

A. Lexical Patterning

   1. *aabb*

Gen 37:8   המלך תמלך עלינו
                          אם משול תמשל בנו

> Will you really reign over us; [*mlk-mlk*]
> Will you really rule us. [*mšl-mšl*]

Isa 66:23   והיה מדי חדש בחדשו
                          ומדי שבת בשבתו

> It will be from one *new moon* to another *new moon*;
> From one *sabbath* to another *sabbath*.

Perhaps the ultimate in this type of patterning is

Isa 28:10, 13   כי צו לצו צו לצו
                          קו לקו קו לקו
                          זעיר שם זעיר שם

> Mutter upon mutter, mutter upon mutter;
> Murmur upon murmur, murmur upon murmur;
> A little here, a little there.

2. *abab*[35]

Ps 33:10–11   ה' הפיר עצת גוים
                          הניא מחשבות עמים
                          עצת ה' לעולם תעמד
                          מחשבות לבו לדר ודר

> YHWH frustrates the *plan* of nations;
> Brings to naught the *designs* of peoples.
> YHWH's *plan* endures forever;
> His heart's *designs*, for eternity.

Note that the semantic pattern is *aabb*, as is the syntactic pattern; but morphologically there is an *abab* alternation between singular and plural
which matches the lexical pattern. Compare also Isa 51:6.

Ex 29:27   . . . את חזה התנופה ואת שוק התרומה
                          . . . אשר הונף ואשר הורם

> . . . the *wave* breast and the *heave* thigh
> which was *waved* and which was *heaved*. . . .[36]

Sometimes the words which are patterned are not word pairs, as in the
following:

Isa 54:7–8   ברגע קטן עזבתיך
                           וברחמים גדלים אקבצך
                  בשצף קצף הסתרתי פני רגע ממך
                        ובחסד עולם רחמתיך . . .

For a small *moment* I forsook you;
But with great *compassion* I will gather you in.
In slight anger I hid my face from you for a *moment*;
But with eternal kindness I will be *compassionate* to you.

Ps 126:5–6   הזרעים בדמעה
                                 ברנה יקצרו
             הלוך ילך ובכה נשא משך הזרע
               בא יבוא ברנה נשא אלמתיו

Those who *sow* in tears;
In *joy* will they reap;
He who indeed goes crying, carrying the *seed*-bag;
Will indeed come *joyfully*, carrying his sheaves.
[*zrᶜ-rnh-zrᶜ-rnh*]

3. *abba*[37]

Jer 17:7   ברוך הגבר אשר יבטח בה'
                             והיה ה' מבטחו

Blessed is the man who is *secure* in *YHWH*;
And *YHWH* will be his *security*.

Ps 132:13–14   כי בחר ה' בציון
                               אוה למושב לו
                           זאת מנוחתי עדי עד
                           פה אשב כי אותיה

For YHWH has chosen Zion;
He has *desired* it for his *seat*.
This is my resting-place for all time;
Here I will *sit*, for I *desire* it.

Notice that here only two lines out of four are involved in the *abba* lexical patterning, yet all four are involved in an *aabb* semantic pattern. There is only partial grammatical correspondence.

B. Grammatical Patterning

1. *aabb*

Ps 126:5–6 has arranged its singulars and plurals in this pattern. Ps
33:10–11 has an *aabb* syntactic pattern.

Ps 33:10–11

ה' הפיר עצת גוים
הניא מחשבות עמים
עצת ה' לעולם תעמד
מחשבות לבו לדר ודר

YHWH frustrates the plan of nations;
Brings to naught the designs of peoples.
YHWH's plan endures forever;
His heart's designs, for eternity.

2. *abab*

Jer 31:16b–17

כי יש שכר לפעלתך נאם ה'
ושבו מארץ אויב
ויש תקוה לאחריתך נאם ה'
ושבו בנים לגבולם

For there is a reward for your labor, says YHWH:
They shall return from the enemy's land;
And there is hope for your future, says YHWH:
The children shall return to their own territory.

The syntactic, lexical, and semantic patterning are in harmony here.

3. *abba*

Ps 137:5–6a

אם אשכחך ירושלם
תשכח ימיני
תדבק לשוני לחכי
אם לא אזכרכי

If I forget you, Jerusalem,
Let my right hand wither;
Let my tongue stick to my palate,
If I do not remember you.

C. Semantic Patterning

In many cases the syntactic and semantic patterns are the same, but
there may be a definite semantic pattern even when a grammatic pattern is
lacking.

1. *aabb*

Joel 1 : 2

שמעו זאת הזקנים
והאזינו כל יושבי הארץ
ההיתה זאת בימיכם
ואם בימי אבתיכם

Hear this, elders;
And listen all dwellers of the land.
Was there ever such a thing in your days;
Or in the days of your fathers.

Cf. also Ps 132 : 13–14; Isa 51 : 6.

2. *abab*

Ps 33 : 20–21

נפשנו חכתה לה'
עזרנו ומגננו הוא
כי בו ישמח לבנו
כי בשם קדשו בטחנו

Our being hopes on YHWH,
Our help and our shield is he;
For in him our heart rejoices,
For in his holy name we trust.[38]

Cf. also Isa 54 : 7–8 and Jer 31 : 16b–17.

3. *abba*

Pr 23 : 15–16

בני אם חכם לבך
ישמח לבי גם אני
ותעלזנה כליותי
בדבר שפתיך מישרים

My son, if your heart is wise,
My own heart will rejoice;
My kidneys will be glad,
When your lips speak rightly.

I have chosen the simplest, most obvious examples of patterning. There
are more intricate ones, too, containing more than two sets of terms or
structured less symmetrically, e.g., *abac*, etc. In a segment involving four
lines it is not uncommon for the last line to break the pattern suggested in
the first three. This often serves as a link to other segments or as a type of
closure.[39]

My purpose in presenting these patterns was to bring once more the lexical, grammatical, and semantic aspects into clearer focus. All of these as-

pects have a role in parallelism. Their patterns may correspond, or they may be different, but all of them add to the effect of the parallelism. Although I have taken pains to separate them for heuristic purposes, they interact with one another in a variety of ways. Parallelism is the result of the effects of its many aspects.

THE SEMANTIC ASPECT

The lexical aspect of parallelism consists of lexical equivalences which, as we saw in the two preceding sections, are not to be confused with semantic equivalences. Let us now turn our attention to the semantic aspect: the relationship between the meanings of parallel lines. But first let us establish a link between the methodology used to describe the lexical aspect and that applied to other aspects of parallelism.

The first part of this chapter showed that lexical equivalences—that is, the equivalence that constitutes word pairs—is best explained as the same equivalence that exists in word associations. The corollary is that the process whereby word associations are generated can be used to explain the generation of word pairs. In doing this we seem to have left the realm of structural linguistics, where we first sought a description of parallelism, to sojourn in an alien linguistic land. In reality, though, we have not traveled far, for while structural linguists and psycholinguists speak different metalanguages and employ different methodologies, at a more profound level they seem to be saying the same thing. Deese, a psycholinguist whose studies are far removed from poetry and parallelism, sums up his work on associations as follows: "The two associative laws may be stated as follows: (1) Elements are associatively related when they may be contrasted in some unique and unambiguous way, and (2) elements are associatively related when they may be grouped because they can be described by two or more characteristics in common" (165). These "contrasting relations and grouping relations" (cf. Deese, 160, 164) are the psycholinguistic equivalents of "equivalence" and "contrast"—the terms which structural linguists find basic to the definition of parallelism. Can association be used to explain parallelism as a whole? Deese's following statement may be viewed as having implications in this direction (although he does not mention parallelism).

A more difficult question, however, is whether or not these same associations have any influence upon the generation of sentences. It is certain that sentences are not merely concatenations of associations. Sentences are composed of syntactic structures, though it is less certain at what level these structures are generated. Class membership which makes assignment of words of different syntactic value possible, however, may well be determined by the same functional properties, namely, contrast and grouping, that determine the patterns among manifest associations. *We can imagine sentences, then, in which the structural properties are syntactic but for which the choice of the particular elements that fit into various positions is determined by associative processes.* Such sentences, of course, would assert very unlikely things. While such sentences do occur in poetry and in similar kinds of writing, they are not ordinary sentences. [167]

In the context of a discussion of biblical parallelism it is not at all difficult to imagine the kind of sentences that Deese describes in the words which I have italicized. Many biblical verses seem to have been composed in just this way.

Deese goes on to quote some data on the generation of sentences by association. A typical response to *The wide road spoiled the park* is *The narrow path hid the beauty.* Thus not only does the second sentence reproduce the syntax of the first—i.e., parallel it grammatically[40]—but, in Deese's words, "the distribution of individual words substituted for particular words in these sentences are remarkably like the distributions of free associations" (169). Deese adds: "Despite semantic constraint, the distribution of verbal elements is very much like what one would expect from simple associative processes. Thus, syntactic and semantic constraint provided by words in ordinary sentences do not eliminate or replace associative processes" (170).

If nothing else, these statements support my contention that parallel word pairs and word associations are one and the same. But I think there *is* something else—namely, that the whole process of paralleling is related in some way to the process of association. Just as any competent speaker can generate a word pair, so any competent speaker can generate a parallel line. Presumably this is done through an associative process similar to that of word association. But is this simply a result of duplicating the grammatical form of the sentence and substituting lexical associates? Or is there an associative process on the semantic level, comparable to the one on the lexical level? This is suggestive, but I know of no psycholinguistic experiment or theory that sheds further light on the matter. So I will not deal with the

semantic aspect from a cognitive perspective but will explore other linguistic avenues.

Let me make clear that the semantic aspect of parallelism does not refer
to the meaning of a line, or even the meaning of the parallelism as a whole.
*The semantic aspect is the relationship between the meaning of one line and its
parallel line.* It is this relationship which Lowth categorized as synonymous, antithetic, or synthetic, and which Kugel described as "A, what's
more, B." My thesis is that parallel lines are in some way linguistically
equivalent. One type of equivalence is semantic equivalence. But how is
semantic equivalence to be defined? Lowth's system is too rigid, basically
limiting equivalence to synonymity or opposition; and Kugel's seems to
exclude equivalence by definition. Equivalence, as I use the term, does not
mean identity or synonymity. Two lines do not have to mean the same thing
in order to be semantically equivalent; semantic equivalence does not imply sameness of meaning any more than lexical equivalence does. Even
a paraphrase, which is one type of equivalence, is not identical with its
original.[41]

The semantic equivalence between parallel lines may be perceived as either paradigmatic or syntagmatic. These are the same categories that were
used to classify word pairs (lexical equivalents), and they are, in fact, the
major binary opposition of structural linguistics. As such, they can, theoretically at least, be used to describe any linguistic aspect of parallelism.[42]
We usually think of semantic parallelism only as paradigmatic—that is,
one thought can substitute for the other. But we should not exclude the
possibility of a syntagmatic semantic relationship where the two lines contain a semantic continuation, a progression of thought.[43] This may be independent of the grammatical relationship of the lines, and of the relationship between word pairs. A semantic syntagm may be expressed in
grammatically paradigmatic or syntagmatic lines, using paradigmatic or
syntagmatic word pairs.

Isa 40:9   על הר גבה עלי לך מבשרת ציון
                     הרימי בכח קולך מבשרת ירושלם

Ascend a high hill, herald to Zion;
Lift your voice aloud, herald to Jerusalem.

The actions of the herald are presented in the order in which they would
naturally occur. Thus I would say that these two lines are syntagmatically
related in their semantic aspect, although the word pair *herald to Zion* and

herald to Jerusalem is paradigmatic. Another syntagmatic semantic pairing
is found in

Isa 16:5   והוכן בחסד כסא
                                 . . . וישב עליו באמת באהל דוד

A throne shall be established in kindness;
And he shall sit on it in faithfulness. . . .

In this verse the lines as a whole are syntagmatic—the chair is first prepared
and then occupied; and the word pairs אמת // חסד and כסא // ישב are also
syntagmatic pairs.

Less easily classified as either paradigmatic or syntagmatic are verses like

Hab 3:3   כסה שמים הודו
                                    ותהלתו מלאה הארץ

His glory covers heaven;
And the earth is full of his praise.
[or: And his praise fills the earth.]

This looks like a merismus and would therefore be paradigmatic. But it
could just as well be interpreted as embodying a cause and result relationship which would make it syntagmatic. Lowth would call it synonymous,
and Kugel would say that B goes beyond A. We will see shortly that this
ambiguity—the tension between the paradigmatic and the syntagmatic—
is at the heart of parallelism, which, after all, imposes similarity upon
contiguity.[44]

Once we allow for equivalences that are more than paraphrases the possibilities multiply and the assignment of a particular verse to a specific
type becomes subjective (as in the case of Hab 3:3). This is so because the
parallelism itself does not always make the relationship between its lines
explicit. It usually juxtaposes them paratactically or joins them with the
multivalent *waw*. It is then up to the reader to decide if the *waw* means
"and," "but," "moreover," etc. This is the crux of the semantic aspect.

The area of linguistics that has the most potential for clarifying the semantic relationship between parallel lines is textlinguistics (or text grammar). Unlike generative grammar and formal semantics, which view the
sentence as the maximum linguistic unit, textlinguistics looks at larger
units and is especially concerned with describing the relationship between
adjacent sentences in a text or discourse, and with global relationships
throughout the discourse. The work that I have found most relevant in this
area is that of Teun van Dijk, even though van Dijk intentionally excludes

parallelism from his studies since he considers it as having a rhetorical or stylistic function but not a purely linguistic function (cf. *Text and Context*, 4). Nevertheless, several of van Dijk's points have a bearing on the semantic aspect of parallelism, especially insofar as they justify the concept of syntagmatic equivalence, and so I will bring them into our discussion.

Van Dijk examines connections and connectives in both compound sentences and sequences of sentences. While he is correct to distinguish between the two, it is immediately apparent that both are included in parallelism. It remains for future studies to see whether this makes a difference in parallelism. But more striking is van Dijk's statement that "Connectedness seems to be a condition imposed upon PAIRS OF SENTENCES" (*Text and Context*, 45). This was said of ordinary discourse, not poetic texts; it applies much more to lines in biblical poetry. In other words, the normal connectedness of ordinary discourse is heightened, or taken to an extreme, in poetry by parallelism.

Van Dijk examines different types of connectives (conjunctions, adverbs, particles, etc.) as well as sentences with no specific connection between them. He concludes that "connection is not dependent on the presence of connectives" and, conversely, "the presence of connectives does not make sentences connected" (*Text and Context*, 46). In other words, there is an inherent semantic connectedness that is perceived in a coherent discourse; in an uncoherent one (as in the isolated sample *We went to the beach and Peter was born in Manchester*) the use of a conjunction or other connective is not enough to generate a semantic connection between the clauses.

There are certain things that help to link two sentences besides specific connectives. Mainly it is a matter of their relating to the "topic of conversation" (the subject of the discourse, the point being made), giving a cause or reason, or making a temporal or local connection. (I oversimplify here.) Van Dijk again emphasizes that "sentential and especially sequential connection need not be expressed by explicit connectives . . . the connections between propositions in sentences and sequences may be 'expressed' by the very co-occurrence of the sentences expressing them" (*Text and Context*, 87).

Parallelism can easily be related to this discussion, for the types of connectives and connectedness between sentences in a discourse also pertain to parallel lines (simply because they are also sentences in a discourse). Some parallel lines are linked by specific linguistic connectives like כי

("for"), some have the ambiguous *waw* (van Dijk notes that "and" is often ambiguous also), and some have no connective at all. Moreover, parallelism itself serves as a rhetorical connective, in addition to the semantic connectedness of coherent discourse. Therefore, parallel lines are doubly connected; once by virtue of their role in a coherent text (with or without connective particles), and again by the linguistic equivalences which constitute parallelism. In the semantic aspect of parallelism, the normal semantic connectedness between sentences is enhanced by other linguistic equivalences so that semantic equivalence is promoted. What I have called semantic equivalence can also be viewed as van Dijk's semantic connectedness.

This discussion may make it seem that all parallel lines are, by definition, semantically equivalent. In a sense this is true, for as mentioned in chapter 2, even lines which have no apparent semantic relationship tend to be perceived as semantically related when they are grammatically equivalent. The question then is: do parallel lines manifest an inherent semantic equivalence aside from that described by van Dijk or projected by the equivalence in other linguistic aspects.

Actually, most of what van Dijk describes as semantic connectedness is the same as what I have called syntagmatic semantic connectedness. This connectedness is merely the result of contiguity—the logical development of coherent discourse. We are still left with the question of paradigmatic semantic equivalence, which is the most obvious type of semantic parallelism and would constitute the "inherent semantic equivalence" sought in the preceding paragraph. For this, the notion of generative semantics may be helpful. Modelled on generative grammar, generative semantics posits a deep semantic structure which may be realized through a number of different surface structures. To take a mundane example, the questions *How are you?*, *How are things?*, *How do you feel?* could be said to be different realizations of the same underlying semantic entity. The notion of paraphrase—that the same thought can be expressed through different words and forms—is based on the existence of a semantic deep structure (cf. van Dijk, *Some Aspects of Text Grammars*, 14). Since most of what is usually considered semantically parallel involves some sort of paraphrase, it is appropriate that we investigate this in greater detail. What needs to be stressed here, as it was in the case of syntactic equivalence, is that the same deep structure can be reflected in different surface structures. In this case it means that the same semantic equivalence can be expressed through dif-

ferent grammatical and lexical choices. Ultimately, what is interesting
about paraphrase—or paradigmatic semantic equivalence—is that it can
take so many different forms.

In order to demonstrate this with as much control as possible, we will
present parallelisms whose first lines are identical (or nearly identical) and
whose second lines are semantically equivalent but differently phrased.
Here it is not a question of the stylistic variation within the same parallelism, but of two completely different parallelisms which have one line in
common.

Ps 39:13   שמעה תפלתי ה'
                                  ושועתי האזינה

                                  Hear my prayer, YHWH;
                                  And give ear to my cry.

Ps 102:2   ה' שמעה תפלתי
                                  ושועתי אליך תבוא

                                  YHWH, hear my prayer;
                                  And let my cry reach you.

Semantically, both verses seem the same, although Ps 39:13 is grammatically identical while Ps 102:2 is grammatically equivalent (subject-
object parallelism).

Ps 55:2   האזינה אלהים תפלתי
                                  ואל תתעלם מתחנתי

                          Give ear, God, to my prayer;
                          And do not hide yourself from my plea.

Ps 86:6   האזינה ה' תפלתי
                                  והקשיבה בקול תחנונותי

                          Give ear, YHWH, to my prayer;
                          And harken to the sound of my pleadings.

This example is similar to the preceding one. The difference between the
verses is grammatical, not semantic. The grammatical equivalence in Ps
55:2 involves positive-negative parallelism; in Ps 86:6 there is a morphologic shift from singular to plural (*prayer // pleadings*).

Pr 10:15   הון עשיר קרית עזו
                                  מחתת דלים רישם

> The wealth of a rich man is his fortress;
> The ruin of the poor is their poverty.

Pr 18:11   הון עשיר קרית עזו
                וכחומה נשגבה במשכיתו

> The wealth of a rich man is his fortress;
> And like a high wall in his fancy.

The semantic equivalence is slightly different in the two verses. In Pr
18:11 there is a semantic extension of *fortress* while in Pr 10:15 there is a
contrast between the two lines. This may sound suspiciously like new labels for old distinctions—Lowth's synonymous and antithetic parallelism—but it is not. The terms "equivalence" and "contrast" are the same
that I have been using throughout this book, and they can be applied to the
semantic aspect as well as to the grammatic. Semantic equivalence is a
much broader term than Lowth's synonymous parallelism, and would include much that he might have considered "synthetic parallelism." "Contrast" is also broader than "antithetic parallelism" and includes not only
semantic opposites but also other types of contrast (which Lowth might
have thought of as synonymous), such as "Water he asked; Milk she gave"
(Jud 5:25).

Note also that the semantic parallels in each of these verses are not only
equally acceptable, neither being "more parallel" than the other, but that
the choice of parallel in each case fits the larger context in which the verse
is situated. Pr 10 contains many other contrasts, between the righteous
and the wicked, the wise and the foolish, and so the contrast between the
rich and the poor is quite at home. Pr 18, on the other hand, is structured
much differently; it is not built on quick contrasts but on more prolonged
images, and v. 11 fits into one of these.

Lam 5:19   אתה ה' לעולם תשב
                כסאך לדור ודור

> You, YHWH, will sit forever;
> Your throne is for eternity.

Ps 102:13   ואתה ה' לעולם תשב
                וזכרך לדר ודר

> You, YHWH, will sit forever;
> Your fame is for eternity.

The parallelisms in these verses are almost identical; only one word differs. But that makes all the difference in meaning—a whole different thought is stressed. And like Pr 10:15 and 18:11, each thought is the appropriate one for its context. Lam 5:19, by pairing *sit* and *throne*, emphasizes the idea of God's sitting enthroned forever as a reigning monarch. This is a fitting antidote in the context of the destruction of Mt. Zion, God's seat of power (cf. Lam 5:18). The second line of Ps 102:13, however, does not direct attention to sitting, but rather to "being, presence."[45] This verse speaks of the permanence of God in contrast to the transience of the psalmist (Ps 102:12). Here semantics gives way to pragmatics; the larger context of the poem determines the form of the semantic equivalence within the parallelism.[46]

We should learn from these examples that generating a semantic parallel is not automatic—a formulaic reflex, as it were. The parallel must fit the semantic and structural context, and, indeed, is fashioned to do so. In the majority of parallelisms this is accomplished by choosing which components to repeat or parallel and which to leave unparalleled. Both Lam 5:19 and Ps 102:13 pair *forever* and *eternity*, for this idea is important to both. Lam 5:19 pairs *sit* and *throne*, thereby confirming the idea of sitting on a throne, while Ps 102:13 pairs *you* and *your fame*, ignoring the sitting aspect and underlining the "being" or "you-ness" aspect. This point about contextual appropriateness has certain implications for understanding semantic parallelism and parallelism as a whole. Not every part of the first line need be paralleled in the second, and, in fact, it rarely is. But it is a mistake to perceive such parallelisms as "incomplete" or otherwise defective. The words which are gapped or left unparalleled are those which the verse wants to deemphasize; the emphasis is on the words that are repeated or paralleled.

A. Disambiguation and Ambiguity

This brings us to one of the main semantic functions of parallelism: disambiguation and ambiguity. One of the functions of the second line of a parallelism is to disambiguate the first, especially if the first does not make clear what the topic of conversation is. This occurs in nonparallelistic discourse as well. Van Dijk gives an example, *Please go to the store and buy me some beer*, in which the first clause does not contain enough information and the second is used to fill in this missing information. The hearer only knows what kind of store is meant after he interprets the second clause (cf. *Text and Context*, 60). The terseness of the poetic line always puts it at risk of being misunderstood, either because information is omitted or because the reader/hearer is unable to focus on the main point (the topic of conversation). This can be partially overcome through parallelism, for the second line directs the interpretation of the first; the first line comes to be understood in terms of the second. On the other hand, the second line may introduce an element of ambiguity into the first. The first line takes on a new shade of meaning when it is read in terms of the second. Both disambiguation and ambiguity coexist in parallelism. Let us see them at work in a passage from Isaiah which Kugel (*Idea*, 9) has explained at some length and which I will explore even further.

Isa 1 : 3

ידע שור קנהו
וחמור אבוס בעליו
ישראל לא ידע
עמי לא התבונן

> An ox knows its owner;
> And an ass its masters' trough.
> Israel does not know;
> My people does not understand itself.

The first line is a relatively straightforward statement, but its exact shade of meaning—i.e., the point that Isaiah wants to make through it—does not become clear until later. Isaiah begins to clarify his point about the ox by bringing in the ass. Now the prophet does not come to praise the ox or denigrate the ass. He uses two examples to make one point. The ox, being a relatively superior animal, but an animal nevertheless, can recognize who its owner is. The ass, an inferior counterpart, at least knows where its feeding trough is. Both animals have primitive, animal knowledge—each in a measure appropriate to its status on the intellectual hierarchy—by which they comprehend that they are controlled and provided for by masters.

A closer look at these lines is in order. The verb *ydᶜ* is gapped, so our attention is withdrawn from it. Whatever kind of knowledge the ox has, the ass has the same. But the object of the knowledge is different: owner vs. masters' trough, which implies that the degree of knowledge is not equal. This contrast within equivalence matches the contrast within equivalence of *ox* and *ass*. On one hand, the two are similar, but on the other hand, they are different.

Of course, these lines are merely paving the way for the clincher in the next two. The progression continues from ox to ass to Israel. If the terms are all counterparts (equivalents) that is bad enough—Israel is situated among the animals. If a progression is intended, then the matter is even worse, for Israel is the stupidest. And here the parallelism becomes an optical illusion, like the picture in psychology books that is both a vase and two profiles. Before, lines 1 and 2 seemed to be a paraphrase; now they suddenly become a progression. Israel is more stupid than an ass because it doesn't *know* anything at all. The verb ידע, which was gapped in the second line reappears in the third; but instead of having an object—that which is known—it occurs without an object, hinting that its object is nothing—"Israel doesn't know (anything)." Even the kind of knowledge that was credited to the animals is lacking in respect to Israel; Israel does not possess even primitive animal knowledge. What is this animal knowledge? A sense of who one's master is. It is this that Israel lacks. This thought reaches its climax in the fourth line. Kugel has made much of the verbal form of התבונן, claiming that the *hitpaᶜel* form intensifies in some vague way, yielding "does not understand at all." It is true, as Kugel notes, that when בון is paired with ידע, it is usually in the *hiphᶜil* (הבין), not the *hitpaᶜel* (התבונן). But the word התבונן, "consider, pay attention to," is not so unusual; it is found a number of times in conjunction with שמע, "to hear" (Isa 52:15; Job 26:14), ראה, "to see" (Jer 2:10; Job 11:11), זכר, "to remember, pay mind to" (Isa 43:18), and ידע, "to know" (Job 11:11; 38:18). If one must find in the choice of the *hitpaᶜel* some extra shade of meaning, it is perhaps best to render it in its common reflexive sense: "does not understand itself." This, I think, is the sense of the line, and it is brought home by the word עמי, "my people." What is it that Israel does not understand? "[Israel] does not understand itself [to be] my people." This is what the first three lines have been building toward: Israel has no sense of who its master is or from whence it receives its sustenance.

What I have called disambiguation is this kind of clarification, redefinition, unfolding of development. I think this is what Kugel often means by his "A, what's more, B." But this should not be understood to mean that B is not equivalent to A. A and B are not independent lines; we read one in terms of the other. They need not be synonymous, of course, but they are certainly equivalent—they correspond semantically, in any one of a number of ways.

The other side of the coin is ambiguity or polysemy, and it is present along with disambiguation. We have seen the tension between the two in the lines involving the ox and the ass; they are the same and yet different, they signify one thing and two things simultaneously. In Hab 3:3, too, which can be viewed as a merismus or as a progression, we waver between the paradigmatic and syntagmatic reading. In parallelism after parallelism we are torn between the similarity of the lines and, at the same time, their dissynonymity. Parallelism is forever poised between redundancy and polysemy.

This is nowhere more evident than in the paralleling of numbers: one // two, three // four, six // seven, and so on. This piques the modern scientific mind no end; how can three be four? Do the two numbers represent the same quantity or different quantities? We feel compelled to choose between "synonymous" and "goes beyond" here just as we do between Lowth and Kugel. But both are correct. Both facets of parallelism coexist. This is a manifestation of what Waugh referred to as *redundancy* vs. *ambiguity*, one of the major dichotomies in linguistic discourse (cf. chapter 1, p. 16). Redundant signs do not provide independent information, but inform about other signs in the text. "They are used in a sense to insure that the given information is provided" (73). This is disambiguation. Ambiguous signs provide more than one interpretation, "even when in context of other signs." A parallel line does both; it insures the delivery of the information in the first line and, even in the context of that first line, it encourages a second view of things, an alternate interpretation. Redundancy and ambiguity (disambiguation and polysemy) are locked in eternal struggle in parallelism. To choose one is to lose the other, and thereby lose the major dialectic tension of parallelism. There is no better way to sum this up than to quote

| Ps 62 : 12 | אחת דבר אלהים |
| | שתים זו שמעתי |

One thing God has spoken;
Two things I have heard.

This verse not only lends itself to discussions of hermeneutics—that one statement has many interpretations—but it also reflects the essence of parallelism. Parallelism is constituted by redundancy and polysemy, disambiguation and ambiguity, contrast within equivalence. Parallelism focuses the message on itself but its vision is binocular. Like human vision it superimposes two slightly different views of the same object and from their convergence it produces a sense of depth.

B. Parallelism as Metaphor

A final facet of semantic equivalence is the metaphoric function of parallelism. I have already discussed the fact that syntactic equivalence promotes the perception of semantic equivalence. Two contiguous lines which have the same syntactic structure tend to be viewed as having some correlation in meaning, and even when there is no obvious semantic connection between them, we seek a correlation through our interpretation (cf. chapter 2, p. 23). In this way one aspect of parallelism affects other aspects. Equivalence in one aspect is projected onto another aspect. The result is that even lines that do not have the same semantic deep structure are considered equivalent. This is one of the ways in which parallelism gains its power and effectiveness: from partial equivalence it creates the illusion of total equivalence. Equivalence is transferred from one aspect to another, and from one line to another. In this sense, parallelism is metaphoric.

Roman Jakobson has elevated this metaphoric function to a principle of parallelism: "anything sequent is a simile" and "metonymy is slightly metaphorical and any metaphor has a metonymical tint" (*LP*, 370). Jakobson uses these terms to explain the mutual effects of similarity and contiguity, and by so doing he broadens "metaphor" to include all parallelism. Francis Landy follows him in saying that "two halves of a clause are juxtaposed and held to be alike; the basic form of parallelism is metaphor" ("Poetics and Parallelism," 80). I do not want to pursue the concept of parallelism as metaphor on such a grand scale, although I appreciate the metaphoric effect of reading any B line after, and in terms of, any A line. Rather, I want to show that parallelistic structuring can become the medium for a comparison, a form for figurative language.[47] Parallel lines always have the potential to be understood metaphorically—this is in the nature of parallelism, as Jakobson has suggested. But only in specific cases is this potential actualized; here parallelism, and parallelism alone, conveys a simile or a metaphor.

This is clearest in proverbial sayings like

Pr 26:9   חוח עלה ביד שכור
                           ומשל בפי כסילים

                    A thorn comes to the hand of a drunkard;
                    And a proverb to the mouth of fools.

The two juxtaposed lines are grammatically equivalent but, on the surface at least, semantically unequivalent. Nevertheless, it is immediately apparent that a semantic relationship is intended. We understand it as an analogy: "Just as a thorn . . . so a proverb. . . ." There is ample support from the text itself for such a reading, for this and other similarly structured verses alternate with verses containing the particles כ . . . כן, "just as . . .

so" throughout Pr 26 (cf. McKane, *Proverbs*, 593–94). Either form, with or without "just as," is equally effective. A simile does not have to be specially marked; it can be conveyed through parallelism.

Ps 125:2   ירושלם הרים סביב לה
                          . . . וה' סביב לעמו

> Jerusalem—mountains surround it;
> And YHWH surrounds his people. . . .

The natural physical protection of Jerusalem serves as the comparison for God's protection of his people. There is no particle "as, like" to mark this as a simile, yet it is immediately understood as such from the structure of the lines. It is not quite a metaphor, in the conventional sense, for God is not identified with the mountains, and Jerusalem is not a metaphor for the people, although it may symbolize them. As mountains protect the city of Jerusalem, so God protects the people in it.

It is but a small step from simile to metaphor.[48] The interpretation of Eccl 7:1 is an interesting case in point.

Eccl 7:1   טוב שם משמן טוב
                  ויום המות מיום הולדו

> Better a name than good oil;
> And one's death-day than one's birth-day.

The verse as a whole is read as an analogy, like Pr 26:5—"Just as a name is better than good oil, so death is better than life." But this verse is more complex than Pr 26:5 because each line contains its own internal comparison. The first line, טוב שם משמן טוב, has all the earmarks of a popular proverb in its form and sound play (compare "Better red than dead"). It is quite plausible, as Gordis has suggested, that Koheleth is quoting a well-known saying and joining to it his own interpretation or application. Presumably, his audience understood the saying, so he could use it as the basis of his analogy to life and death. If one accepts the first premise, then one must accept the second. In order for the analogy to work, it must proceed from the known to the unknown; the second line makes sense only when it is read in light of the first.

Now just the opposite happens when a modern reader approaches this verse. He, too, understands that there is an analogy being made between the two lines, but, unlike Koheleth's audience, he is not familiar with the comparison in the first line. How can a name be contrasted with oil?[49]

Since there is an inherent comparison in this line, the reader seeks to understand how the two things are related. He may see them as a contrast between the physical and the nonphysical, the ephemeral and the lasting, or the cosmetic appearance and the true essence of a person. But there is nothing to tell him which of these, if any, is correct. In Eccl 7 : 1, however, something else enters the picture: the second line of the verse—which is immediately used to solve the riddle of the first line. The modern reader *reads the first line in light of the second.* He reads the analogy from back to front, and in doing so he makes the first line a metaphor (or to be more correct, a metonymy) for the second. Oil is equated with birth (oil is rubbed on the newborn) and a name (all that remains when life is finished) is equated with death.[50] I am not sure that this is the correct interpretation of "Better a name than good oil." As an independent proverb it may have had no connection with life and death. But I am reasonably certain that this interpretation owes its existence to the parallel structure of the lines and the urge to make sense of their combination. In the modern reading of Eccl 7 : 1 parallelism has indeed become metaphorical.

I have attempted to explain the semantic aspect of parallelism in terms of semantic equivalences ranging from paraphrase to progression to metaphor. When it comes to the semantic aspect, which is dependent on, yet separate from, the formal constructions within a text, the boundary between what is equivalent and what is not is hard to draw; for it is usually possible to find some relationship in meaning between two lines. That relationship is both enhanced and inhibited in poetry. We expect a poem to have a unity of theme and we expect its parts to relate to one another—and parallelism contributes to the unity of the parts. But at the same time the terseness of the poem and the parataxis of parallel lines do not permit the unity among the parts to be spelled out directly. So we are left very often with ambiguity or polysemy in regard to semantic relationships. But this, after all, is the core of poeticalness and the crux of poetic interpretation.

V

THE PHONOLOGIC ASPECT: SOUND PAIRS

Just as parallelism activates the grammatical, lexical, and semantic aspects of language, so, too, it activates the phonologic aspect. Phonologic equivalences and contrasts are often present in parallel lines and they contribute to the perception of correspondence between the lines.

Scholars of literature and linguistics have discussed many types of phonologic equivalence in language, especially in poetry. The most common in the English literary tradition are alliteration and rhyme. Biblical scholars, on their part, recognized long ago the Bible's penchant for wordplay or punning, and have taken note of various kinds of phonologic repetition in a wide variety of passages. These phenomena are generally subsumed under the term paronomasia.[1] My discussion will not be concerned with the many types of phonologic repetition in the Bible, nor with the importance of sound in biblical poetry; it will be limited to the repetition and contrast of sounds in parallel lines. More specifically, I will deal with sound pairs.

WHAT IS A SOUND PAIR?

Linguists speak of assonance and consonance. While the former term is sometimes applied to all types of sound repetition, it is properly confined to the repetition of like vowels or diphthongs. Consonance designates the repetition of the same or a similar sequence of consonants with a change in the intervening vowels. An example is ". . . and what says / My *conceal'd* lady to our *cancell'd* love" (*Romeo and Juliet*, act 3, scene 3). This line from Shakespeare, however, could not be said to contain a parallel sound pair because the consonance is not distributed over grammatically or semantically parallel phrases or lines.[2] An example of a consonant sound pair is: "In the northern hemisphere it was a *burnished* autumn; in the southern, a *burgeoning* spring" (James Michener, *Space* [New York: Random House, 1982], 3). But if we look closely, we find that although the two members of the sound pair have the same or similar (*š* and *j̃*) consonants, they are not in exactly the same order: *b-r-n-š*; *b-r-j̃-n*. Some might argue whether this meets the criterion for consonance, but it is precisely the kind of sound pairing that is found in biblical parallelism. I define a sound pair as *the repetition in parallel words or lines of the same or similar consonants in any order within close proximity*. For instance:

Mic 5:9   והכרתי סוסיך מקרבך
                                   והאבדתי מרכבתיך

        I will cut off your horses from your midst [*mqrbk*];
        I will destroy your chariots [*mrkbtyk*].

I have limited the definition of sound pairs to consonants for two reasons: 1) in biblical Hebrew only the consonants were originally written, and there exists among scholars some doubt about the original pronunciation of the vowels,[3] 2) Hebrew is often thought of as a consonantal language—that is, the meaning of the word is carried in the root consisting only of consonants. I do not mean to suggest that the vowels were not important in creating the effects of biblical diction—after all, without them the words are unpronounceable—but the fact remains that in biblical wordplay it is the consonants that are called into action; the vowels have but a minor role, if any. The priority of consonants over vowels has been taken for granted in the classic studies of paronomasia[4] and is made explicit in a more recent study by W. L. Holladay: "In Hebrew poetry such word-play is, so far as we can tell, primarily a matter of similarity in *combinations of consonants* between the words or phrases in question, whether the same consonants or like consonants (sibilants, for example, or voiced-unvoiced correlatives) appear in the same order or in a different order" (*VT* 20, 157).

Because there are only twenty-two consonants, some amount of repetition is inevitable, even within a space of two lines, and may therefore not appear to be linguistically or stylistically significant. In order to reduce the effect of random repetition and to control to some degree the subjectivity involved in the perception of sound correspondence, I would qualify the definition proposed above in the following ways: 1) at least two sets of consonants must be involved, 2) the sets must be in close proximity, within a word or adjacent words in both lines, 3) "same or similar consonant" means the identical phoneme, an allophone (e.g., ב and כ), or two phonemes which are articulated similarly (e.g., nasals: *m* and *n*; fricatives: *s* and *š*).

It should be made clear at the outset that the use of sound pairs can and should be distinguished from the use of lexical pairs. Previously I showed that lexical pairing is not identical with semantic pairing; the two may co-occur (i.e., a lexical pair may also be a semantic pair) or may be independent of one another (the lexical pair is not the semantic pair). So, too, in the case of sound pairs we find that some sound pairs may also be lexical or semantic pairs, but more often sound pairs occur in addition to, or in the absence of, lexical or semantic pairs. There is one striking illustration of the independence of sound pairs from word pairs, and of the ability of a sound pair to replace a word pair. We are fortunate to have three "versions" of virtually the same parallelism:

2 Sam 22:32	כי מי אל מבלעדי ה'
	ומי צור מבלעדי אלהינו

> For who is a god *except* YHWH?
> And who is a rock *except* our God?

Ps 18:32	כי מי אלוה מבלעדי ה'
	ומי צור זולתי אלהינו

> For who is a god *except* YHWH?
> And who is a rock *besides* our God?

Isa 44:8b	היש אלוה מבלעדי
	ואין צור בל ידעתי

> Is there a god *except me* [*blᶜdy*]?
> And there is no rock, *I know none* [*bl ydᶜty*].

It is not a question here of which is the "more original" or "better" parallelism; the fact is that all three are acceptable and all illustrate different types of pairings. In the first verse the term מבלעדי is repeated in the parallel line; in the second it is paralleled by זולתי, a lexical and semantic pair; and in the third it is paired with בל ידעתי, a phrase more distant semantically but very close phonologically. Isa 44:8b uses a sound pair instead of a word pair.[5]

Such sound pairs are occasionally commented upon in passing in some biblical commentaries, but to my knowledge the only scholar to grant these pairings the status of a distinct phenomenon is John Kselman, who collected thirteen examples of what he called "semantic-sonant chiasmus."[6] These are verses containing one word pair and one sound pair arranged chiastically, as in

Gen 27 : 36   את בכרתי לקח
                                          והנה עתה לקח ברכתי

My birthright [*bkrty*] he took;
And now he has taken my blessing [*brkty*].

What Kselman discovered is just the tip of the iceberg. There are many examples of sound pairs in the Bible, not only in chiastic combinations with word pairs, but with or without word pairs and in multiple sets of different patterns. This chapter will cite a large selection of illustrations and discuss how the activation of this phonologic aspect affects parallelism.

SOUND PAIRS AS WORD PAIRS

In chapter 4 I explained word pairs as the products of normal linguistic association, and cited a number of principles underlying specific pairs. It is possible that, in addition to those principles already mentioned, sound plays a part in certain lexical combinations. Certainly the phonologic equivalence is foregrounded in such English idioms as *flip-flop*, *forgive and forget*, and it may even be responsible for the formation of the idiom in the first place. Besides these and similar idioms there are several lexical associates listed by Deese which, although they can be explained by other principles, seem to have a phonologic dimension to their association: *daisy-pansy*; *depression-recession*; *rayon-nylon*; *auditorium-gymnasium*. These are word pairs which can also be considered sound pairs. Hebrew, too, has a few word pairs which show phonologic correspondence: עפר־אפר, *ʿpr-ʾpr*, *dust-ashes* (cf. Gen 18:27; Job 30:19; 42:6; Ezek 27:30); מדבר־ערבה, *mdbr-ʿrbh, desert-wilderness* (cf. Jer 2:6; 50:12; Job 24:5; Isa 35:6; 40:3); תהו־בהו, *thw-bhw, emptiness-chaos* (cf. Gen 1:2; Isa 34:11; Jer 4:23); פח־פחד־פחת, *ph-phd-pht, terror-pit-trap* (cf. Isa 24:17–18; Jer 48:43; Job 22:10; Lam 3:47). Besides these pairs, which are common enough to be considered word pairs, there are several verses with semantically related sound pairs. It is not clear to me whether these are sound pairs which are also word pairs, or pairings based on sound alone—not lexical associates. The uncertainty arises from the fact that these pairings are rare, in most cases occurring only once. In combinations like בור // באר, *bwr // b'r*, *cistern // well* (Pr 5:15)[7] and שלום // שלוה, *šlwm // šlwh*, *peace // tranquility* (Ps 122:7), there seems a good chance that lexical association is involved. But this is less obvious in pairs like כף נחת // חפנים, *kp nḥt // ḥpnym*, *a handful of gratification // two fistfuls* (Eccl 4:6).

The following are sound pairs which also manifest grammatical and semantic equivalence.

Gen 7:11b   נבקעו כל מעינת תהום רבה
             וארבת השמים נפתחו

All the fountains of the great deep burst [*nbq 'w*];
And the floodgates of the sky opened [*npthw*].[8]

Isa 31:9   אשר אור לו בציון
            ותנור לו בירושלם

Who has a fire [*'wr lw*] in Zion;
Has an oven [*tnwr lw*] in Jerusalem.

Ps 122:7   יהי שלום בחילך
            שלוה בארמנותיך

May there be peace [*šlwm*] in your ramparts;
Tranquility [*šlwh*] in your citadels. [cf. Ps 122:6.]

Pr 5:15   שתה מים מבורך
           ונזלים מתוך בארך

Drink water from your cistern [*bwrk*];
Running water from out of your well [*b'rk*].

Pr 6:15   על כן פתאם יבוא אידו
           פתע ישבר ואין מרפא

Therefore suddenly [*pt'm*] calamity will come upon him;
In a flash [*pt'*] he will be broken with none to mend.[9]

Ps 32:1   אשרי נשוי פשע
           כסוי חטאה

Happy is he whose transgression is borne [*nśwy*];
Whose sin is covered [*kswy*].[10]

Pr 26:3   שוט לסוס מתג לחמור
           ושבט לגו כסילים

A whip [šwṭ] for a horse, and a bridle for a donkey;
And a rod [šbṭ] for the back of fools.

Eccl 4:6   טוב מלא כף נחת
                              ממלא חפנים עמל ורעות רוח

Better is a handful of gratification [kp nḥt];
Than two fistfuls [ḥpnym] of toil and pursuit of wind.

Two sound pairs occur in

Job 8:11   היגאה גמא בלא בצה
                              ישגה אחו בלי מים

Can papyrus thrive [hygʾh] not in [blʾ] a marsh?
Can rushes grow [yśgh] without [bly] water?

Less similar semantically, but still within range, are the pairs in

Ps 37:6   והוציא כאור צדקך
                              ומשפטך כצהרים

He will cause to shine like light [whwṣyʾ kʾwr] your vindication;
And your justice like the noon [kṣhrym].

Isa 40:12a   מי מדד בשעלו מים
                              ושמים בזרת תכן

Who measured in the hollow of his hand the waters [mym];
And the sky [šmym] with a span gauged.[11]

Yet the same pair, mym // šmym, occurs in Jud 5:4b but here it is not grammatically or semantically equivalent:

Jud 5:4b   ארץ רעשה
                              גם שמים נטפו
                              גם עבים נטפו מים

The earth trembled;
Also the sky dripped;
Also the clouds dripped water.[12]

SOUND PAIRS WHICH ARE NOT WORD PAIRS

As in Jud 5:4, there are many cases in which the sound pair is not
lexically-semantically equivalent, but occurs in addition to a word pair or

in place of one. (This is analogous to examples of lexical pairs which are not semantic pairs—cf. chapter 4, p. 81ff.)

Ex 34:3   . . . וגם איש אל ירא בכל ההר
גם הצאן והבקר אל ירעו אל מול ההר ההוא

. . . no one else shall be seen [*yr*ʾ] anywhere on the mountain; neither shall flocks and herds graze [*yrʿw*] at the foot of this mountain.

Isa 58:8   אז יבקע כשחר אורך
וארכתך מהרה תצמח

Then shall your light [ʾ*wrk*] burst through like the dawn;
And your healing [ʾ*rktk*] spring up quickly.

Ps 69:13   ישיחו בי ישבי שער
ונגינות שותי שכר

The sitters at the gate [*šr*] discuss me;
[I am] the taunts of drinkers of strong drink [*škr*].

Ps 104:19   עשה ירח למועדים
שמש ידע מבואו

He made the moon for time-markers [*mwʿdym*];
The sun knows its setting [*ydʿ mbwʾw*].[13]

Job 3:8   יקבהו אררי יום
העתידים ערר לויתן

May the spell-casters [ʾ*rry*] of the day/sea damn it;
Those prepared to stir up [ʿ*rr*] the Leviathan.[14]

Job 26:2   מה עזרת ללא כח
הושעת זרוע לא עז

How can you help [ʿ*zrt*] with no strength;
Save with an arm [*zrwʿ*] with no power [ʿ*z*].

Job 28:20   והחכמה מאין תבוא
ואי זה מקום בינה

And wisdom, from where does it come [*mʾyn tbwʾ*];
And whence is the place of understanding [-*wm bynh*].[15]

Job 31:37   מספר צעדי אגידנו
כמו נגיד אקרבנו

An account of my steps I would tell him [ʾ*gydnw*];
As to a prince [*ngyd*] I would offer it.

Job 36:15   יחלץ עני בעניו
                                 ויגל בלחץ אזנם

    He rescues [yḥlṣ] the afflicted through their affliction;
    And reveals their ear through oppression [blḥṣ].

Job 37:24   לכן יראוהו אנשים
                                 לא יראה כל חכמי לב

    Therefore men fear him [yrʾwhw];
    Whom all the wise hearted cannot see [yrʾh].[16]

Job 38:27   להשביע שאה ומשאה
                                 ולהצמיח מצא דשא

    To satisfy [lhśbyʿ] the desolate wasteland;
    And to make sprout [lhṣmyḥ] the crop of grass.[17]

Song 4:2b   שכלם מתאימות
                                 ושכלה אין בהם

    Of which all [šklm] are perfectly matched;
    There is none missing [šklh] from them.

Lam 3:4   בלה בשרי ועורי
                                 שבר עצמותי

    He has wasted my flesh and my skin [bśry wʿwry];
    He has shattered my bones [šbr ʿ-].

Several other verses containing sound pairs, which have been noted by
Kselman, should be included here.

Ps 72:7   יפרח בימיו צדיק
                                 ורב שלום עד בלי ירח

    The righteous may flourish [yprḥ] in his day;
    And well-being abound till the moon [yrḥ] is no more.[18]

Ps 78:33   ויכל בהבל ימיהם
                                 ושנותם בבהלה

    He made their days end in futility [bhbl];
    Their years in trouble [bbhlh].

Ps 147:13   כי חזק בריחי שעריך
                                 ברך בניך בקרבך

    For he made firm the bars [bryḥy] of your gates;
    He blessed [brk] your children in your midst [bqrbk].

The list is already long enough to suggest that sound pairing is more than coincidental—and there are yet more examples to come in subsequent sections. Although some sound pairs are also word pairs, the majority are unrelated lexically or semantically, and occur only once. Unlike word pairs, they are not automatic responses to stimuli, but a one-time nexus between sound and sense. It is precisely the unexpectedness of these combinations that creates their effect. And it is by virtue of their nonequivalence with the grammatical and semantic aspects of the parallelism that an artistic tension among linguistic aspects is produced. As I. M. Casanowicz put it: "The charm and effect of paronomasia lie . . . in the union of similarity of sound with dissimilarity of sense" (26).

THE EFFECT OF SOUND PAIRS ON PARALLELISM

In a sequence, where similarity is superimposed on contiguity, two similar phonemic sequences near to each other are prone to assume a paronomastic function. Words similar in sound are drawn together in meaning. [*LP*, 371]

Jakobson did not intend for this statement to apply only to what I have designated as sound pairs, but it has obvious relevance to the type of phonologic correspondence that I am discussing. We have seen that some sound pairs are "natural" semantic pairs; but we have also seen that many sound pairs are not equivalent on other linguistic levels. In what sense, then, are "words similar in sound drawn together in meaning"? I would argue that it is not the individual words that are drawn together (their meanings remain charmingly dissimilar, as Casanowicz's statement says) so much as the lines of which they are a part. Sound pairing enhances the perception of correspondence between the lines. When the sound pair is also a lexical-semantic pair, the bond between them is reinforced; when the sound pair is not a lexical-semantic pair, it can be said to replace such a pair. Even when there are other word pairs in the parallelism, the sound pair plays a crucial role in forging the union between the lines. In this way the sound pair helps to superimpose similarity upon the contiguity of the lines. A good illustration is

Ps 104:19   עשה ירח למועדים
                                שמש ידע מבואו

He made the moon for time-markers [$mw^c dym$];
The sun knows its setting [$yd^c\ mbw^\jmath w$].

Despite the word pair *moon // sun* (in an order reversed from normal), and
the expectation of parallelism (since it is pervasive throughout the psalm),
the semantic relationship between the lines, and hence their meaning, is
not immediately apparent, at least to the modern reader. But the phonologic equivalence of מועדים and ידע מבואו pulls the lines together and suggests that equivalence of sound signifies equivalence of sense. The psalm is
speaking here of the nighttime world and the verse says that the moon was
made to mark the onset of night, as does the setting of the sun.[19] I mentioned earlier (chapter 2) that a similarity in syntactic structure leads to the
perception of a correspondence in meaning. The same is true for phonologic structure; phonologic similarity or equivalence promotes the perception of semantic equivalence.

The converse is also true: similarity in syntactic or semantic structure
foregrounds phonologic similarity.[20] This can be seen in

Isa 54:7   ברגע קטן עזבתיך
                                   וברחמים גדלים אקבצך

> For a small moment (*rgʿ*) I forsook you;
> But with great mercy (*rhmym*) I will gather you up.

There are three pairs here. Two are lexical-semantic pairs: גדלים // קטן,
"small // great," and עזבתיך // אקבצך, "I forsook you // I will gather
you." The third, רחמים // רגע, "moment // mercy," has no semantic relationship but a strong phonologic correspondence. In addition, both members of this sound pair are located in the same position in terms of word
order, and both are grammatically similar in that they are preceded by the
same preposition. In this case, the extensive grammatical and lexical-
semantic equivalence in the two lines acts to heighten the perception of
phonologic equivalence between רגע and רחמים. The more equivalences
there are in all linguistic aspects, the stronger any one equivalence tends to
appear. The phonologic aspect of parallelism both adds to the perception
of these equivalences and is itself perceived because of them.

THE PATTERNING OF SOUND PAIRS

Until now I have cited verses which, for the most part, contain only one
sound pair. There are many which have two or more, and the sound pairs

are arranged in the same patterns used for word pairs: *aabb*; *abab*; *abba*.
I have included in this section verses containing two or more sound pairs,
or one sound pair and one repeated root. The repetition of the same word
or root was shown to be a response in psycholinguistic word association
(cf. chapter 4), but it also fits my definition of a sound pair. In fact, it is
sound equivalence par excellence.

The transliteration that accompanies the citations is designed to focus
attention on the sounds involved in the patterning. A hyphen indicates that
only part of a word is involved.

A. aabb

Isa 5:1

אשירה נא לידידי
שירת דודי לכרמו
כרם היה לידידי
בקרן בן שמן

Let me sing for my beloved,	*ydydy*
A song of my lover for his vineyard.	*dwdy*
My beloved had a vineyard	*krm*
On a fruitful hill [?].	*qrn*

This verse employs word patterning as well as sound patterning, and while
there is some overlap between them, they are not congruent. The repeated
words are ידידי (lines 1, 3), שיר (lines 1, 2), and כרם (lines 2, 3). The sound
pattern involves two of these and links them with two different words with
similar phonemes.[21]

Isa 34:10

לילה ויומם לא תכבה
לעולם יעלה עשנה
מדור לדור תחרב
לנצח נצחים אין עבר בה

Night and day it shall not go out;	*lylh wywm*
Forever shall its smoke rise;	*l^cwlm y^clh*
From generation to generation it shall be ruined;	*ḥrb*
For all eternity none shall traverse it.	*^cbr*

It appears that the more common order, *day and night*, was reversed for
phonologic effect. Again, this passage contains a complex interplay between words, grammar, and sound. Note the negative-positive-positive-
negative grammatical pattern and the subject-object-subject-object pattern
as well as the feminine-masculine-feminine-masculine pattern.

Isa 35:6   אז ידלג כאיל פסח
                                  ותרן לשון אלם
                                  כי נבקעו במדבר מים
                                  ונחלים בערבה

    Then the lame shall leap like a deer;   *'yl*
    And the tongue of the dumb shall shout.   *'lm*
    For waters shall burst forth in the desert;   *bmdbr*
    And streams in the wilderness.   *b'rbh*

The first pair, *'yl* (*deer*) and *'lm* (*dumb*), are a sound pair, not a semantic pair; the second pair, *mdbr* (*desert*) and *'rbh* (*wilderness*), are both a semantic and a phonetic pair.

Zeph 1:13   והיה חילם למשסה
                                  ובתיהם לשממה
                                  ובנו בתים ולא ישבו
                                  ונטעו כרמים ולא ישתו את יינם

    Their wealth shall become plunder;   *lmšsh*
    And their houses a wasteland.   *lšmmh*
    They shall build houses and not dwell [in them];   *wl' yšbw*
    They shall plant vineyards and not drink their wine.   *wl' yštw*

"Building" and "planting," i.e., establishing a settlement, co-occur frequently (e.g., Isa 65:21; Jer 1:10 and passim; Eccl 2:4), but here they are given phonologic equivalence through the addition of *wl' yšbw* and *wl' yštw*—compare also Amos 5:11 and 9:14.

B. abab

In this and the following section I will first list verses containing one sound pair and one repeated root, and then verses containing two sound pairs.

Isa 54:4   אל תיראי כי לא תבושי
                                  ואל תכלמי כי לא תחפירי
                                  כי בשת עלומיך תשכחי
                                  וחרפת אלמנותיך לא תזכרי עוד

    Do not fear for you shall not be ashamed;   *tbwšy*
    And do not be confounded for you shall not be disgraced.   *thpyry*
    For the shame of your youth you shall forget;   *-y bšt*
    And the embarrassment of your widowhood you shall   *whrpt*
      no longer remember.

The syntax and semantics of the verse is structured on an *aabb* pattern
while the sound pairs occur in an *abab* arrangement.[22]

Ps 35:22   ראיתה ה' אל תחרש
                       אדני אל תרחק ממני

    You have seen, YHWH, do not be silent;   *ʾl tḥrš*
    Lord, do not be distant from me.   *ʾl trḥq*

If 'ה and אדני are pronounced the same there is an additional pair. The surrounding verses continue the sound play of *tḥrš-trḥq* with ראתה, וירחיבו
(v. 21), and העירה (v. 23).

Ezek 36:34
                       והארץ הנשמה תעבד
                  תחת אשר היתה שממה לעיני כל עובר

    And the desolate land will be tilled,   *hnšmh tʿbd*
    instead of having been a wasteland to the   *šmmh*
    eyes of every passer-by.   *ʿwbr*

Job 5:2-3   כי לאויל יהרג כעש
                      ופתה תמית קנאה
                   אני ראיתי אויל משריש
                      ואקוב נוהו פתאם

    For vexation kills the fool;   *ʾwyl*
    Passion slays the simpleton.   *wpth*
    I myself have seen a fool strike roots;   *ʾwyl*
    I cursed his home suddenly.[23]   *ptʾm*

Ps 56:9   נדי ספרתה אתה
                      שימה דמעתי בנאדך
                      הלא בספרתך

    You keep account of my wanderings;   *ndy sprth*
    Put my tears in your flask,   *nʾdk*
    Are they not in your account-book?   *sprtk*

Ps 139:7   אנה אלך מרוחך
                      ואנה מפניך אברח

    Where can I get away from your spirit;   *ʾnh mrwḥk*
    And where from your presence can I flee?   *ʾnh -k ʾbrḥ*

This verse sets up the same kind of false equation with sound pairs as Ps
105:6 and Ps 49:5 do with word pairs (cf. chapter 3, p. 62). The sound
pairs occupy identical positions in respect to word order, but they do not

correlate with the syntactic-semantic equivalents which are *ʾlk // ʾbrḥ*, "I go // I flee," and *mrwḥk // mpnyk*, "from your spirit // from your presence."

Jud 5:4a   ה' בצאתך משעיר
בצעדך משדי אדום

> YHWH, when you came forth from Seir;   *bṣ ʾtk mś-*
> When you strode from the plains of Edom.[24]   *bṣʿdk mś-*

Isa 34:6b   כי זבח לה' בבצרה
וטבח גדול בארץ אדום

> For there is a sacrifice for YHWH in Bozrah;   *zbḥ bbṣrh*
> A great slaughter in the land of Edom.   *ṭbḥ bʾrṣ*

Isa 35:5   אז תפקחנה עיני עורים
ואזני חרשים תפתחנה

> Then the eyes of the blind shall be opened;   *ʾz tpqḥnh*
> And the ears of the deaf shall be unstopped.   *ʾz- tpthnh*

Isa 40:12b   וכל בשלש עפר הארץ
ושקל בפלס הרים

> And meted the earth's dust with a measure;   *wkl bšlš*
> And weighed the mountains with a scale.   *wškl bpls*

Other segments of this verse were discussed above. The whole verse represents a complex intertwining of words, sounds, and meaning.

Isa 42:16   והולכתי עורים בדרך לא ידעו
בנתיבות לא ידעו אדריכם
אשים מחשך לפניהם לאור
ומעקשים למישור

> I will make the blind walk by a road they knew not;
> On paths they knew not I will lead them;
> I will turn darkness before them to light;
> And rough places to level ground.

The first half of the verse contains two repeated roots in chiastic order: *drk-ydʿ-ydʿ-drk*. The second half contains two sound pairs in an *abab* order: *mḥšk-lʾwr-mʿqš-lmyšwr*.

Ps 46:10   משבית מלחמות עד קצה הארץ
קשת ישבר וקצץ חנית עגלות ישרף באש

> He makes cease wars to the end of the earth,   *mšbyt qšh*
> Breaking the bow, snapping the spear,   *yšbr qṣṣ*
> burning wagons in fire.

The roots *šbt* and *šbr* occur in juxtaposition in Ezek 6:6, also for reasons of sound (cf. Saydon, *Biblica* 36, 292). Additional consonance is in ‐יִשְׂרֹף קֶשֶׁת‐קִצֵּץ and יְשַׁבֵּר.

Ps 147:15

השלח אמרתו ארץ
עד מהרה ירוץ דברו

He sends forth his word to the earth;   *'mrth 'rṣ*
Swiftly runs his command.   *mhrh yrwṣ*

Pr 23:9

באזני כסיל אל תדבר
כי יבוז לשכל מליך

Into the ears of a fool do not speak,   *b'zny ksyl*
For he will disdain the good sense of your words.   *ybwz śkl*

Pr 24:22

כי פתאם יקום אידם
ופיד שניהם מי יודע

For suddenly their disaster arises;   *pt'm 'ydm*
The doom of both of them who can know.[25]   *wpyd my ywdᶜ*

Job 4:11

ליש אבד מבלי טרף
ובני לביא יתפרדו

A lion perishes without prey,   *mbly ṭrp*
And the lion cubs are scattered.   *lby' ytprdw*

Job 6:6

היאכל תפל מבלי מלח
אם יש טעם בריר חלמות

Can tasteless [food] be eaten without salt?   *mbly mlḥ*
Does . . . have flavor?   *-m bryr ḥlm-*

Job 8:11

היגאה גמא בלא בצה
ישגה אחו בלי מים

Can papyrus thrive not in a marsh?   *hyg'h bl'*
Can rushes grow without water?   *yśgh bly*

Job 9:33

לא יש בינינו מוכיח
ישת ידו על שנינו

There is no arbiter between us   *yš bynynw*
To put his hand on both of us.   *yšt šnynw*

לא יֵשׁ is something of an oddity, and some commentators prefer to read לֻא יֵשׁ, "if only there were."[26] If the vocalization of the MT is correct, perhaps this peculiar construction was chosen because it creates a phonetic parallelism with *yšt*.

C. abba

Isa 34:9

ונהפכו נחליה לזפת
ועפרה לגפרית
והיתה ארצה לזפת בערה

Its streams shall be turned to pitch,	*lzpt*
And its soil to sulfur;	*ʿprh gpryt*
Its land shall become burning pitch.	*lzpt bʿrh*

This can be analyzed as *abab*: זפת‑עפרה‑לזפת‑בערה or as *abba*:
לזפת‑עפרה‑גפרית‑לזפת.

Isa 42:13

ה׳ כגבור יצא
כאיש מלחמות יעיר קנאה
יריע אף יצריח
על איביו יתגבר

YHWH like a valiant goes forth;	*gbwr*
Like a man of wars he stirs up [his] rage;	*yʿyr*
He yells, he roars aloud;	*yryʿ*
Upon his enemies he prevails.	*ytgbr*

Ps 64:5

לירות במסתרים תם
פתאם ירהו ולא ייראו

To shoot from hiding at the blameless,	*lyrwt tm*
Suddenly they shoot him and they do not fear.	*ptʾm yrhw/yyrʾw*

Ps 107:36

ויושב שם רעבים
ויכוננו עיר מושב

He settles the hungry there;	*ywšb*	*rʿbym*
And they establish a city settlement.	*ʿyr*	*mwšb*

Ps 139:1b–2

ה׳ חקרתני ותדע
אתה ידעת שבתי וקומי
בנתה לרעי מרחוק

YHWH, you have examined me and know,	*hqrtny wtdʿ*
You know when I sit down and get up,	*ydʿt*
You discern my thoughts from afar.	*rhwq*

Job 4:14

פחד קראני ורעדה
ורב עצמותי הפחיד

Fear came upon me, and trembling,	*phd rʿ-*
Causing all my bones to fear.	*rb ʿ- hphyd*

Job 37:16   התדע על מפלשי עב
                             מפלאות תמים דעים

        Do you know about the suspending [?] of the clouds,   *tdᶜ mplśy*
        The wonders of the one perfect in knowledge?   *mplʾwt dᶜym*

Four verses noted by Kselman (*Biblica* 58) should be included in this category.

Gen 27:36	בכרתי־לקח־לקח־ברכתי	, *bkrty-lqh-lqh-brkty*
2 Sam 1:21b	שם־מגן־מגן־שמן	, *šm-mgn-mgn-šmn*
Eccl 7:1a	טוב־שם־שמן־טוב	, *twb-šm-šmn-twb*[27]
Ezek 22:2	אדם־התשפט־התשפט־דמים	, *ʾdm-htšpṭ-htšpṭ-dmym*[28]

In his list of chiastic word patterns, A. Ceresko (*CBQ* 38) has included eight which involve sound pairs in combination with repeated roots. Although they are not in all cases distributed over parallel lines, they manifest the same phenomenon that we are discussing.

Isa 29:17	ושב־כרמל־כרמל־יחשב	, *wšb-krml-krml-yḥšb*
Jer 25:5	שובו־הרעה־מרע־ושבו	, *šwbw-hrᶜh-mrᶜ-wšbw*
Job 14:6-7	ויחדל־עד־עוד־תחדל	, *wyḥdl-ᶜd-ᶜwd-tḥdl*
Job 21:29-30	עוברי־ליום־ליום־עברות	, *ᶜwbry-lywm-lywm-ᶜbrwt*
Job 31:9	נפתה־על־על־פתח	, *npth-ᶜl-ᶜl-ptḥ*
Job 32:13-14	תאמרו־אל־לא־לא־אלי־באמריכם	
	tʾmrw-ʾl-lʾ-lʾ-ʾly-bʾmrykm	
Job 33:12-13	אענך־ירבה־ריבות־יענה	
	ʾᶜnk-yrbh-rybwt-yᶜnh [cf. Ceresko, *UF* 7, 86]	
Job 37:13-17	לארצו־נפלאות־התדע־התדע־מפלאות־ארץ	
	lʾrṣw-nplʾwt-htdᶜ-htdᶜ-mplʾwt-ʾrṣ	

I now present verses containing two sets of sound pairs (not repeated roots) in the *abba* pattern.

Isa 24:12   נשאר בעיר שמה
                         ושאיה יכת שער

        Left in the town is desolation;   *nšʾr šmh*
        And the gate is battered to ruins.   *šʾyh šᶜr*

Isa 31:8b   ונס לו מפני חרב
                                       ובחוריו למס יהיו

    He shall flee before the sword;   *ns ḥrb*
    And his young men shall become forced labor.   *bḥwryw ms*

Isa 40:4b   והיה העקב למישור
                                         והרכסים לבקעה

    The depression shall become level;   *hᶜqb myšwr*
    And the ridges a plain.[29]   *hrksym bqᶜh*

Ps 37:19   לא יבשו בעת רעה
                                     ובימי רעבון ישבעו

    They shall not be shamed in bad times;   *ybšw rᶜh*
    In days of famine they shall be sated.   *rᶜ- yśbᶜw*

Ps 46:2   אלהים לנו מחסה ועז
                                       עזרה בצרות נמצא מאד

    God is for us a refuge and stronghold;   *mḥsh ᶜz*
    A help in trouble, very much present.[30]   *ᶜz- nmṣʾ*

Ps 60:5   הראיתה עמך קשה
                                     השקיתנו יין תרעלה

    You have shown your people harshness;   *hrʾyth qšh*
    You have given us bitter wine to drink.   *hšqyt- trᶜlh*

Ps 60:10   מואב סיר רחצי
                                     על אדום אשליך נעלי
                                   עלי פלשת התרעעי

    Moab would be my washbasin;   *rḥṣy*
    On Edom I would cast my shoe;   *nᶜly*
    Acclaim me, Philistia.   *ᶜly htrᶜᶜy*
           [cf. Ps 108:10]

Ps 109:29   ילבשו שוטני כלמה
                                    ויעטו כמעיל בשתם

    My accusers shall be clothed in disgrace;   *ylbšw klmh*
    They shall be wrapped in their shame as in a robe.[31] *kmᶜyl bštm*

Pr 14:4   באין אלפים אבוס בר
                                     ורב תבואות בכח שור

    If there are no oxen the crib is bare;   *ʾbws br*
    But a rich harvest comes through the strength   *rb tbwʾwt*
      of the ox.

Job 3:9

יחשכו כוכבי נשפו
יקו לאור ואין
ואל יראה בעפעפי שחר

May its twilight stars remain dark; -hš-
May it hope for light and have none; l'wr
May it not see the glimmerings of the dawn. 'l yr'h šh-

Job 22:24

ושית על עפר בצר
ובצור נחלים אופיר

If you regard treasure as dirt; ʿpr bṣr
Ophir-gold as stones of the wadi. bṣwr 'wpyr

Job 33:26a

יעתר אל אלוה וירצהו
וירא פניו בתרועה

He entreats God and He accepts him; yʿtr wyrṣhw
He sees His face with shouts of joy. wyr' trwʿh

D. Multiple Sound Pairs

In several cases a parallelism contains more than two sets of sound pairs (and/or repeated roots). This increases the possible permutations in their patterning, but I have not found enough examples to categorize them. I still consider these verses to contain phonologic equivalence on the level of the word, but as more and more words become involved we move closer to phonologic equivalence on the level of the line as a whole (cf. chapter 2, p. 29). True phonologic equivalence of entire lines occurs very rarely; only in cases of the actual repetition of a line or a large part of it (e.g., Ps 115:9–11; Ps 118:25) or in a verse like

Ps 150:2

הללוהו בגבורתיו
הללוהו כרב גדלו

Praise him for his mightiness;
Praise him as befits his exceeding greatness.

hllwhw bgbwrtyw
hllwhw krb gdlw

Verses having a great amount of sound and word repetition are

Jud 5:30

הלא ימצאו יחלקו שלל
רחם רחמתים לראש גבר
שלל צבעים לסיסרא
שלל צבעים רקמה
צבע רקמתים לצוארי שלל

> Have they not found, divided the spoil,
> A damsel or two for each man,
> Spoil of dyed [cloths] for Sisera,
> Spoil of dyed embroidery,
> A piece or two of dyed embroidery,
> For every neck as spoil.

In addition to repeated words: *šll* (4 times); *ṣbʿ* (3 times), and the duplication in *rḥm rḥmtym* and *rqmh . . . rqmtym*, there is also sound correspondence between the last mentioned sets as well as between *lrʾš // lsysrʾ // lṣwʾry*. The blending of sound repetitions creates a vivid poetic effect: the plundering is sustained (*šll* over and over again) and the things plundered merge in sound as well as visually; the men swirl women about their heads (לראש גבר) and colored cloths around their necks—so that the women and their colorful clothing become one image.

2 Sam 1:24

המלבשכם שני עם עדנים
המעלה עדי זהב על לבושכן

> Who clothed you in crimson with finery;
> Who decked your clothes with golden jewels.

Both lines begin with *hm-* and contain the pairs *mlbškm // lbwškn* and *ʿdnym // ʿdy*.[32]

Jer 17:13

מקוה ישראל ה'
כל עזביך יבשו
יסורי בארץ יכתבו
כי עזבו מקור מים חיים את ה'

> The hope [or: pool] of Israel is YHWH,
> All who forsake you shall be confounded [or: dried up];
> Those in the land who turn away shall be inscribed [?],
> For they forsook the source of living water—YHWH.

This verse plays on water imagery and the double entendre which I have indicated in the translation. The sound pairs are *mqwh // mqwr*, *yśrʾl // ʾrṣ*, *YHWH // YHWH*, *ʿzbyk // ʿzbw*.

Jer 17:22

ולא תוציאו משא מבתיכם ביום השבת
וכל מלאכה לא תעשו
וקדשתם את יום השבת כאשר צויתי את אבותיכם

> You should not take a burden out of your house on the Sabbath day,
> And you should not perform any work.
> You should sanctify the Sabbath day as I commanded your fathers.

This rather prosaic sounding verse contains the sound pairs *twṣy*w // ṣwyty*, *btykm // *bwtykm, ywm šbt // ywm hšbt*.

Ps 51:19

זבחי אלהים רוח נשברה
לב נשבר ונדכה אלהים לא תבזה

> [True] sacrifice to God is a contrite spirit;
> A contrite and crushed heart, God, you will not disdain.

The pairs here are *zbḥy // tbzh, nšbrh // nšbr, *lhym // *lhym*.

E. Other Occurrences of Sound Pairs

There are other possibilities for activating the phonologic aspect of the language in parallel lines. One is the use of sound pairs in place of a repeated pair. Some examples already cited may show evidence of this, but it is especially obvious in Ps 103:11-13, where the structure of the lines seems to demand word repetition, but where sound repetition is substituted in the first set of lines: *kgbh // gbr*.

Ps 103:11-13

כי כגבה שמים על הארץ
גבר חסדו על יראיו
כרחק מזרח ממערב
הרחיק ממנו את פשעינו
כרחם אב על בנים
רחם ה' על יראיו

> For as high as is the sky over the earth,
> So does his faithful love prevail over those who fear him;
> As distant as east is from west,
> So does he distance from us our sins;
> As a father has compassion on children,
> So does YHWH have compassion on those who fear him.

In Job 33:31-33 there is a similar usage, though it is less noticeable.

Job 33:31-33

הקשב איוב שמע לי
החרש ואנכי אדבר
אם יש מלין השיבני
דבר כי חפצתי צדקך
אם אין אתה שמע לי
החרש ואאלפך חכמה

> Listen, Job, heed me,
> Be silent and I will speak.
> If you have words, answer me,

> Speak, for I am eager for your vindication.
> But if not, you heed me,
> Be silent and I will teach you wisdom.

Elihu uses four verbs in verse 31; three of these, *šmᶜ*, *ḥrš*, and *dbr* recur in the next verses. But *ḥqšb* is not left unpaired; its partner can be found in the consonant *ḥšybny*. Note, too, that the semantic equivalents are not the same as the phonologic equivalents in all cases. אדבר, "I will speak" is echoed semantically in אאלפך חכמה, "I will teach you wisdom."

Just as a repeated verse may substitute a lexical pair instead of repeating a word (cf. chapter 4, p. 70), so occasionally we find a repeated verse in which a term is replaced by its sound pair, for example,

Ps 49:13   ואדם ביקר בל ילין
                  נמשל כבהמות נדמו

          Man does *not abide* in honor;   *bl ylyn*
          He is like the beasts that perish.

Ps 49:21   אדם ביקר ולא יבין
                  נמשל כבהמות נדמו

          Man does *not understand* honor;   *lᵓ ybyn*
          He is like the beasts that perish.

There can be an element of sound play in an *inclusio*, as in

Ps 90:1   . . . אדני מעון אתה היית לנו

          Lord, you have been our refuge. . . .

          ᵓdny mᶜwn . . . hyyt

Ps 90:17   . . . ויהי נעם אדני אלהינו עלינו

          May the favor of the Lord our God be upon us. . . .

          wyhy nᶜm ᵓdny. . . .

Finally, a different kind of substitution involving sound. The word pair תהו // בהו, "emptiness // chaos," is a common associate (cf. Gen 1:2; Isa 34:11; Jer 4:23) which itself has a phonologic dimension. But it seems to me that in Isa 24:10 the prophet subverted the expectation that תהו would produce בהו and put in its place a different word that sounds like בהו , namely, בוא , "entry." That is, only one member of the sound pair בוא // בהו is manifest in the verse. The missing member is present in the mind of the reader because of the strong association that it has with תהו.

Isa 24:10   נשברה קרית תהו
                              סגר כל בית מבוא

         The town is broken, *chaotic*;   *thw*
         Every house is closed to *entry*.   *mbw*ᵓ

The fact that both *thw* and *mbw*ᵓ occupy the same position in the word
order of their respective lines further strengthens the feeling that they have
some relationship. But, again, the relationship is not a direct one—there is
no linguistic correspondence between *thw* and *mbw*ᵓ; but there is a phonologic correspondence between *mbw*ᵓ and the unrealized lexical associate
of *thw*.

There is always a risk of subjectivity in identifying sound correspondence. What rings loudly in my ears may only echo silence in the ears of
others. I can only hope that out of the large number of illustrations that I
have brought, a sufficient number will be acceptable proof that sound must
also be considered an aspect of parallelism. Some of my illustrations have
been noted by sensitive textual commentators and investigators of paronomasia and other rhetorical devices. My purpose is to underscore the
role of sound correspondence in parallelism. Although some of this correspondence may have been accidental, just as some of the grammatical contrasts discussed in chapter 3 may have been accidental, the quantity of examples strongly suggests that sound pairing is no less significant than are
other types of linguistic equivalence. The desire for phonologic correspondence might be so important in certain cases that it could override grammar or normative expression (cf. Ps 32:1, where the form of נשוי may have
been influenced by כסוי; Isa 34:10—the reversal of "night and day"; Job
9:33—the anomalous לא יש). Sound, like the other linguistic aspects, par-
ticipates in and is enhanced by the placing of similar things in contiguity.
The occurrence in contiguous lines of equivalent or contrasting sounds is
the phonologic aspect of parallelism.

APPENDIX: SOUND PAIRS IN *A MIDSUMMER NIGHT'S DREAM*

The type of phonologic correspondence that I have been discussing is
not limited to the Bible. Indeed, at the beginning of the chapter I cited an
English example, and Kselman (*Biblica* 58, 219) has also observed one in
George Herbert's sonnet "The Sonne":

How neatly do we give one onely name
To parent's issue and the *sunne*'s bright starre!
A *sonne* is light and fruit; a fruitful flame
Chasing the father's dimnesse. . . .

One could doubtlessly find many more examples throughout English literature, but it is nevertheless interesting to note the moderate frequency of sound pairs in *A Midsummer Night's Dream*,[33] even though they do not occur in the kind of parallelism found in the Bible. Although some of these pairs resulted from the desire to rhyme, others do not. Like the biblical pairs, they employ repeated words as well as consonant words (cf. "fruit" and "fruitful" in "The Sonne"), and occur in similar patterns.

abab

Churl, upon thy eyes I *throw*
All the power this *charm* do*th owe*.
[act 2, sc. 2, lines 78–79]

The will of man is by his *reason sway'd*;
And *reason says* you are the worthier maid.
[act 2, sc. 2, lines 115–16]

And I in *fury* hither *followed* them,
Fair Helena in fancy *following* me.
[act 4, sc. 1, lines 162–63]

That *hatred* is so *far* from jealousy,
To sleep by *hate*, and *fear* no enmity?
[act 4, sc.1, lines 144–45]

I *frown* upon him; yet he loves me *still*.
O that your *frowns* would teach my smiles such *skill*!
[act 1, sc. 1, lines 194–95]

abba

Farewell, sweet *play*fellow; *pray* thou *for* us;
[act 1, sc. 1, line 220]
[Note also *farewell* and *fellow*.]

I *followed fast*, but *faster* he did *fly*.
[act 3, sc. 2, line 416]

This is he, my master said,
Despised the Athenian *maid*;
And here the *maiden*, *sleep*ing sound,
On the dank and dirty ground.
[act 2, sc. 2, lines 72–75]

VI

PARALLELISM AND THE TEXT

THE VARIETY OF PARALLELISMS

For heuristic purposes we have isolated four aspects of language, the grammatical, the lexical, the semantic, and the phonologic, in order to show how these aspects of language are activated in parallelism. But one should be aware that these aspects usually occur in combination; for example, a parallelism may contain equivalences and/or contrasts in its grammar and in its semantic content (this is quite usual). We have also cited verses that show tension among the aspects (cf. pp. 81–88) such that grammatical equivalences may be patterned in one way while lexical or phonologic equivalences may be arranged in a different pattern. With so many aspects of language capable of being activated (there may be more than four), and so many possibilities for types of equivalence or contrast in each, it would seem that the number of possible parallelisms for any given line is enormous—perhaps infinite. In support of this statement I list here eleven parallelisms from the Book of Psalms containing the idea of God's hearing the psalmist's prayer. All of the verses employ at least one of several verbs meaning "to hear" and/or the noun "prayer" or one of its synonyms. This is such a common theme in Psalms that one might expect the expression of it to have become a standardized formula, but, surprisingly, it did not. Not only is the wording of "God, hear my prayer" varied extensively, but in all of the twenty-nine cases that I have found,[1] no two parallelisms are identical.

Ps 54:4   אלהים שמע תפלתי
האזינה לאמרי פי

God, hear my prayer;
Harken to the words of my mouth.

Ps 61:2   שמעה אלהים רנתי
                                 הקשיבה תפלתי

Hear, God, my song;
Harken [to] my prayer.

Ps 66:19   אכן שמע אלהים
                                 הקשיב בקול תפלתי

Indeed God heard;
He harkened to the sound of my prayer.

Ps 84:9   ה' אלהים צבאות שמעה תפלתי
                                 האזינה אלהי יעקב סלה

YHWH, the God of Hosts, hear my prayer;
Harken, God of Jacob, Selah.

The differences among these four verses result mainly from varying the
lexical pairs, the word order, and the ellipsis. There is a slight grammatical
contrast in Ps 54:4 and 66:19, where the second line contains a prepositional phrase making the object of the verb indirect instead of direct. (This
is usually dependent on the verb—some verbs take direct objects and
some do not—but notice that הקשיב can be used with either. Ps 61:2 uses
it with a direct object.)

Ps 102:2   ה' שמעה תפלתי
                                 ושועתי אליך תבוא

YHWH, hear my prayer;
And may my cry come to you.

Ps 88:3   תבוא לפניך תפלתי
                                 הטה אזנך לרנתי

May my prayer come before you;
Incline your ear to my song.

Ps 88:14   ואני אליך ה' שועתי
                                 ובבקר תפלתי תקדמך

As for me, to you, YHWH, I cry;
And at morning my prayer greets you.

These verses speak of the prayer reaching God. Ps 102:2 and 88:3 contain
subject-object alternation: "my prayer" is the grammatical subject in one

line and the object in the parallel line. Yet again, because of word choice and arrangement, they are different. Ps 88:14 is a more complex form involving the transformation of the verbal phrase "I cry" into the nominal "my prayer."

Ps 4:2

בקראי עונני אלהי צדקי
בצר הרחבת לי
חונני ושמע תפלתי

When I call, answer me, my righteous God;
In dire straits you eased [things] for me;
Be gracious to me and hear my prayer.

Ps 71:2

בצדקתך תצילני ותפלטני
הטה אלי אזנך והושיעני

According to your righteousness save me and rescue me;
Incline your ear to me and deliver me.

Ps 119:149

קולי שמעה כחסדך
ה' כמשפטך חיני

Hear my voice as befits your loyalty;
YHWH, as befits your justness preserve me.

Ps 143:1

ה' שמע תפלתי
האזינה אל תחנוני באמנתך
עונני בצדקתך

YHWH, hear my prayer;
Give ear to my pleadings in your steadfastness;
Answer me in your righteousness.

These four verses are more complex because their semantic content is greater, and this provides more potential elements to be paralleled. I have grouped them together because they all contain the idea of God's justice or loyalty. There is more syntagmatic equivalence here than in the previous examples, such as Ps 119:149: "Hear my voice" and the consequence, "Preserve me."

Given such variety, with the potential for much more, it is no wonder that attempts to define parallelism by limiting it to one form or another have failed. All of the foregoing examples contain parallelism, but it is exceedingly difficult to write a single formula that would account for all of them. The purpose of this book has not been to reduce parallelism to a simple linguistic formula, but rather to show the enormous linguistic complexity of parallelism. It is certainly not just a matter of repeating a thought in different words, or repeating the same syntactic structure; and "A, what's more B" is so nebulous as to be useless as a definition. Parallelism is, rather, a matter of intertwining a number of linguistic equivalences and contrasts.

By the same token it is impossible to evaluate parallelisms. There are no "better" or "poorer" parallelisms, and there are no "complete" or "incomplete" parallelisms. Needless to say, the practice of emending the text in order to create "better" parallelism has no basis, and even deriving the meaning of an unknown word from its word pair is fraught with danger. We must adopt a broader view of parallelism, taking into account the wide range of linguistic possibilities for its construction. I have tried in this book to indicate some of these possibilities, to suggest some guidelines for explaining how parallelism works from a linguistic perspective. But this "grammar of parallelism" is still very primitive. As in the case of other generative grammars, we are still a long way from a complete set of rules for generating all and only acceptable parallelisms in biblical Hebrew.

PERCEPTIBILITY AND INTERESTINGNESS

In order for parallelism to serve the poetic function—to focus on the message for its own sake—it must be perceptible (cf. chapter 1, p. 10). But since perceptibility is to some extent subjective, it is never easy to decide what is perceptible and why or how it is perceived. This was one of the weak points in Jakobson's argument; Jakobson seems to have felt that any linguistic equivalence was potentially perceptible, and hence meaningful, but his critics were hesitant to grant all equivalences equal status and chided Jakobson for his own selectivity in interpreting them. Jakobson's problem was, first of all, that he perceived equivalences that others before him had not, and, secondly, that once the equivalences were perceived he felt constrained to make them relevant to the interpretation of the meaning of the poem. Let us separate these two issues: the perceptibility of parallelism (which I will discuss here), and the effect of parallelism (which I will discuss in the following section).

Unlike many of the examples that Jakobson and his colleagues analyzed, and despite the element of subjectivity involved in matters of perception, the Bible contains many obvious parallelisms. When it comes to biblical parallelism involving two or more consecutive lines there is ample evidence that others besides the present writer perceive it (even though we

may not agree on how to define it). What is it that makes biblical parallelism perceptible to a modern, if not to an ancient, reader?[2] In other
words, what allows us to recognize that parallelism exists, to recognize the
equivalences present in the two lines? This is a problem for psycholinguists. But since, to my knowledge, there are no cognitive studies on the
perception of parallelism, I would venture, however tentatively, to propose
several formal principles which *may* make parallelisms perceptible to a
reader. These principles are the result of personal experience and logical
deduction; they represent an untested hypothesis about the cognitive processing of parallelism.

The most obvious kind of parallelism, it seems to me, is total equivalence repeated many times, as in כי לעולם חסדו, "For his loyalty is forever,"
at the end of every verse in Ps 136;[3] or הללוהו, "Praise him," at the beginning of almost every verse in Ps 150. But this kind of identical repetition is
rare; most cases of biblical parallelism are not so obvious, but are nevertheless easily recognized as parallel. There are four principles which may
account for this—four principles which tend to make parallelisms more
perceptible: proximity of the linguistic equivalences, the similarity of their
surface structures, the number of linguistic equivalences involved, and the
expectation of equivalence.

A. Proximity

Jakobson's analyses uncovered linguistic equivalences scattered throughout a text, but biblical parallelism usually involves equivalences in close
proximity—adjacent words, phrases, or sentences. The less intervening
material there is between the parts of the parallelism, the more perceptible
it will be. This may be true even when identical repetition is involved;
thus the repetition of

ישראל / בית אהרן / יראי ה' / בטח[ו]ן בה'
עזרם ומגנם הוא

Israel / House of Aaron / Fearers of YHWH trust in YHWH;
He is their help and shield.

in Ps 115:9–11 would be more immediately perceptible than the repetition of איך נפלו גבורים, "How heroes have fallen" in 2 Sam 1:19, 25, 27. It
is my impression that the Bible often goes out of its way to place parallelisms close together. It does this by paralleling each part of a sentence

rather than the sentence as a whole. For example, 2 Sam 1:20 could have read

*אל תגידו בגת
פן תשמחנה בנות פלשתים
אל תבשרו בחוצת אשקלון
פן תעלזנה בנות הערלים

but instead it reads

אל תגידו בגת
אל תבשרו בחוצת אשקלון
פן תשמחנה בנות פלשתים
פן תעלזנה בנות הערלים

> Don't tell it in Gath;
> Don't announce it in the environs of Ashkelon,
> Lest the daughters of the Philistines be happy;
> Lest the daughters of the uncircumcised be glad.

To be sure, there are many parallel lines arranged in the pattern designated here by the asterisk (*abab*), but I would claim that the parallelism in the *aabb* pattern (as in 2 Sam 1:20) is more easily perceived than the *abab* pattern. An *abcabc* pattern would be still less perceptible. This is not to suggest that the *aabb* pattern is always preferable, however, for there are other factors at work in a text besides ease of perception.[4]

The greatest distance between parallel parts is found in *inclusios*, and, in fact, these are less readily perceived than parallelisms in consecutive lines. *Inclusios*, however, serve a slightly different function from other parallelisms; by framing the text they provide cohesion and unity for the text as a whole.

B. Similarity of Surface Structure

Lines with similar surface structures are more readily perceived as parallel than lines with different surface structures. This suggests that parallelisms using repeated words are more perceptible than those using word pairs, and that those with the same syntactic surface structure are more perceptible than those with different surface structure (even though the deep structure is the same). An example with repeated words, sounds, and syntactic surface structure is

Gen 27:36b   את בכרתי לקח
                                והנה עתה לקח ברכתי

My birthright he took;
And look, now he took my blessing.

A parallelism like

Ps 61:2   שמעה אלהים רנתי
                                הקשיבה תפלתי

Hear, God, my song;
Harken [to] my prayer.

would be more perceptible than

Ps 102:2   ה' שמעה תפלתי
                                ושועתי אליך תבוא

YHWH, hear my prayer;
And may my cry come to you.

since in the former the surface structure is the same while the latter involves a transformation.

C. Number of Linguistic Equivalences

The more linguistic equivalences present, the greater the perceptibility of the parallelism. A parallelism with only syntactic equivalence is less perceptible than one with syntactic and semantic equivalence. The use of word pairs and/or sound pairs heightens the perceptibility. In Ps 105:17, even though the deep structure of the lines is the same, there are few linguistic equivalences:

שלח לפניהם איש
לעבד נמכר יוסף

He sent before them a man;
As a slave was Joseph sold.

whereas

Ps 105:35   ויאכל כל עשב בארצם
                                ויאכל פרי אדמתם

It ate all the grass in their land;
It ate the fruit of their ground.

whose deep structure is different, has a similar surface structure: one repeated word, two lexical associates, and a semantic equivalence. Ps 105:35
is therefore more easily perceived as parallel than is Ps 105:17.

D. Expectation of Parallelism

In a text formally structured on binary sentences, or on any form of pervasive parallelism, one tends to find parallelism even in lines which have
few or no linguistic equivalences. For instance, in a nonparallel context a
verse like

Ps 94:11   ה׳ ידע מחשבות אדם
                                  כי המה הבל

YHWH knows the thoughts of man
That they are futile.

would probably not be thought to contain a parallelism, but in its present
context, surrounded by parallelistic verses, the tendency is to read this
verse, too, as a binary sentence. Just as syntactic equivalence promotes
the perception of semantic equivalence, so here, too, equivalence in one
area spills over into other areas. When parallelism becomes the constructive device of the text as a whole, then all of its parts begin to be viewed as
participating in some way in the parallelism.

Again, for heuristic purposes, I have isolated four principles which do
not occur in isolation. They are all at work together in greater or lesser
measure. Nor should the order in which I have listed them be taken
as their rank of importance. Proximity, for example, may or may not be
more significant than similarity of surface structure in making parallelism
perceptible.

I have used "perceptibility" as a rough equivalent of "ease of processing," that is, ease in recognizing the existence of a parallelism. But ease of
cognitive processing is not always the highest desideratum of literature, especially poetry. For, as textlinguists have noted, something processed
easily, which matches the reader's knowledge or expectation perfectly, possesses low "informativity" and is therefore devoid of "interest" (cf. de
Beaugrande and Dressler, 9, 213). Informativity may relate to factual
knowledge of the world or to linguistic expectation. When a poem reverses
normal syntax, its level of informativity rises, and it becomes correspond-
ingly more interesting. If we apply this to parallelism we see that, for in-

stance, changing the surface structure of a parallel line makes it more
interesting, so that while Ps 61:2 may be more perceptible, Ps 102:2 is
more interesting.[5] For this reason the principles that I have enunciated
here are often violated: exact repetition and identical surface structure are
avoided in favor of a variety of equivalent forms of expression. In the most
interesting parallelisms even the deep structure of the lines may be different. It is also my feeling that the lack of correspondence among aspects of
parallelism (illustrated on pp. 30, 62) and the resulting tension is calculated to raise the level of interest. The extra bit of effort required to process
such parallelisms is rewarded by their higher level of interest. A text must
create a balance between informativity and ease of processing.

THE EFFECT OF PARALLELISM

To perceive parallelism is not necessarily to understand the effect it has
in a text. Most of us are aware that, say, Ps 61 : 2 contains a parallelism, but
we would be hard pressed to describe what effect that parallelism has on
our reading of the psalm. Let me make clear at once that parallelism in
itself does not have meaning. The analysis of the parallelism in Ps 61:2,
the fact that it uses the lexical pair שמע // הקשיב and that the syntax of the
two lines is the same, tells us nothing about the meaning of the verse. As
J. Culler said: "Linguistics is not hermeneutics. It does not discover what a
sequence means or produce a new interpretation of it. . . ." (*Structuralist
Poetics*, 31). But parallelism, like other formal features in a text, *does* help
to structure the text and thereby has an impact on how its meaning is arrived at.

Parallelism sets up relationships of equivalence or opposition between
two propositions. Sometimes the effect of the equivalence or opposition is
striking. For instance, when Esau says in

Gen 27:36   הכי קרא שמו יעקב
ויעקבני זה פעמים
את בכרתי לקח
והנה עתה לקח ברכתי

> Truly he is named Jacob;
> and he has deceived me ["Jacobed me"] twice now:
> my birthright he took;
> and look, now he took my blessing.

he and the reader suddenly see the relationship between two separate narrative sequences. Jacob's acquiring of the rights of the firstborn (Gen 25) is
equated with his acquiring the blessing in Gen 27. Furthermore, Jacob's
name is now understood as relating to his actions; his name is equivalent to
his nature.

Two different narrative sequences are joined in

Ps 114:3   הים ראה וינס
                                            הירדן יסב לאחור

                          The sea saw and fled;
                          The Jordan turned backward.

This parallelism operates on two levels: it utilizes the common associated
pair ים // נהר, *sea* // *river*,[6] but, by specifying the river as the Jordan, it
makes the connection between the splitting of the Reed Sea (Ex 14, 15)
and the splitting of the Jordan (Josh 3), two comparable events which
frame the Exodus narrative.

Opposition, not equivalence, is promoted when Naomi contrasts her
former and present states in

Ruth 1:21a   אני מלאה הלכתי
                                            וריקם השיבני ה'

                          I went out full;
                          and YHWH brought me back empty.

This parallelism captures an important opposition in the story: emptiness
vs. fullness (so well explicated by D. F. Rauber).

Sometimes we can see how a particular *form* of parallelism has a particular effect. For instance, varying the syntactic surface structure of a parallel
line may create an additional effect, just as any stylistic feature may inject
nuances of meaning. The verse just cited, Ruth 1:21a, is a case of subject-
object parallelism; the "I" of the first line becomes "me" in the second
(cf. chapter 3, p. 57). As a result, the second line has a different grammatical subject from the first, and this adds a dimension to the meaning
that is conveyed. For besides the opposition between "then-fullness" and
"now-emptiness" there is also an opposition between "I" and "YHWH."
This, too, is an important opposition in the story which is reconciled at the
end: "Blessed be YHWH who has not withheld from you a *goel*" (Ruth
4:14).

Other forms of parallelism may have other effects. The *qtl-yqtl* alternation may have the effect of a merismus in

Ps 26:4   לא ישבתי עם מתי שוא
                                               ועם נעלמים לא אבוא

Translations generally equate the tenses of the two lines:

> I *do not* consort with scoundrels;
> And with hypocrites I *do not* associate.

But it is possible that the verse suggests something stronger:

> I *have never* consorted with scoundrels;
> And with hypocrites I *will never* associate.

Isa 54:7 expresses comfort by the opposition between the smallness of God's abandonment and the greatness of his gathering in of the people.

Isa 54:7   ברגע קטן עזבתיך
                                               וברחמים גדלים אקבצך

> For a small moment I abandoned you;
> But with great mercy I will gather you up.

The contrast is present semantically in the words "small" and "great," but it is reinforced grammatically by the opposition of the singular of "small" and the plural of "great."

The choice of a word pair can also have an effect on meaning. In chapter 4 I discussed word pairs as the products of normal lexical association, but one should not conclude from this that the pairing of terms in parallel lines is a kind of reflex action. An author always has options when it comes to pairing words, and it is important to note which one of the possible associates he chose and what difference an alternative choice would have made. For example, in Isa 1:3b "Israel" is paired with "my people."

Isa 1:3b   ישראל לא ידע
                                               עמי לא התבונן

> Israel does not know;
> My people does not understand itself.

I would suggest that the choice of "my people," instead of another associate for Israel (e.g., "Ephraim," "House of Jacob," etc.) has an impact on the meaning of the verse. This phrase adds an emotional tone, a closeness to God, and the irony that God's people does not realize that it is God's people.

These have been examples of specific parallelisms in specific contexts. I am not suggesting that parallelism always equates two separate narrative sequences, or that the *qtl-yqtl* alternation always produces a merismus, and so on. As these examples show, and as I suggested toward the end of chapter 4, parallelism must be viewed in light of its context. Each parallelism is designed to fit into its own context, to partake of the meaning of the text as a whole and to contribute to it. Parallelism itself does not have meaning; but it structures the meaning of the signs of which it is composed. I have commented at various points throughout the book on how this structuring of meaning is achieved; I noted how semantic relationships can be superimposed on syntactic relationships (chapter 2, p. 23), or on phonologic relationships (chapter 5, p. 112), and I observed how parallelism may provide ambiguity or disambiguation or serve a metaphoric function (chapter 4, pp. 96–102).

Thus far I have been discussing specific effects of specific parallelisms, but what of the effect of parallelism per se? I inquire here not about the effect of individual parallelisms, but the more diffuse effect of a text employing pervasive parallelism—a text whose constructive device is parallelism. With this we return to the issue with which we began: the relationship between parallelism and poetry, or, more precisely, the poetic function.

Drawing again on Jakobson's concept as elaborated by Waugh (cf. chapter 1, p. 11), we can define a poetic text as one that manifests a predominance of the linguistic equivalences that we call parallelism—that is, a text that is constructed on linguistic equivalences. These linguistic equivalences work toward promoting thematic or conceptual equivalences as the text is read. The result is that the elements in the text, which of necessity occur in a linear sequence (contiguity), are then perceived as equivalent or contrasted (similarity). This is vividly exemplified in Ps 136, which is a narrative turned into a poem. The psalm preserves its narrative sequence (the list of events in the order in which they occurred), but the poetic function has been superimposed on it. The poet has taken a linear sequence and restructured it as a series of equivalences. A few verses suffice to make the point:

Ps 136:10–15

למכה מצרים בבכוריהם
כי לעולם חסדו
ויוצא ישראל מתוכם
כי לעולם חסדו
ביד חזקה ובזרוע נטויה

כי לעולם חסדו
לגזר ים סוף לגזרים
כי לעולם חסדו
והעביר ישראל בתוכו
כי לעולם חסדו
ונער פרעה וחילו בים סוף
כי לעולם חסדו

Who struck Egypt through their firstborn;
For his loyalty is forever;
And brought Israel out of their midst;
For his loyalty is forever;
With a strong hand and an outstretched arm;
For his loyalty is forever;
Who split apart the Reed Sea;
For his loyalty is forever;
And made Israel pass through it;
For his loyalty is forever;
Who hurled Pharaoh and his army into the Reed Sea;
For his loyalty is forever.

The psalm is almost entirely composed of a chronological list of God's actions during creation and the exodus and settlement. The list is broken up
into clauses or phrases, many of which contain parallelism;[7] and additional
parallelism of a more obvious nature (exact repetition) is inserted after
each item on the list. This repetition causes the end of every verse to sound
and mean the same. It superimposes similarity (of an extreme type) upon
contiguity. The effect then spreads to the first parts of the verses, which
already have a certain amount of similarity from their own parallelisms. As
a result, the actions enumerated in the list appear to be equated: smiting
the Egyptian firstborn is like splitting the Reed Sea is like leading the Israel-
ites through the wilderness, and so forth.[8] In what sense are all these actions alike? In the sense that they result from God's eternal loyalty, כי
לעולם חסדו. All of the actions derived from one actor for one purpose. The
poet has "made sense" out of "history."[9] Through a set of linguistic equiva-
alences he has concisely organized a series of discrete events into a meaningful pattern. Although Ps 136 is admittedly an extreme example, since
all of its verses are parallel, the same effect in varying intensity can be felt
wherever parallelism is the constructive device.

    I have been speaking here of poetry, but of course poetry is not the only
genre, ancient or modern, that employs parallelism as its constructive device. In the Bible, one finds it also in legal passages, proverbs, prophetic
speech, speculative thought (e.g., Ecclesiastes), and even some sections of

narrative. It is not a question of forcing all of these texts into one genre called "poetry," but rather that there may be several types of texts which are structured on relationships of equivalence or opposition. What all of these texts have in common is the dominance of the poetic function. These texts all focus the message on itself; they draw attention to the relationships which they impose on their linguistic signs. They organize, or reorganize, the world into equivalences and oppositions by their form of expression. It should not surprise us that the Bible contains so much parallelism, for in the ancient near eastern milieu from which it emerged most formal verbal expression was parallelistic. This was, and still is, a most effective way to give heightened awareness of the message to its receivers.

Let me conclude by summing up what I have shown parallelism to be. Following Roman Jakobson, I have accepted that parallelism is to be equated with the poetic function, which "projects the principle of equivalence from the axis of selection into the axis of combination" or, in other words, that "similarity is superimposed on contiguity." This book has provided extensive illustration of how this is accomplished in biblical parallelism. Similarity in morphology consists of drawing on words of the same word class; or of different word classes that serve the same syntactic function. Syntactic similarity consists of clauses with the same deep syntactic structure. Lexical similarity consists of words which are lexically associated, either paradigmatically or syntagmatically. Likewise, semantic similarity consists of expressions which are either close in meaning or are syntagmatically related in meaning. Phonological similarity consists of repeating the same or similar group of sounds. All of these types of similarity, and perhaps others which I have not investigated, are brought into play in biblical parallelism. Two or more similar elements are combined in contiguous expressions; that is, similarity is superimposed on contiguity.

"Similarity" implies "equivalence." I have used "equivalence" in the sense of "belonging to the same linguistic category or paradigm, or to the same sequence or syntagm." Parallel elements (words, sounds, grammatical constructions, etc.) are linguistically equivalent in some way. However, in addition to the equivalence that underlies all forms of parallelism there is often a contrast. For after all, equivalent elements are not identical, and their lack of identity—i.e., their difference—shows up all the more clearly when they are placed in contiguity. Thus one can conclude with L. Waugh that parallelism manifests a "strong linkage of contrast with equivalence." [10] In biblical parallelism this contrast can be seen in lexical associates, in morphological alternations (e.g., singular // plural; definite // indefinite, etc.), in syntactic transformations, in the semantic relationships of parallel lines, and in the rearrangements and substitutions of phonemes in sound pairs.

Parallelism, then, consists of a network of equivalences and/or contrasts involving many aspects and levels of language. Moreover, by means of these linguistic equivalences and contrasts, parallelism calls attention to itself and to the message which it bears. Parallelism embodies the poetic function, and the poetic function heightens the focus on the message.

NOTES

I. PARALLELISM AND POETRY

1. On Lowth's forerunners see Kugel, *Idea*, 96–286; Cooper, 17–19, 150–62; Lundbom, 121–27.

2. This point is made by Dennis Pardee in two unpublished papers.

3. Biblicists are divided on the question of whether biblical poetry has meter, and if so, how it is to be measured. For a summary of metric studies see Stuart, 1–49; Cooper, 11–33, 147–49; Kugel, *Idea*, 287–304; O'Connor, *HVS*, 29–41. For a discussion of the tension between parallelism and meter in Ugaritic studies see S. Parker in *UF* 6 (1974), 283–94.

4. Kugel's definition of parallelism is broader than the semantic one in most earlier biblical studies. He calls parallelism a style in which syntax, morphology, and meaning establish a feeling of correspondence between the two parts (*Idea*, 2). Although he begins to examine the nature of certain correspondences, his criteria for recognizing parallelism are not always clear. In the end, his insistence that the essence of parallelism is that B goes beyond A, seconds it, contrasts with it, etc., and that parallelism does not consist of "stringing together clauses that bear some semantic, syntactic, or phonetic resemblance" (*Idea*, 53) threatens to reduce parallelism once again to a semantic correspondence.

5. Cf. *Idea*, 85: "It may strike the reader as perverse to refuse simply to call the relative concentration of heightening factors 'poetry' and their relative absence 'prose.'" Actually, Kugel is opposed to the polarity, the all-or-nothingness, that the use of these terms generates. "To see biblical style through the split lens of prose or poetry is to distort the view."

6. Compare Segert, in reference to Ugaritic poetry: "Features known as parallelistic may also occur in prose texts. . . . This criterion alone cannot determine whether the text is poetry or prose" (*UF* 11, 730). Still, on p. 731 he says: "The most prominent feature of Ugaritic poetry is its parallelistic structure." See also Dahood, *RSP* III, p. 5.

7. Cf. Geller, "Theory and Method," 75–77. This issue was the subject of a piece by Kugel in *Prooftexts* 1 (1981), 217–36 and my response in *Prooftexts* 2 (1982), 323–32.

8. Thus Whallon's attempt to find a distinction between prose and poetic parallelism (*Formula*, 196–99) seems misguided.

9. Kugel puts the same idea somewhat differently: "The fact is that very often there *is* little connection between one verse and the next, and when such a connection does exist, quite often it is left to the reader or listener to figure it out" (*Idea*, 92).

10. Cf. Hrushovski: "These basic units are not equal; all attempts to correct the text in order to achieve strict numbers make no sense from any textual point of view. . . . But there is no need of this. The rhythmic impression persists in spite of all 'irregularities.' The basic units almost never consist of one or of more than four stresses, that is, they are simple groups of two, three, or four stresses . . . the stresses are strong, being major stresses of words . . . and being reinforced by the

syntactic repetition. Thus the groups can be felt as similar, simple, correlated units. As the number of stresses in such a unit is small, they become conspicuous, giving special weight to the words" ("On Free Rhythms," 189).

11. Michael O'Connor has reminded me (in a private communication) that such lists may also occur in poetry—e.g., "Shiloh, Antietam, Malvern Hill, Bull Run" in Allen Tate's "Ode to the Confederate Dead"; the names at the end of Book II of the *Iliad*; and, I would add, the names of Marduk at the end of *Enuma Elish*.

12. Parallelism was defined in this study as 1) the repetition of two or more words of the same form-class or 2) the repetition of two or more constructions of the same grammatical classification in 3) the same functional or syntactic situation (Hiatt, 118).

13. Erlich, 12, uses the term "literarily active."

14. This could also be shown in Ex 2:1–7 as compared with Ps 106:29–34, two passages which Kugel finds to be "structurally identical" (*Idea*, 60–61).

15. Kugel, *Idea*, 43, hesitates to accept the two-action interpretation but bases this reluctance on the possibility that יתד and הלמות are the same weapon. He is not able to decide if יד / / ימין "was always equative," but if it were this would strengthen his one-action interpretation. My view is the reverse: I see יד / / ימין as "equative" but would still allow that two weapons, and two actions, are present.

16. This view is most frequently associated with Dahood (cf. *Psalms* III, 281; *RSP* I, 195–96) but Pope points out in *JBL* 85 (1966), 458 that there are antecedents for this view in rabbinic exegesis.

2. THE LINGUISTIC STUDY OF BIBLICAL PARALLELISM

1. This survey does not attempt to be a comprehensive presentation of all that these studies contain; it will concentrate on their use of linguistics for describing parallelism. There are, of course, many other studies of particular phenomena that occur in parallelism—e.g., word pairs, certain verbal patterns, chiasm, etc. These are far too numerous to be reviewed here (consult the bibliography); relevant studies will be mentioned in the appropriate places in subsequent chapters. It should be noted, however, that most of these studies represent a continuation of older approaches to parallelism and are not linguistically oriented. This does not mean that they are wrong or useless; on the contrary, they have done much to improve our powers of textual observation. This book will combine the insights of these studies with the broader framework provided by a linguistic approach, and thereby integrate a number of apparently different features into a more unified picture of parallelism.

2. Collins omits from consideration nominal sentences and sentences with any tense of the verb "to be."

3. Unfortunately, Geller's method is terribly cumbersome, and because it includes semantics and analyzes all of the surface permutations in detail, it directs attention away from the fact that grammatical parallelism involves grammatical equivalences.

4. "By parallelism . . . is understood the regularly recurring juxtaposition of symmetrically constructed sentences" ("Parallelism in Hebrew Poetry," *Jewish Encyclopedia* 9:520b—quoted in Greenstein, 45).

5. This was also my assumption in *HUCA* 50 (1979), 35 note 46. I showed there a number of specific transformations that occur in parallel lines.

6. I should also mention here the work of R. Sappan. Unlike the studies by Geller and Greenstein, which are studies of parallelism that utilize grammatical

analysis, Sappan's is primarily a study of the grammar of biblical poetry that includes a consideration of parallelism. Sappan considers as parallel those lines that are *semantically* parallel and then proceeds to examine their grammatical structure. He finds that semantically parallel lines often do not have the identical grammatical structure, but that in most cases there is some degree of structural correspondence between them (V). He discusses the levels on which these correspondences may be found (there is some overlap here with the methods of Geller and Greenstein). His conclusion, derived from the work of S. Levin, is that "instances of parallelism of all types are generally characterized by the special structural feature that corresponding semantic units usually occur at equivalent positions . . . [as defined by Sappan] in their respective syntactical frame" (XI).

7. Collins finds that his Type II sentences (i.e., matching without gapping) account for about one-fourth of his corpus, and his Type III sentences (matching with gapping) account for approximately the same percentage. He does not, however, give percentages in terms of parallelism.

8. Cf. T'sou, 319, and Pardee, "Types and Distribution" and "Ugaritic and Hebrew Poetry: Parallelism."

9. Dahood included words in juxtaposition and collocation only if they also occur in parallelism elsewhere (in Hebrew or Ugaritic). He does not list words which occur in juxtaposition only. His lists are descriptive, based on attested occurrences, not on a theory of linguistic correspondences. I would theoretically include combinations that do not actually occur in parallel lines if they manifest the same kinds of linguistic correspondences as those that do. However, in practice I will refrain from this since there is more than enough material in parallel lines to illustrate the linguistic correspondences that I wish to demonstrate.

10. They may be part of a series, joined with a connective or not, or part of a continuous grammatical unit (e.g., a noun and its verb), or two nouns in construct (cf. Avishur, *The Construct State*).

11. Actually, the grammatic relationship here is a displacement of the one that obtains in Ps 78:55 and Ps 120:5.

3. THE GRAMMATICAL ASPECT

1. Many of these grammatical equivalences were first presented in Berlin, *HUCA* 50. Kugel (*Idea*), Geller (*Parallelism in Early Biblical Poetry*), and Sappan independently put forth a few of the same and others. I will here combine and enlarge upon all of these studies.

2. A relative clause is not a morphological element; a relative pronoun is. But since the relative pronoun is often omitted in poetry, I will speak of relative clauses. This is actually more correct, for it is the whole clause, not just the pronoun, which is equivalent to the noun in the parallel line.

3. The lexical pair עבד // בחר has been conventionalized, occurring in different parts of speech in Isa 41:8, 9; 42:1; 43:10; 44:1, 2; 65:9, 15 (noted in Watters, 174) and also in Ps 89:4; 105:6 and perhaps Hag 2:23.

4. יומם is more often paired with לילה, which serves as the adverbial form—compare, for example, Ex 13:21, 22; Isa 4:5. But an adverb can be introduced by a preposition—cf. Blau, *Grammar*, 103.

5. Cf. Cassuto, *Biblical and Oriental Studies* II, 58–59; Held, "The YQTL-QTL (QTL-YQTL) Sequence of Identical Verbs in Biblical Hebrew and in Ugaritic"; Dahood, *Psalms* III, 420–23.

6. Cf. Yoder, *Fixed Word Pairs*, p. 9, n.21.

7. Cf. Cross and Freedman, *Studies in Ancient Yahwistic Poetry*, 127–28; D. N. Freedman, *Pottery, Poetry, and Prophecy*, 210; Clines, *I, He, We*, 47–48.

8. I have limited this section to verbs from the same root because different verbal roots occur in different conjugations. Therefore, the pairing of, say, *bqš* in the *piʿel* with *mṣʾ* in the *qal* is not a strong morphological contrast because these are simply the conjugations in which these verbs are used. The contrast is most perceptible when different conjugations of the same root are paired. (This pairing also adds a lexical and phonetic dimension to the parallelism.)

9. *The Goddess Anath*, 47–48 = *Biblical and Oriental Studies*, II, 58–59 (original: *Tarbiz* 14, 1–10).

10. *Psalms* III, 414. Dahood also lists Ps 29:5; 38:3; 69:15.

11. The verses listed by Cassuto and Held are: Isa 6:11 (?); Jer 15:19; 17:14; 20:7; 31:3, 17; Ps 19:13–14; 24:7; 69:15; Lam 5:21. Held hesitates to include Isa 6:11 because many modern commentators, following the reading of the LXX, emend תשאה to תשאר. This emendation, notes Held, seems to be supported by Isa 24:12 (*JBL* 84, 275, n. 2). However, while it is true that Isa 24:12 contains the same idea and many of the same terms found in 6:11, this does not mean that all of the terms need be identical. The word נשאר may have been used in 24:12 because it makes a good phonologic complement to the word שער at the end of the verse. The phonetic pattern in 6:11 is entirely different. Here one might see an ABBA pattern composed of שאו־אדם־אדמה־תשאה. In my opinion emending תשאה is unnecessary; the verbs תשאה and שאו exemplify a contrast in tense, conjugation, and number.

12. Cf. Kselman, *JBL* 97, 168. There is no need to change יולד to אולד or to explain the *lamed* as emphatic, as Kselman does. The syntax of the two parallel lines need not be identical—see below, Syntactic Parallelism.

13. *The Goddess Anath*, 44–46 = *Biblical and Oriental Studies*, II, 66–68 (original: *Lešonenu* 15, 97–102). Cf. also Watson, *JBL* 99 and Watson, *UF* 13.

14. The pair *Jerusalem // Judah* also creates a merismus by employing a part and its whole. The effect of totality is emphasized by the chiastic word order. The verbs also constitute a totality since both verbs can apply to both subjects: Jerusalem and Judah have stumbled and fallen. This is a distributional reading, something warned against by Kugel (*Idea* 40–41). Heeding the warning, and influenced by Kugel's discussion of "sharpness" (*Idea*, 7–11), I would go on to see an even more dramatic picture of totality in Isaiah's words: Jerusalem's stumbling will lead to Judah's fall. Thus the grammatical and the lexical parallelisms work toward the same end.

15. A person has only one father but more than one elder (or perhaps even "grandfather"—cf. Pr 17:6).

16. This follows the rule for paralleling numbers: x // x +1.

17. Watters has also observed the paralleling of a singular with a plural, but explains the phenomenon as being necessary for metric reasons: "By so varying the singular-plural aspect of the words in pair, the lines are balanced in more uniform lengths" (105). Cf. Kugel, *Idea*, 20–21.

18. On אחדים cf. Ezek 37:17.

19. ברגע and ברחמים are not normally considered word pairs, but can be construed here as such because they each occupy the same position in their respective lines. The fact that they are phonologically similar, and that both are modified by similar adjectives, adds to the impression that they are parallel terms.

20. Cassuto comments on this verse: "The difference between the plural *those*

who bless you and the singular *him who curses you* was introduced, it seems, for the sake of diversification and variation in the parallelism, for which reason a change was also made in the order of the words of the two clauses" (*From Noah to Abraham*, 315).

21. For a similar approach to textual traditions see S. Talmon, "The Textual Study of the Bible—A New Outlook."

22. Cf. D. N. Freedman, *Pottery, Poetry, and Prophecy*, 2 and now F. I. Andersen and A. D. Forbes, "'Prose Particle' Counts of the Hebrew Bible."

23. Cf. Andersen, *Job*, 101, where the correspondence between the indefinite and definite is recognized in this verse.

24. The pair מעון תנים and מבלי יושב are neither lexically nor grammatically parallel, but they are phonologically similar (both begin with *mem* and have the same number of syllables and accent pattern), and they occupy the same position in otherwise parallel lines.

25. Greenstein ("How Does Parallelism Mean?") defines parallelism in terms of this syntactic equivalence (see above, chapter 2). I would allow for the possibility of other kinds of parallelism in which the syntax is not equivalent. (Cf. chapter 4, note 42.)

26. Both clauses are verbal but there is still the contrast between *yšlm* (a verb) and *šlmh* (an adjective).

27. Most positive rhetorical questions imply a negative answer, and vice versa. For exceptions see R. Gordis, "A Rhetorical Use of Interrogative Sentences in Biblical Hebrew," *The Word and the Book*, 152–57.

28. The jussive and the imperfect indicative are indistinguishable in form in most cases, so the identification is based on the context. The sequence of imperative followed by jussive (or other similar combinations) often has a causal nuance: "Do X so that he may do Y." For various combinations see Andersen, *The Sentence*, 112–13. The combinations in parallel lines are the same as those found in prose sentences.

29. This transformational grammar model is for the purpose of analysis only. I am not suggesting that the biblical author consciously performed these transformations when composing parallelisms any more than we do when we form interrogative or passive sentences. The legitimacy of such an analysis, however, is reinforced by Jakobson when he says that "the analysis of grammatical transformations and of their import should include the poetic function of language, because the core of this function is to push transformations into the foreground. It is the purposeful poetic use of lexical and grammatical tropes and figures that brings the creative power of language to its summit" ("Verbal Communication," 80).

4. THE LEXICAL AND SEMANTIC ASPECTS

1. The scholar primarily associated with this enterprise in recent years was M. Dahood. Cf. *Psalms* III, 445–56; *RSP* I, 71–382; *RSP* II, 1–39; *RSP* III, 1–206. The list of others who have contributed in this area is too long to cite here; for summaries of the early work on word pairs see Yoder, *Fixed Word Pairs and the Composition of Hebrew Poetry*, 2–10 and Watters, 20–38. For specific articles consult the bibliography.

2. There was at least one attempt to show that actual formulas existed in Hebrew poetry—cf. Culley, *Oral Formulaic Language in the Biblical Psalms*—but this was refuted by Yoder (*Fixed Word Pairs and the Composition of Hebrew Poetry*), who reasserted that it was indeed the word pairs (not formulas) that made oral composi-

tion possible. The issue was again raised by Watters, who questioned the assumption of oral composition and the role of word pairs in it.

3. Cf. Kugel, *Idea*, 30, 34. This argument has been voiced before. Defenders of the oral theory usually respond that written poetry preserved the conventions of its oral forerunner.

4. The total number of pairs listed in *RSP*, I, II, III is 1019.

5. On pairs in construct see Avishur, *The Construct State of Synonyms in Biblical Rhetoric*.

6. The same unevenness of attestation pertains even among fixed pairs—some are more common than others. This has always been one of the problems in defining a fixed pair. How many times must it occur? At least twice? Three or more? Are pairs that occur ten times more "fixed" than those that occur five times? Biblical scholarship, sensing the arbitrariness of this numbers game, has settled in to viewing any pair that occurs in both Hebrew and Ugaritic as fixed. Pairs that occur in only one or the other seem to have an indeterminate status. In recent years, even the term "fixed" is employed less often; scholars simply speak of "parallel pairs."

7. Cf. Clark: "Word associations should be thought of as a consequence of linguistic competence" (272).

8. Watters adds to this the strange idea that "word pairs which *repeat* are common associations fostered by limited vocabulary" (78). That is, certain combinations recur because the choice for different combinations was limited by a paucity of words in the Hebrew language. This is linguistically untenable for two reasons: 1) A language would not develop a device for which it had "too few words"—a language's vocabulary is presumably adequate for its needs. 2) There is no evidence that languages with larger vocabularies have fewer recurring associations.

9. *UF* 11 (1979), 135–40.

10. *UF* 11, 136. See also Craigie's articles in *Semitics* 5 and in *Ugarit in Retrospect*.

11. Cf. O'Connor: "Most parallelistic usages result from ordinary facts of language, not specific poetic features" (*HVS*, 101). In a similar vein Kugel states: "There is nothing 'poetic' or literary in the pairs per se" (*Idea*, 33–34).

12. The idea that texts once circulated in slightly different but equally valid forms is gaining support. S. Talmon cites many examples suggesting stylistic fluidity and discusses the implication this has for textual study ("The Textual Study of the Bible—A New Outlook"—cf. also his earlier article, "Synonymous Readings in the Old Testament").

13. Based both on responses from a number of different players and on multiple responses from one player.

14. On the ordering of Hebrew word pairs see Boling, *JSS* 5; Watson, *UF* 13. Dahood discusses this matter briefly in *RSP* I, pp. 77–78 and his lists carefully note the order of the paired terms. O'Connor, *HVS*, 97–102 presents the linguistic criteria for the ordering.

15. On particularizing see Berlin, *JANES* 10.

16. See above, chapter 3, p. 36. This would also include shifts to other conjugations and other causative transformations involving different verbal roots.

17. Clark, 281–82, explains how this accounts for the fact that nouns usually elicit other nouns (i.e., are paradigmatic), while other parts of speech produce more syntagmatic responses.

18. This scheme corresponds approximately to what O'Connor calls the tropes of coloration: binomination, coordination, and combination (*HVS*, 112–15). However, I would specify the conventionalized status of the coordinates in my first cate-

gory. And I do not agree with many of O'Connor's examples of "combination." See below, note 23.

19. Cf. Melamed in *Sefer Segal* and in *Scripta* VIII.

20. This of course, is true for all word associates. To think of them as synonyms occasionally puts one into the kind of bind that Talmon found himself in when, observing that the verbs השליך and מאס are associates, he felt compelled to add: "In spite of the difference in meaning between the two verbs . . . , they were apparently used synonymously" (*Scripta* VIII, 353). Much misunderstanding has been promoted by scholars who, less sensitive than Talmon, forced certain word pairs to mean the same thing.

21. "Binomination" is a term close to "binomial"—a linguistic term employed somewhat differently. "Binomial" has been defined as "the sequence of two words pertaining to the same form-class, placed on an identical level of syntactic hierarchy, and ordinarily connected by some kind of lexical link" (Malkiel, 311). Theoretically, this would then include any word pair used in juxtaposition. To the extent that the binomial has become formulaic or idiomatic, it would be included in my category of conventionalized coordinates (and O'Connor's "coordination," which involves two parts of a basic pair—*HVS*, 114). Binomination, as it is being used here, is a much more restricted term.

22. It may be that יהודה // ירושלם is also a case of binomination; cf. Jer 4:3–5 and passim; Isa 3:8 and passim. This is different from ערי יהודה // ירושלם which was discussed above. *Jerusalem-Judah* seems similar to *Edinburgh-Scotland* and *Oxford-England*, both listed by Deese as word associations. I consider them to be syntagmatic responses, although they might be considered superordinates.

23. I feel that O'Connor goes much too far in finding examples of "the rupture of the construct relation" (*HVS*, 114). Combinations like *mdbr* // *yšymwn* (Ps 107:4); *rwh* // *sᶜrh* (Ps 107:25) and many others that O'Connor perceives as broken constructs (*HVS*, 380–82) could just as easily have been paradigmatic associates. The same is true of his adjectival combinations (*HVS*, 384) and his appositional combinations (*HVS*, 385).

24. Even though עמל is singular and מרי נפש is plural. This would be an example of both syntagmatic and paradigmatic (singular // plural) pairing.

The recognition that such word pairs may be syntagmatic is not to suggest that we should reunite them into the continuous expressions whence they came. It is the ingeniousness of biblical parallelism that allows such breakups to be made and such linguistic ambiguity to be sustained. The urge to read syntagmatic pairs distributively should be held in check, for, as Kugel (*Idea*, 40–45) has noted, this does violence to the form of the parallelism. Job 3:20 may have meant something like "Why did he give the light of life to the embittered toiler," but a translation like that would suck the blood out of the poem.

25. Word pairs may figure over sections larger than a verse or two; compare for example, the play involving *day* and *night* in Job 3:3–9. Talmon has shown that word pairs can substitute for one another in similar contexts, even though only one of them is present at a time. For instance, the pair איש־אדם alternates in Ps 105:14 (לא הניח אדם לעשקם) and 1 Chr 16:21 (לא הניח לאיש לעשקם). The two appear together as a parallel pair in Isa 31:8 and elsewhere. Cf. Talmon, "The Textual Study of the Bible—A New Outlook," 338, and also *Scripta* VIII.

26. Thus it is misleading to say, as Dahood did in *RSP* III, that "the Canaanite scribes and poets apparently thought in binomials" (5). Everyone, in every language group, thinks in binomials.

27. The methodology of word association has been applied to the study of cultural views by Szalay and Deese in *Subjective Meaning and Culture: An Assessment Through Word Associations.*

28. On this pair see O'Connor, *HVS*, 115, 384. He views the pair פלשתים // הערלים in 2 Sam 1:20 as the breakup of the phrase "the uncircumcised Philistines," i.e., an example of "combination" of a noun and an adjective, which would place it in my third category of syntagmatic pairings. However, I see no compelling reason to view it as such. It could possibly be a case of conventionalized coordinates—cf. 1 Sam 17:26, 36; Jud 14:3—but O'Connor does not use this argument. It is more likely, though, that this is a normal paradigmatic association. (O'Connor, *HVS*, 115, states that "appositional combination most closely approximates ordinary dyading.") An American analogy is *Russian-Communist*. Now we know that not all Russians are Communists, and not all Communists are Russian, but this remains a strong association nevertheless. Therefore, just because not all uncircumcised persons are Philistines (O'Connor's argument), it does not mean that the two words cannot be considered paradigmatically associated. This example illustrates my main point, namely that parallel word pairs are best understood as word associations, regardless of whether we can classify them as synonyms, stereotyped phrases, superordinates, or any other subcategory.

29. *Parallelism in Early Biblical Poetry*, 31–42. Geller's basic categories are synonym, list, antonym, merism, epithet, proper noun // common noun, pronoun // antecedent, whole // part, concrete // abstract, numerical, identity, metaphor.

30. But the reverse is true when it comes to the penalties for seduction and adultery, for, from a legal point of view, illicit sex with a married woman is a greater offense than with an unmarried one.

31. The first to do this, as far as I am aware, was Perry Yoder who, in his 1970 dissertation, excluded semantics from his definition of word pairs. He defined them as "any two terms having the same grammatical class which occur more than once in parallelism" (40). Yoder stressed that "it is recurrence, not semantic relationship, which is decisive in defining a 'fixed pair'" (41). The distance between semantics and fixed pairs grows wider later on: "Not only may a traditional formula [= fixed word pair] be used regardless of context, but it may also be used regardless of the semantic content of the A word itself" (106), and "formulas exist to meet formal, not semantic, exigencies" (107).

It is important to understand why Yoder said this, for his view of word pairs is not the same as mine, and the distinction that he made is therefore different from the one that I am making. Yoder viewed word pairs as serving the same function in Hebrew poetry as formulas did in Homeric poetry—they existed as aids in oral composition. In order to prove this, Yoder had to demonstrate that the use of word pairs was automatic under certain circumstances; that is, they were not chosen for their semantic value but rather for their prosodic value. I seriously question Yoder's premise and conclusions, but I see here an important insight nevertheless. Yoder realized that the pairing of certain terms had nothing to do with their similarity in meaning, and that the lexical aspect of the parallelism could be divorced from its semantic aspect.

32. Another facet of the life of word pairs is "metathetic parallelism," discussed by Bronznick.

33. This technique of using word order to create the illusion of lexical, syntactic, or semantic equivalence is not uncommon, and it is effective in increasing the perception of parallelism. It is primarily their positions in Isa 54:7 that permit an

equation between ברגע and ברחמים. Likewise word order is responsible for the syntactic illusion in Ps 105:6 and Ps 49:5. Cf. also מעון תנים and מבלי יושב in Jer 9:10.

34. On chiastic word patterning see the articles by Ceresko; on chiasm in general see di Marco.

35. Cf. Berlin, *JANES* 10, 40–41; Gordis, *Poets, Prophets, and Sages*, 79–82.

36. See Gordis, *Poets, Prophets, and Sages*, 79.

37. Ceresko occasionally mixes morphological patterns with his lexical patterning.

38. Cf. *Gordis, Poets, Prophets, and Sages*, 79.

39. Greenstein ("How Does Parallelism Mean?") mentions this among various types of closure involving parallelism.

40. Compare the discussion of Greenstein in chapter 2, p. 22. Greenstein stressed only the similarity in syntax in such sentences since that was what interested him. Deese stresses the words that are used to fill in the syntactic structure.

41. Compare the statement in G. Steiner, *After Babel*, 261: "Inside a language synonymy is only very rarely complete equivalence. 'Rewording' unavoidably produces 'something more or less'; definition through rephrasing is approximate and reflexive."

42. All of the grammatical equivalences presented in chapter 3 are paradigmatic (cf. Holenstein, 142). In a syntagmatic grammatical construction one line would not replace the other but would be a grammatical continuation of it, as in

Ps 115:18   ואנחנו נברך יה
                                   מעתה ועד עולם

But we will bless YH
From now until eternity.

These two lines constitute one syntactic unit—one sentence. The question is: can we consider such lines to be grammatically equivalent or parallel? One might argue against this equivalence by saying that a syntagmatic relation in the grammatical aspect (and also in the phonological aspect) is not the same as in the lexical and semantic aspects. In grammar, the syntagmatic is not equivalent—it is simply contiguous. In the lexical and semantic aspects the syntagmatic may be considered equivalent in that both parts come from one "thought-mass" or contain entities that would be grouped together. Grammar provides the structure of the parallelism. This structure can itself project equivalence onto contiguity through grammatical parallelism; or it can simply provide the contiguity and allow the lexical and semantic elements to project their equivalences onto it.

This is somewhat opposed to Jakobson's view; he seems to permit both semantic and grammatical syntagms to be called parallel. "On the semantic level, we observed that parallels may be either metaphoric or metonymic, based on similarity and contiguity respectively. Likewise the syntactic aspect of parallelism offers two types of pairs: either the second line presents a pattern SIMILAR to the preceding one, or the lines complement each other as two CONTIGUOUS constituents of one grammatical construction" (*GPRF*, 428).

Theoretically, then, a definition of grammatical parallelism could accept as parallel those lines which manifest a grammatically syntagmatic relationship, such as two parts of one sentence. But from a practical viewpoint this runs the risk of stretching the definition of grammatical parallelism beyond meaningfulness. (Since this is mainly applicable to verse, the discussion should take into account at this point what constitutes a line of verse, but this issue is beyond our scope and therefore the discussion of syntagmatic grammatical parallelism will not be pursued.)

43. This syntagmatic relationship underlies some of Lowth's "synthetic parallelism." He did not have our linguistic model or terminology and therefore could not formulate a definition for this term that would seem rigorous enough for us. But despite the criticism of Lowth's third category of parallelism, I would not be so quick to dismiss it as a worthless catchall. Compare also P. D. Miller's "synonymous-sequential parallelism" (*Biblica* 61) which is a subspecies of syntagmatic semantic parallelism.

44. Tension between grammatical paradigm and syntagm is present in a verse like

Ps 135:5   כי אני ידעתי כי גדול ה'
                              ואדנינו מכל אלהים

For I know that YHWH is great;
And our lord than all gods.

Is this verse one sentence: "I know that YHWH, our lord, is greater than all gods"? (cf. Freedman in Gray, XXX). Or is it two sentences: "I know that YHWH is great. Our lord [is greater] than all gods"?

45. It is difficult to find a proper rendering for *zkr*. It has the range of meaning that includes "name, appellation, mention, that which is invoked."

46. Greenstein makes a similar point in "The Phenomenology of Parallelism." Textlinguistics, too, is always conscious of context, of the fact that the form and meaning of any textual segment are dependent on the text as a whole and on the place of that segment within the text.

47. Cf. Caird, *The Language and Imagery of the Bible*, 150.

48. Kugel, *Idea*, 11, introduces a metaphor-like interpretation into Pr 26:9 with his "sharp" reading.
Isaiah moves from a simile to a metaphor in his use of Sodom and Gomorrah in 1:9–10: "We were like Sodom. . . . Listen, captains of Sodom. . . ." There is a wonderful "play on imagery" in these verses, for in the simile Sodom and Gomorrah represent completely destroyed cities, but in the metaphor they take on their other connotation—completely corrupt cities. Isaiah has successfully "set up" his audience; if they accept their likeness to Sodom in the first instance they must accept it also in the second.

49. Cf. Song 1:3 which equates *name* and *oil*.

50. Commentator after commentator attempts to make a connection between oil and birth and name and death. On oil used to rub the newborn see Scott, *Proverbs, Ecclesiastes*, 235 and Gordis, *Koheleth*, 267. Zer-Kavod ("Koheleth," 38 in *Hamesh Megillot*) suggests that "name" refers to the eulogy for the righteous at the time of his death. Gordis cites other links between "name" and "death." Landy ("Poetics and Parallelism," 62–63), improving on Kugel (*Idea*, 10), interprets the metaphor as "the day of death leaves us with but a name, while at the day of birth we are entirely physical, fragrant with possibility, but nameless."

5. THE PHONOLOGIC ASPECT: SOUND PAIRS

1. The classic study in English on biblical paronomasia is Immanuel M. Casanowicz, *Paronomasia in the Old Testament*. Casanowicz lists the following types of paronomasia: alliteration, rime, assonance, epanastrophe, play on words, play on proper names. See also J. M. Sasson, "Wordplay in the OT," *IDB Suppl.*, 968–70. Adopting the terminology of J. Glück (*Semitics* I, 50–78), Sasson lists: equivocal, metaphonic, parasonancy, farrago, assonance, onomatopoeia, antanaclasis. Glück himself, in "Assonance in Ancient Hebrew Poetry," further subdivides what is often called assonance into assonance, consonance, dissonance, and alliteration. For a discussion citing the medieval Hebrew and Arabic terms see A. Diez Macho, "La Homonimia o Paronomasia," *Sefarad* 8 and 9. Other major studies include Gustav Boström, *Paronomasi i den äldre hebreiska maschallitteraturen med särskild hänsyn till Proverbia* and H. Reckendorf, *Über Paronomasie in den semitischen Sprachen*. See also L. Alonso-Schökel, *Estudios de Poética Hebrea*, 71–117; A. Strus, *Nomen-Omen* and "La poétique sonore des récits de la Genèse."

A number of verses presented in this chapter are cited by Casanowicz, Boström, and/or other scholars (e.g., Dahood and Gordis), but none of these scholars recognize them as manifestations of the phonologic aspect *of parallelism*.

2. I make the assumption here that phonologic correspondence alone does not constitute parallelism, but that it occurs along with other linguistic correspondences.

3. S. Morag counters the prevailing view of discounting the vocalization with the following: "The vocalization was definitely not invented when the vocalization signs were created. The vocalization signs are to be regarded . . . as a system of graphemic notation for those phonemic and phonetic entities that had been transmitted orally for generations in the various liturgical reading-traditions of Hebrew" (*JAOS* 94 [1974], 307). Cf. also E. J. Revell, *VT* 31 (1981), especially p. 198.

Moreover, even if the vocalization system does not preserve the "original" pronunciation, it does convey how the words were heard at a certain period in time. G. Gerleman's observation can be applied to pronunciation as well as to meaning: "The sense of the Massoretic text as it stands, what meaning the Massoretes themselves made of it, is a point too often absent from discussion by those eager to make brilliant conjectures" (*VT* I [1951], 168).

4. For example, Casanowicz, 33, states: "Of the subtle assonance there are in Hebrew, in which the consonantal element predominates, hardly any instances, except perhaps. . . ."

5. This sound pair accords well with the phonologic repetition throughout this passage—cf. v. 6 (ומבלעדי אין אלהים) and v. 9 (בל יועילו and ובל ידעו).

6. *Biblica* 58 (1977), 219–23. The verses that Kselman identified are: Gen 27:36; 2 Sam 1:21b; Ezek 22:2; Eccl 7:1a; Lam 3:22; Ps 37:6; Ps 51:19; Ps 78:33; Ps 147:15; Jer 2:7b; Pr 14:4; Gen 7:11; Ps 72:7.

7. These two words may well derive from the same word.

8. Cf. Kselman, *CBQ* 35 and Weinfeld, *Die Welt des Orients* IX.

9. פתע and פתאם may be a lexical pair as well as a sound pair—cf. Isa 29:5; Isa 30:13. See Pr 24:22, where פתאם has a different sound pair.

10. The form of נשוי could be due to the desire for sound play. Cf. Casanowicz, 43 and 67, no. 271 with note 92; and Dahood, *Psalms* I, 194.

11. In this verse שמים may be serving as a double-duty term, paralleling מים in

the first line and ארץ in the third (וכל בשלש עפר הארץ). While שמים־ארץ are common lexical associates, the pair מים // שמים is rare. On purely semantic grounds one might have expected here שמים // ימים (*sky // seas*), and indeed this is a known lexical pair (cf. *RSP* I, #555). Interestingly, 1QIsaᵃ (first copy of Isa from Qumran cave 1) reads *mey yam* in Isa 40:12 instead of *mayim* (cf. Gitay, *Prophecy and Persuasion*, 96, note 31). But the MT's *mayim* is better phonologically and is still semantically acceptable. The sound correspondence of שמים and מים is emphasized and complemented by מאזנים at the end of the verse.

12. The lexical-semantic pair is שמים // עבים. מים // שמים is a sound pair which is present in addition to the semantic pair. It gives the parallelism a phonologic dimension. D. Stuart, *Studies in Early Hebrew Meter*, omits *mym* and notes that it is "suspect but not clearly superfluous. Perhaps it entered the text through a misunderstanding of the parallelism" (133). According to my interpretation the misunderstanding is Stuart's; *mym* is there for phonologic reasons, and also because this is a type of incremental parallelism in which each line is rhythmically longer than the preceding one.

13. Cf. Berlin, *Prooftexts* 3, 237.

14. Gordis (*The Book of Job*, 35) emends the first line to עררי ים, which creates word repetition, not just sound correspondence. The words יום and לויתן are also consonant.

15. Compare

Job 28:12   והחכמה מאין תמצא
                              ואי זה מקום בינה

in which the sound pair is *tmṣ*ʾ and *ʾy zh m-*.

16. This verse is difficult. Scholars are divided on whether we have here two consonant roots, *yr*ʾ and *r*ʾ*h*, or a repetition of the root *yr*ʾ. Gordis (*The Book of Job*, 434) and Andersen (*Job*, 268) find *yr*ʾ in both lines, and draw support from the LXX and the Peshitta. The MT writing takes the verb in the second line as *r*ʾ*h* and this is followed by Pope (*Job*, 279, 283) and Tur-Sinai (*Sefer Iyyob*, 314).

17. Cf. Berlin, *Prooftexts* 3, 237.

18. Cf. Kselman, *BASOR* 220, 79.

19. I pointed out in *Prooftexts* 3, 237 with note 9 that indeed this verse has been mistranslated because the relationship between its parts, as well as its relationship to the rest of the poem, was not correctly perceived. Dahood (*Psalms* III, 42–43) was troubled by what he viewed as the poor syntactic match between the two parts, and therefore construed them as having the same syntactic structure. But as I have shown in chapter 3, two parallel lines need not have the same syntactic surface structure. I consider this verse an example of object-subject parallelism.

20. Cf. Levin, *Linguistic Structures in Poetry*, 35.

21. For an analysis of this passage see G. Schramm, "Poetic Patterning in Biblical Hebrew," 181–83.

22. Note the additional sound correspondence in עלומיך and אלמנותיך.

23. Gordis (*The Book of Job*, 43, 53) revocalizes to פְּתָאם and translates "I declare folly's dwelling to be cursed"—thus replacing the sound pair with a repeated term. Cf. above, note 14.

24. Cf. Ps 68:8 which also contains בצאתך and בצעדך. If 'ה is pronounced אדני then there is an additional sound correspondence with this and אדום.

25. A. Ceresko (*CBQ* 38, 311) finds an *abba* phonologic pattern in Pr 24:21–22: שונים־פתאם־ופיד־שניהם.

26. Ancient versions and modern scholars are divided on whether to read לֹא or
לָא. The negative expression לֹא יֵשׁ can be defended on the basis of Aramaic לָא אִית,
and the similar construction in Ps 135:17—אֵין יֵשׁ. Cf. Tur-Sinai, *Sefer Iyyob*, 105.

27. For שֶׁמֶן־שֵׁם cf. Song 1:3.

28. דָּם, אָדָם, and אֲדָמָה also figure in Gen 4:1–2, 10–11; 9:6; Isa 6:11; 15:19,
and perhaps Pr 28:17.

29. Cf. Berlin, *HAR* 3.

30. Cf. M. Weiss, *Biblica* 42.

31. Boström, 258, notes the sound correspondence between *lbš* and *bšt* in Job
8:22, where they both occur in the same line.

32. For an analysis of 2 Sam 1 see Holladay, *VT* 20.

33. G. Blakemore Evans, ed., *The Riverside Shakespeare* (Boston: Houghton
Mifflin, 1974).

6. PARALLELISM AND THE TEXT

1. In addition to the verses presented below, compare Ps 5:2–3; 6:9–10; 17:
1,6; 27:7; 28:2; 30:11; 31:3; 39:13; 55:2–3; 64:2; 69:14; 86:1,6; 119:169–
170; 130:2; 141:2–3; 142:7.

2. On the "forgetting" of parallelism by the rabbinic exegetes see Kugel, *Idea*,
96–134. Kugel points out that while the Rabbis seemed blind to parallelism in
their exegesis, they used it in their own poems. The inability of the Rabbis to perceive parallelism in the biblical text was largely due to their refusal to admit that
the text contained any type of redundancy. As I discussed in chapter 4, parallelism
is poised between redundancy and polysemy; to accept only one of these facets—
polysemy as the Rabbis did or redundancy as modern scholars did—is to risk a
misperception of parallelism.

3. It makes no difference if this is considered to be a refrain or communal response; the effect is the same.

4. I would draw an analogy between this and the perceptibility of rhyme schemes
in English poetry. Rhyme is most easily perceived when it appears in consecutive
lines (*aabb*), slightly less perceptible in every second line (*abab*), etc. The rhyme in
Robert Browning's "Song from Pippa Passes" is more distantly spaced (*abcdabcd*)
and it takes the reader longer to become aware of it.

> The year's at the spring
> And day's at the morn;
> Morning's at seven;
> The hillside's dew-pearled;
>
> The lark's on the wing;
> The snail's on the thorn;
> God's in his heaven—
> All's right with the world!

5. Greenstein ("How Does Parallelism Mean," 54) makes a similar observation.

6. Cf. *RSP* I #233.

7. For example, the similar syntax of 10a and 13a; the similar syntax and word
repetition in 11a and 14a; the grammatical and semantic equivalences in the two
parts of 12a.

8. This may also explain other poetic lists—cf. chapter 1, note 11.

9. On a larger scale, the Bible as a whole has "made sense of history," that is, it has given pattern and significance to historical events. But the way it is done in Ps 136 is much terser.

Poetry that gives meaning to history is, of course, not confined to one time or place. American readers recognize it in "The Battle Hymn of the Republic," which suggests that the Civil War is the battle par excellence, the apocalyptic Battle of Armageddon: "Mine eyes have seen the glory of the coming of the Lord." But more apropos to our discussion, the last stanza of this poem contains a parallelism which, like Gen 27:36, Ps 114:3, and Ps 136, equates two separate events: "As He died to make men holy, let us die to make men free." By means of this parallelism the deaths of the Civil War soldiers are equated with the death of Jesus, thereby giving the highest significance (to a Christian) to the lives lost in this war. Moreover, not only are their deaths like Jesus' death, but freedom is equated with holiness; the purpose for which the soldiers died is no less exalted than the purpose for which Jesus died. This line, like the poem as a whole, embodies an American blend of patriotism and religion. Notice that the parallelism not only utilizes lexical and syntactic repetition, but actualizes the metaphoric function of parallelism through the word "as."

10. Waugh, 65—cf. above, chapter 1, p. 11. Holenstein also discusses contrast, although somewhat more cryptically: "Jakobson's structural definition of poetry within the framework of the theory of the two axes can be extended as follows. Besides the projection of the principle of similarity from the axis of selection into that of combination, there also occurs in poetry a projection of the principle of contrast from its usual level of latent prerequisite for linguistic relations into the level of an obvious, 'palpable' form" (152).

GLOSSARY

aspect of parallelism: the linguistic aspect—e.g., lexical, grammatical, semantic, phonologic—involved in the parallelism.

binomination: the splitting up, in parallel lines, of the components of one personal or geographic name.

collocation: the occurrence of the parts of a pair or set at an unspecified distance within the same passage.

constitutive device: the formal device on which the text is structured; constructive device.

constructive device: the formal device on which the text is constructed.

contiguity: the combining of linguistic elements in a sequential or linear order.

contrast: the stressing of the difference between comparable terms; opposition.

conventionalized coordinates: terms which are members of common expressions or idioms, e.g., "horse" and "driver"; the use of such terms in parallel lines is also known as the breakup of stereotyped phrases.

deep structure: the underlying level of structural organization; in generative grammar, the abstract syntactic representation of a sentence; the opposite of surface structure.

equivalence: the stressing of the sameness of comparable terms; belonging to the same category or paradigm, or to the same sequence or syntagm.

gapping: the deletion of a repeated verb in conjoined clauses.

grammatical: the structural organization of language; morphology and syntax.

informativity: the concept of a text's presenting new factual information or unusual linguistic constructions; the opposite of contextual or linguistic redundancy.

juxtaposition: the occurrence of the parts of a pair next to each other or within the same phrase.

level of parallelism: the amount of textual structure—word, line, clause—involved in the parallelism.

lexical: having to do with the words, the vocabulary, of a language as distinct from its grammar.

lexical associate: the product of word association similar to that elicited by psycholinguists in word association games; word pair.

linearity: the chain of actions or events characteristic of narrative; the placement of one thing after another in a sequence.

morphological: relating to the form of words.

opposition: the stressing of the differences between comparable terms; contrast.

paradigmatic: pertaining to members of a linguistic class available for selection in a given context (e.g., all words that can serve as subject).

parallelism: the activation of linguistic equivalences and/or contrasts within or among words, phrases, lines, or entire texts.

parataxis: the linking of constructions solely through juxtaposition, not through the use of conjunctions.

perceptibility: the ease in recognizing the existence of a phenomenon; ease in processing it.

phonological: relating to the sounds of a language.

poetic function: focus on the message for its own sake.

pragmatics: the study of language from the point of view of the user, his audience, and the context of the communication.

psycholinguistics: the study of the correlation between linguistic behavior and the cognitive processes underlying that behavior.

semantic: relating to meaning in language.

similarity: see equivalence.

sound pair: a set of phonologically equivalent terms in a parallelism.

structural linguistics: an approach to linguistics stressing the description of linguistic features in terms of structures and systems; in structural linguistics language is considered to consist of an underlying network of relationships.

surface structure: the form of the phrase or sentence as it occurs in the text; in generative grammar, the final stage in the syntactic representation of a sentence; the opposite of deep structure.

syntactic: relating to the way words are combined to form sentences.

syntagmatic: referring to the sequential relationships of linguistic elements; a combination based on the linear sequence of linguistic terms; cf. contiguity.

textlinguistics: the study of linguistics above the level of the sentence; the relationship of the linguistic elements throughout an entire text.

transformation: a formal linguistic operation showing the process whereby one moves from surface structure to deep structure or vice versa.

word pair: a pair of lexically equivalent terms in a parallelism; lexical associate.

BIBLIOGRAPHY

The works listed below are those from the fields of biblical studies, linguistics, and poetics which are most relevant to the present study. Many discussions of biblical poetry, linguistic theory, and specific parallelistic texts have not been cited.

Abrams, M. H., *A Glossary of Literary Terms* (fourth edition) (New York: Holt, Rinehart, Winston), 1981.

Adams, P. G., "The Historical Importance of Assonance to Poets," *Publications of the Modern Language Association* 88 (1973), 8–18.

Adar, Z., *Sefer Tehillim* (Tel Aviv: Cherikover), 1976.

Albright, W. F., "The Psalm of Habakkuk," *Studies in Old Testament Prophecy Presented to Theodore H. Robinson*, ed. H. H. Rowley (Edinburgh: Clark), 1950, 1–18.

Alonso-Schökel, L., *Estudios de Poética Hebrea* (Barcelona: Juan Flors), 1963.

———, *The Inspired Word* (London: Burns and Gates), 1965.

———, "Die stilistische Analyse bei den Propheten," *VT* Supplement 7 (1959), 154–64.

Alonso-Schökel, L., and Strus, A., "Salmo 122: Canto al nombre de Jerusalén," *Biblica* 61 (1980), 234–50.

Alter, R., "The Dynamics of Parallelism," *Hebrew University Studies in Literature and the Arts,* 11/1 (1983), 71–101.

———, "From Line to Story in Biblical Verse," *Poetics Today* 4 (1983), 615–37.

Andersen, F. I., *The Hebrew Verbless Clause in the Pentateuch, JBL* Monograph Series 14 (Nashville: Abingdon), 1970.

———, *Job* (Tyndale O. T. Commentaries, London: Intervarsity Press), 1976.

———, "Orthography in Repetitive Parallelism," *JBL* 89 (1970), 343–44.

———, "Passive and Ergative in Hebrew," *Near Eastern Studies in Honor of William Foxwell Albright*, ed. H. Goedicke (Baltimore: The Johns Hopkins Press), 1971, 1–16.

———, *The Sentence in Biblical Hebrew* (The Hague: Mouton), 1974.

Andersen, F. I., and Forbes, A. D., "'Prose Particle' Counts of the Hebrew Bible," *The Word of the Lord Shall Go Forth*, ed. C. Meyers and M. O'Connor, 165–83.

apRoberts, R., "Old Testament Poetry: The Translatable Structure," *Publications of the Modern Language Association* 92 (1977), 987–1004.

Armstrong, D., and van Schooneveld, C., *Roman Jakobson. Echoes of His Scholarship* (Lisse: Peter de Ridder), 1977.

Auffret, P., *The Literary Structure of Psalm 2, JSOT* Supplement Series, 3 (Sheffield: JSOT Press), 1977.

Austerlitz, R., *Ob-Ugric Metrics* (Folklore Fellows Communications 174, Helsinki: Academia Scientiarum Fennica), 1958.

———, "Parallelismus," *Poetics, Poetyka, Poetika*, ed. D. Davie et al., 439–44.

Avishur, Y., "Addenda to the Expanded Colon in Ugaritic and Biblical Verse," *UF* 4 (1972), 1–10.

——, *The Construct State of Synonyms in Biblical Rhetoric* (Jerusalem: Kiryat Sepher), 1977 [Hebrew].

——, "Studies of Stylistic Features Common to the Phoenician Inscriptions and the Bible," *UF* 8 (1976), 1–12.

——, "Stylistic Common Elements Between Ugaritic Literature and Song of Songs," *Beth Mikra* 59 (1974), 508–25 [Hebrew].

——, "Word Pairs Common to Phoenician and Biblical Hebrew," *UF* 7 (1975), 13–47.

Baker, A., "Parallelism: England's Contribution to Biblical Studies," *CBQ* 35 (1973), 429–40.

Barr, J., *The Semantics of Biblical Language* (London: Oxford University Press), 1962.

de Beaugrande, R., "Semantic evaluation of grammar in poetry," *PTL* 3 (1978), 315–25.

——, "Towards a general theory of creativity," *Poetics* 8 (1979), 269–306.

de Beaugrande, R., and Dressler, W., *Introduction to Textlinguistics* (London: Longman), 1980.

Bennett, W., "An Applied Linguistic View of the Function of Poetic Form," *Journal of Literary Semantics* 6 (1977), 29–48.

——, "Linguistics and the Evaluation of Poetic Style," *Journal of Literary Semantics* 10 (1981), 95–103.

Berlin, A., "Grammatical Aspects of Biblical Parallelism," *HUCA* 50 (1979), 17–43.

——, "Isaiah 40:4: Etymological and Poetic Considerations," *HAR* 3 (1979), 1–6.

——, "Motif and Creativity in Biblical Poetry," *Prooftexts* 3 (1983), 231–41.

——, "On the Bible as Literature," *Prooftexts* 2 (1982), 323–27.

——, "Parallel Word Pairs: A Linguistic Explanation," *UF* 15 (1983), 7–16.

——, "Shared Rhetorical Features in Biblical and Sumerian Literature," *JANES* 10 (1978), 35–42.

——, "Review of M. O'Connor, *Hebrew Verse Structure*," *JAOS* 102 (1982), 392–93.

Beyer, K., "Althebräische Syntax in Prosa und Poesie," *Tradition und Glaube*, ed. G. Jeremias et al. (Göttingen: Van den Hoeck and Ruprecht), 1971, 76–96.

Blau, J., *A Grammar of Biblical Hebrew* (Wiesbaden: Harrassowitz), 1976.

Blenkinsopp, J., "Ballad Style and Psalm Style in the Song of Deborah," *Biblica* 42 (1961), 61–76.

——, "Stylistics of Old Testament Poetry," *Biblica* 44 (1963), 352–58.

Blommerde, A., *Northwest Semitic Grammar and Job* (Rome: Pontifical Biblical Institute), 1969.

Boadt, L., "Textual Problems in Ezekiel and Poetic Analysis of Paired Words," *JBL* 97 (1978), 489–99.

Boling, R., "'Synonymous' Parallelism in the Psalms," *JSS* 5 (1960), 221–55.

Bolinger, D. L., "Rime, Assonance and Morpheme Analysis," *Word* 6 (1950), 117–40.

Boström, G., *Paronomasi i den äldre hebreiska Maschallitteraturen med särskild hänsyn till Proverbia* (Lund: C. W. K. Gleerup), 1928.

Bream, H. N., Heim, R. D., and Moore, C. A., ed., *A Light unto My Path—Old Testament Studies in Honor of Jacob M. Myers* (Philadelphia: Temple University Press), 1974.

Briggs, C. A., *The Book of Psalms* (International Critical Commentary, New York: Charles Scribner's Sons), 1906.

Bronznick, N., "'Metathetic Parallelism'—An Unrecognized Subtype of Synonymous Parallelism," *HAR* 3 (1979), 25–39.

Buhlmann, W. and Scherer, K., *Stilfiguren der Bibel* (Biblische Beitrage 10, Freibourg: Schweizerisches Katholisches Bibelwerk), 1973.

Bullinger, E. W., *Figures of Speech Used in the Bible* (Grand Rapids, Mich.: Baker Book House), 1969.

Buttenwieser, M., *The Psalms* (New York: Ktav), 1969 [Orig. pub. 1938].

Caird, G. B., *The Language and Imagery of the Bible* (Philadelphia: Westminster), 1980.

Casanowicz, I. M., "Parallelism in Hebrew Poetry," *Jewish Encyclopedia* 9 : 520–22.

———, *Paronomasia in the Old Testament* (Boston: Norwood), 1894.

Cassuto, U., *Biblical and Oriental Studies*, Vol. I (Jerusalem: Magnes), 1973, Vol. II, 1975.

———, *From Noah to Abraham—A Commentary on the Book of Genesis, Part II* (Jerusalem: Magnes), 1964.

———, *The Goddess Anath* (Jerusalem: Magnes), 1971.

Ceresko, A., "The A:B::B:A Word Pattern in Hebrew and Northwest Semitic with Special Reference to the Book of Job," *UF* 7 (1975), 73–88.

———, "The Chiastic Word Pattern in Hebrew," *CBQ* 38 (1976), 303–11.

———, "The Function of Antanaclasis (*mṣ'* 'to find' // *mṣ'* 'to reach, overtake, grasp') in Hebrew Poetry, Especially in the Book of Qoheleth," *CBQ* 44 (1982), 551–69.

———, "The Function of Chiasmus in Hebrew Poetry," *CBQ* 40 (1978), 1–10.

Chatman, S., "Comparing Metrical Styles," *Style in Language*, ed. T. Sebeok, 149–72.

———, ed., *Approaches to Poetics* (New York: Columbia University Press), 1973.

———, ed., *Literary Style: A Symposium* (London: Oxford University Press), 1971.

Chatman, S., and Levin, S., ed., *Essays on the Language of Literature* (Boston: Houghton Mifflin), 1967.

Clark, H. H., "Word Associations and Linguistic Theory," *New Horizons in Linguistics*, ed. J. Lyons, 271–86.

Clines, D., *I, He, We and They: A Literary Approach to Isaiah 53*, *JSOT* Supplement Series, 1 (Sheffield: JSOT Press), 1976.

Collins, T., *Line-Forms in Hebrew Poetry* (Rome: Biblical Institute Press), 1978.

———, "Line-Forms in Hebrew Poetry," *JSS* 23 (1978), 228–44.

Cooper, A., *Biblical Poetics: A Linguistic Approach* (Ph.D. Dissertation, Yale University), 1976.

Coulthard, M., *An Introduction to Discourse Analysis* (London: Longman), 1977.

Craigie, P. C., "A Note on 'Fixed Pairs' in Ugaritic and Early Hebrew Poetry," *Journal of Theological Studies* 22 (1971), 140–43.

———, "Parallel Word Pairs in Ugaritic Poetry: A Critical Evaluation of their Relevance for Ps 29," *UF* 11 (1979), 135–40.

———, "The Problem of Parallel Word Pairs in Ugaritic and Hebrew Poetry," *Semitics* 5 (1979), 48–58.

———, "The Song of Deborah and the Epic of Tukulti-Ninurta," *JBL* 88 (1969), 253–65.

———, "Ugarit and the Bible," *Ugarit in Retrospect*, ed. G. D. Young, 99–111.

Cross, F. M., "Studies in the Structure of Hebrew Verse: The Prosody of Lamentations 1:1–22," *The Word of the Lord Shall Go Forth*, ed. C. Meyers and M. O'Connor, 129–55.

Cross, F. M., and Freedman, D. N., *Studies in Ancient Yahwistic Poetry* (Missoula, Mont.: Scholars Press), 1975.

Cross, F. M., and Talmon, S., ed., *Qumran and the History of the Biblical Text* (Cambridge, Mass.: Harvard University Press), 1975.

Cruse, D. A., "The Pragmatics of Lexical Specificity," *Journal of Linguistics* 13 (1977), 153–64.

Crystal, D., *A First Dictionary of Linguistics and Phonetics* (Boulder, Colo.: Westview), 1980.

Culler, J., "Jakobson and the Linguistic Analysis of Literary Texts," *Language and Style* 5 (1971), 53–66.

———, *Structural Poetics: Structuralism, Linguistics, and the Study of Literature* (Ithaca, N.Y.: Cornell University Press), 1975.

Culley, R. C, "An Approach to the Problem of Oral Tradition," *VT* 13 (1963), 113–25.

———, "Metrical Analysis of Classical Hebrew Poetry," *Essays on the Ancient Semitic World*, ed. J. W. Wevers and D. B. Redford (Toronto: University of Toronto Press), 1970, 12–28.

———, *Oral Formulaic Language in the Biblical Psalms* (Toronto: University of Toronto Press), 1967.

Dahood, M., "Chiasmus in Job: A Text-Critical and Philological Criterion," *A Light unto My Path*, ed. H. N. Bream et al., 119–30.

———, "Congruity of Metaphors," *Hebräische Wortforschung*, *VT* Supplement 16, (Leiden: Brill), 1967, 40–49.

———, "A New Metrical Pattern in Biblical Poetry," *CBQ* 29 (1967), 574–79.

———, "Poetic Devices in the Book of Proverbs," *Studies in Bible and the Ancient Near East Presented to Samuel E. Loewenstamm*, ed. Y. Avishur and J. Blau (Jerusalem: Rubenstein), 1978, 7–17.

———, "Poetry," *IDB* Supplement (Nashville, Tenn.: Abingdon), 1976, 669–72.

———, *Psalms I* (Anchor Bible, Garden City: Doubleday), 1966; *Psalms II*, 1968; *Psalms III*, 1970.

———, "Ugaritic-Hebrew Parallel Pairs," *RSP* I, ed. L. Fisher, 71–382; *RSP* II, ed. L. Fisher, 1–39; *RSP* III, ed. S. Rummel, 1–206.

———, "Ugaritic-Hebrew Syntax and Style," *UF* 1 (1969), 15–36.

Davie, D. et al., ed., *Poetics, Poetyka, Poetika. Proceedings of the First International Conference of Work in Progress Devoted to the Problems of Poetics* (Warsaw and The Hague: Panstwowe Wydawntwo Naukowe and Mouton), 1961.

Deese, J. E., *The Structure of Associations in Language and Thought* (Baltimore: The Johns Hopkins Press), 1965.

de Moor, J. C., "The Art of Versification in Ugarit and Israel," *Studies in Bible and the Ancient Near East Presented to Samuel E. Loewenstamm*, ed. Y. Avishur and J. Blau (Jerusalem: Rubenstein), 1978, 119–39.

———, "The Art of Versification in Ugarit and Israel II: The Formal Structure," *UF* 10 (1978), 187–217.

———, "The Art of Versification in Ugarit and Israel III: Further Illustrations of the Principle of Expansion," *UF* 12 (1980), 311–15.

Diez Macho, A., "La Homonimia o Paronomasia," *Sefarad* 8 (1948), 293–321; *Sefarad* 9 (1949), 269–309.

van Dijk, T. A., "On the Foundations of Poetics: Methodological Prolegomena to a Generative Grammar of Literary Texts," *Poetics* 1 (1972), 89–123.

———, *Some Aspects of Text Grammar* (The Hague: Mouton), 1972.

———, *Text and Context. Explorations in the Semantics and Pragmatics of Discourse* (London: Longman), 1980.

———, ed., *The Future of Structural Poetics*, *Poetics* 8 (1979), 497–608.

———, ed., *Pragmatics of Language and Literature* (Amsterdam: North Holland), 1976.

di Marco, A., "Der Chiasmus in der Bibel," *Linguistica Biblica* 36 (1975), 21–79; 37 (1976), 49–68.

Donald, T., *Parallelism in Akkadian, Hebrew and Ugaritic* (Ph.D. Dissertation, Manchester University), 1966 [this work was unavailable to me].

Doron, P., "Paronomasia in the Prophecies to the Nations," *Hebrew Studies* 20–21 (1979–80), 36–43.

Dressler, W., ed., *Current Trends in Textlinguistics* (Berlin: Walter de Gruyter), 1977.

Driver, G. R., "Hebrew Poetic Diction," *VT* Supplement 1 (1953), 26–39.

Ehrlich, A. B., *Mikrâ Ki-Pheshutô* (New York: Ktav), 1969 [orig. pub. 1900— Hebrew].

Eitan, I., "La Repetition de la Racine en Hebreu," *Journal of the Palestinian Oriental Society* 1 (1921), 171–86.

Empson, W., *Seven Types of Ambiguity* (London: New Directions), 1947.

Erlich, V., "Roman Jakobson: Grammar of Poetry and Poetry of Grammar," *Approaches to Poetics*, ed. S. Chatman, 1–27.

Finnegan, R., *Oral Poetry* (Cambridge: Cambridge University Press), 1977.

Fisher, L., ed., *Ras Shamra Parallels* I (Rome: Pontifical Biblical Institute), 1972; II, 1975.

Fitzgerald, A., "Hebrew Poetry," *Jerome Biblical Commentary*, ed. R. E. Brown, J. A. Fitzmyer, and R. E. Murphy (Englewood Cliffs, N.J.: Prentice Hall), 1968, 238–44.

———, "The Interchange of L, N, and R in Biblical Hebrew," *JBL* 97 (1978), 481–88.

Fodor, J. D., *Semantics: Theories of Meaning in Generative Grammar* (Cambridge, Mass.: Harvard University Press), 1980.

Fodor, J. D., and Katz, J., ed., *The Structure of Language: Readings in the Philosophy of Language* (Englewood Cliffs, N.J.: Prentice Hall), 1964.

Fokkelman, J., "Review of W. Watters, *Formula Criticism and the Poetry of the Old Testament*," *Bibliotheca Orientalis* 34 (1977), 212–13.

Fowler, R., "Linguistics and, and Versus, Poetics," *Journal of Literary Semantics* 8 (1979), 3–21.

———, "Preliminaries to a Sociolinguistic Theory of Literary Discourse," *Poetics* 8 (1979), 531–56.

———, ed., *Essays on Style and Language* (New York: Humanities Press), 1966.

Fox, J., "Roman Jakobson and the Comparative Study of Parallelism," *Roman Jakobson. Echoes of His Scholarship*, ed. D. Armstrong and C. van Schooneveld, 59–90.

Freedman, D. N., *Pottery, Poetry, and Prophecy. Collected Essays on Hebrew Poetry* (Winona Lake, Ind.: Eisenbrauns), 1980.

Freedman, D. N., and Hyland, C. F., "Psalm 29: A Structural Analysis," *Harvard Theological Review* 66 (1973), 237–56.

Freeman, D. C., ed., *Linguistics and Literary Style* (New York: Holt, Rinehart, Winston), 1970.

Geller, S., "The Dynamics of Parallel Verse. A Poetic Analysis of Deut 32:6–12," *Harvard Theological Review* 75 (1982), 35–56.

———, *Parallelism in Early Biblical Poetry* (Missoula, Mont.: Scholars Press), 1979.

———, "Review of J. Kugel, *The Idea of Biblical Poetry. Parallelism and Its History*," *JBL* 102 (1983), 625–26.

———, "Theory and Method in the Study of Biblical Poetry," *JQR* 73 (1982), 65–77.

Gerleman, G., "The Song of Deborah in the Light of Stylistics," *VT* 1 (1951), 168–80.

Gevirtz, S., "On Canaanite Rhetoric. The Evidence of the Amarna Letters from Tyre," *Orientalia* 42 (1973), 162–77.

———, *Patterns in the Early Poetry of Israel* (Chicago: Oriental Institute), 1963.

Ginsberg, H. L., "The Rebellion and Death of Ba'lu," *Orientalia* NS 5 (1936), 161–98.

Gitay, Y., "Deutero-Isaiah: Oral or Written?" *JBL* 99 (1980), 185–97.

———, *Prophecy and Persuasion. A Study of Isaiah 40–48* (Bonn: Linguistica Biblica), 1981.

Globe, A., "The Literary Structure and Unity of the Song of Deborah," *JBL* 93 (1974), 493–512.

Gluck, J., "Assonance in Ancient Hebrew Poetry: Sound Patterns as a Literary Device," *De Fructu Oris Sui, Essays in Honour of Adrianus van Selms,* ed I. H. Eybers, F. C. Fensham, and C. J. Labuschagne (Leiden: Brill), 1971, 69–84.

———, "Paronomasia in Biblical Literature," *Semitics* 1 (1970), 50–78.

Gonda, J., *Stylistic Repetition in the Veda* (Amsterdam: Noord–Hollandsche Uitgevers Maatschappij), 1959.

Gordis, R., *The Book of Job: Commentary, New Translation and Special Studies* (New York: Ktav), 1978.

———, *Koheleth, The Man and His World* (New York: Schocken), 1971.

———, "The Structure of Biblical Poetry," *Poets, Prophets, and Sages* (Bloomington: Indiana University Press), 1971, 61–94.

———, *The Word and the Book. Studies in Biblical Language and Literature* (New York: Ktav), 1976.

Gottwald, N., "Poetry, Hebrew," *IDB*, vol. 3 (Nashville, Tenn.: Abingdon), 1962, 829–38.

Gray, G. B., *The Forms of Hebrew Poetry* (New York: Ktav), 1972 [orig. pub. 1915].

Greenstein, E., "How Does Parallelism Mean?" *A Sense of Text, JQR Supplement* (Winona Lake, Ind.: Eisenbrauns), 1982, 41–70.

———, "One More Step on the Staircase," *UF* 9 (1977), 77–86.

———, "The Phenomenology of Parallelism," Paper read at the Annual Meeting of the Society of Biblical Literature, New York, 1982.

———, "Two Variations of Grammatical Parallelism in Canaanite Poetry and Their Psycholinguistic Background," *JANES* 6 (1974), 87–105.

Grossberg, D., "Nominalization in Biblical Hebrew," *Hebrew Studies* 20–21 (1979–80), 29–33.

Grzedzielska, M., "Les tendances à atténuer la distinction entre le vers et la prose," *Poetics, Poetyka, Poetika,* ed. D. Davie et al., 281–92.

Guillaume, A., "Paronomasia in the Old Testament," *JSS* 9 (1964), 282–90.
———, *Studies in the Book of Job* (Leiden: Brill), 1968.
Halle, M., and McCarthy, J. J., "The Metrical Structure of Psalm 137," *JBL* 100 (1981), 161–67.
Halpern, B., "Doctrine by Misadventure. Between the Israelite Source and the Biblical Historian," *The Poet and the Historian. Essays in Literary and Historical Biblical Criticism*, ed. R. E. Friedman (Chico, Calif.: Scholars Press), 1983, 41–73.
Hammond, M., "Poetic Syntax," *Poetics, Poetyka, Poetika*, ed. D. Davie et al., 475–82.
Hauser, A., "Judges 5: Parataxis in Hebrew Poetry," *JBL* 99 (1980), 23–41.
Held, M., "The Action-Result (Factitive-Passive) Sequence of Identical Verbs in Biblical Hebrew and Ugaritic," *JBL* 84 (1965), 272–82.
———, "Additional Pairs of Words in Synonymous Parallelism in Biblical Hebrew and in Ugaritic," *Lešonenu* 18 (1953), 144–60.
———, "Rhetorical Questions in Ugaritic and Biblical Hebrew," *Eretz Israel* 9 (1969), 71–79.
———, "The YQTL-QTL (QTL-YQTL) Sequence of Identical Verbs in Biblical Hebrew and in Ugaritic," *Studies and Essays in Honor of Abraham A. Neuman*, ed. M. Ben-Horin et al. (Leiden: Brill), 1962, 281–90.
Hendricks, W., "Three Models for the Description of Poetry," *Journal of Linguistics* 5 (1969), 1–22.
Hiatt, M., "The Prevalence of Parallelism: A Preliminary Investigation by Computer," *Language and Style* 6 (1973), 117–26.
Hillers, D. R., *Lamentations* (Anchor Bible, Garden City: Doubleday), 1972.
———, "Observations on Syntax and Meter in Lamentations," *A Light unto My Path*, ed. H. N. Bream et al., 265–70.
Holenstein, E., *Roman Jakobson's Approach to Language: Phenomenological Structuralism* (Bloomington: Indiana University Press), 1976.
Holladay, W. L., "Form and Word-Play in David's Lament over Saul and Jonathan," *VT* 20 (1970), 153–89.
———, "Prototype and Copies: A New Approach to the Poetry-Prose Problem in the Book of Jeremiah," *JBL* 79 (1960), 351–67.
———, "The Recovery of Poetic Passages of Jeremiah," *JBL* 85 (1966), 401–35.
Honeyman, A. M., "Merismus in Biblical Hebrew," *JBL* 71 (1952), 11–18.
Hrabák, J., "Remarques sur les corrélations entre le vers et la prose, surtout sur les soi-disant formes de transition," *Poetics, Poetyka, Poetika*, ed. D. Davie et al., 239–48.
Hrushovski, B., "Do Sounds Have Meaning? The Problem of Expressiveness of Sound Patterns in Poetry," *Hasifrut* 1 (1968–69), 410–20 [Hebrew].
———, "The Meaning of Sound Patterns in Poetry," *Poetics Today* 2 (1980), 39–56.
———, "On Free Rhythms in Modern Poetry," *Style in Language*, ed. T. Sebeok, 173–90.
———, "Prosody, Hebrew," *Encyclopedia Judaica* 13: 1195–1203.
Jakobson, R., "Grammatical Parallelism and its Russian Facet," *Language* 42 (1966), 399–429.
———, "Linguistics and Poetics," *Style in Language*, ed. T. Sebeok, 350–77.
———, "On Poetic Intentions and Linguistic Devices in Poetry. A Discussion

with Professors and Students at the University of Cologne," *Poetics Today* 2 (1980), 87–96.

————, "Poetry of Grammar and Grammar of Poetry," *Lingua* 21 (1968), 597–609.

————, "A Postscript to the Discussion on Grammar of Poetry," *diacritics* 10/1 (1980), 22–35.

————, "Subliminal Verbal Patterning in Poetry," *Poetics Today* 2 (1980), 127–36.

————, "Two Aspects of Language and Two Types of Aphasic Disturbances," *Selected Writings*, vol. II (The Hague: Mouton), 1971, 239–59.

————, "Verbal Communication," *Scientific American* 227/3 (1972), 73–80.

Jakobson, R. and Levi-Strauss, C., "'Les Chats' de Charles Baudelaire," *L'Homme* 2 (1962), 5–21.

Jebb, J., *Sacred Literature* (London: James Duncan), 1820.

Joüon, P., *Grammaire de l'hébreu biblique* (Rome: Pontifical Biblical Institute), 1923.

Kaddari, M. Z., "A Semantic Approach to Biblical Parallelism," *Journal of Jewish Studies* 24 (1973), 167–75.

————, "On Semantic Parallelism in Biblical Hebrew," *Lešonenu* 32 (1968), 37–45 [Hebrew].

Katz, J., and Fodor, J., "The Structure of a Semantic Theory," *The Structure of Language*, ed. J. Fodor and J. Katz, 479–518.

Katz, J., and Postal, P., *An Integrated Theory of Linguistic Descriptions* (Cambridge, Mass.: M.I.T. Press), 1964.

Kiparsky, P., "Metrics and Morphophonemics in the Kalevala," *Linguistics and Literary Style*, ed. D. C. Freeman, 165–81.

————, "The Role of Linguistics in a Theory of Poetry," *Daedalus* 102/3 (1973), 231–44.

Kosmala, H., "Form and Structure in Ancient Hebrew Poetry," *VT* 14 (1964), 423–45; *VT* 16 (1966), 152–80.

Krašovec, J., "Merism—Polar Expression in Biblical Hebrew," *Biblica* 64 (1983), 231–39.

Kselman, J. S., "The ABCB Pattern: Further Examples," *VT* 32 (1982), 224–29.

————, "A Note on Gen 7:11," *CBQ* 35 (1973), 491–93.

————, "Psalm 72: Some Observations on Structure," *BASOR* 220 (1975), 77–81.

————, "RB // KBD: A New Hebrew-Akkadian Formulaic Pair," *VT* 29 (1978), 110–13.

————, "The Recovery of Poetic Fragments from the Pentateuchal Priestly Source," *JBL* 97 (1978), 161–73.

————, "Semantic-Sonant Chiasmus in Biblical Poetry," *Biblica* 58 (1977), 219–23.

Kugel, J., *The Idea of Biblical Poetry. Parallelism and Its History* (New Haven: Yale University Press), 1981.

————, "On the Bible and Literary Criticism," *Prooftexts* 1 (1981), 217–36.

————, "Some Thoughts on Future Research into Biblical Style: Addenda to *The Idea of Biblical Poetry*," *JSOT* 28 (1984), 107–17.

Labov, W., *Language in the Inner City. Studies in the Black English Vernacular* (Philadelphia: University of Pennsylvania Press), 1972.

Landy, F., "Poetics and Parallelism: Some Comments on James Kugel's *The Idea of Biblical Poetry*," *JSOT* 28 (1984), 61–87.

Langer, K., "Some Suggestive Uses of Alliteration in Sanskrit Court Poetry," *JAOS* 98 (1978), 438–45.

Levin, S., "Concerning What Kind of Speech Act a Poem Is," *Pragmatics of Language and Literature*, ed. T. van Dijk, 141–60.

———, "The Conventions of Poetry," *Literary Style: A Symposium*, ed. S. Chatman, 177–96.

———, "Coupling in a Shakespeare Sonnet," *Linguistics and Literary Style*, ed. D. C. Freeman, 197–208.

———, *Linguistic Structures in Poetry* (The Hague: Mouton), 1962.

Lewis, R., "Old English Poetry: Alliteration and Structural Interlace," *Language and Style* 6 (1973), 196–205.

Loewenstamm, S. E., "The Expanded Colon Reconsidered," *UF* 7 (1975), 261–64.

———, "Remarks on Stylistic Patterns in Biblical and Ugaritic Literatures," *Lešonenu* 32 (1968), 27–36.

Loretz, O., "Die Analyse der ugaritischen und hebräischen Poesie mittels Stichometrie und Konsonantenzählung," *UF* 7 (1975), 265–70.

———, "Jeremia 18 ^{14}: stichometrie und parallelismus membrorum," *UF* 4 (1972), 170–71.

Lotman, J., *Analysis of the Poetic Text* (Ann Arbor: Ardis), 1976.

———, *The Structure of the Artistic Text* (Ann Arbor: University of Michigan Press), 1977.

Lowth, R., *Isaiah. A New Translation with a Preliminary Dissertation and Notes* (London: Wm. Tegg), 1848 [Orig. pub. 1778].

———, *Lectures on the Sacred Poetry of the Hebrews* (London: T. Tegg and Son), 1835 [Orig. pub. 1753].

Lundbom, J. R., *Jeremiah. A Study in Ancient Hebrew Rhetoric* (Missoula, Mont.: Scholars Press), 1975.

Lyons, J., ed., *New Horizons in Linguistics* (Baltimore: Penguin), 1970.

McKane, W., *Proverbs* (Philadelphia: Westminster), 1975.

McNeill, D., "A Study of Word Association," *Journal of Verbal Learning and Verbal Behavior* 5 (1966), 548–57.

Malkiel, Y., "Studies in Irreversible Binomials," *Essays on Linguistic Themes* (Berkeley: University of California Press), 1968, 311–55.

Margalit, B., "Alliteration in Ugaritic Poetry: Its Role in Composition and Analysis," *UF* 11 (1979), 537–57.

———, "Studia Ugaritica I: Introduction to Ugaritic Prosody," *UF* 7 (1975), 289–314.

Masson, D. I., "Sound-Repetition Terms," *Poetics, Poetyka, Poetika*, ed. D. Davie et al., 189–99.

Mayenowa, M. R., "Quelques differences entre un texte versifié et non-versifié," *Poetics, Poetyka, Poetika*, ed. D. Davie et al., 369–71.

Melamed, E. Z., "Break-up of Stereotype Phrases," *Scripta Hierosolymitana* 8 (1961), 115–53.

———, "Break-up of Stereotype Phrases as an Artistic Device in Biblical Poetry," *Sefer Segal. Studies in the Bible presented to Professor M. H. Segal by his colleagues and students*, ed. Y. Grintz (Jerusalem: Kiryat Sefer), 1964, 188–219 [Hebrew].

Meyers, C., and O'Connor, M., ed., *The Word of the Lord Shall Go Forth. Essays in Honor of David Noel Freedman in Celebration of His Sixtieth Birthday* (Winona Lake, Ind.: Eisenbrauns), 1983.

Milic, L. T., "Rhetorical Choice and Stylistic Option: The Conscious and Unconscious Poles," *Literary Style: A Symposium*, ed. S. Chatman, 77–94.

Miller, P. J., "Review of *Hebrew Verse Structure* by M. O'Connor," *JBL* 102 (1983), 628–29.

———, "Studies in Hebrew Word Patterns," *Harvard Theological Review* 73 (1980), 79–89.

———, "Synonymous-Sequential Parallelism in the Psalms," *Biblica* 61 (1980), 256–60.

———, "Meter, Parallelism, and Tropes: The Search for Poetic Style," *JSOT* 28 (1984), 99–106.

Morag, S., "On the Historical Validity of the Vocalization of the Hebrew Bible," *JAOS* 94 (1974), 307–15.

Muilenburg, J., "Form Criticism and Beyond," *JBL* 88 (1969), 1–18.

———, "Poetry," *Encyclopedia Judaica* 13: 670–81.

———, "A Study in Hebrew Rhetoric: Repetition and Style," *VT* Supplement 1 (1953), 97–111.

Mukarovsky, J., *On Poetic Language* (Lisse: Peter de Ridder), 1976.

———, "Standard Language and Poetic Language," *Linguistics and Literary Style*, ed. D. C. Freeman, 40–56.

Myers, J. M., *The Linguistic and Literary Form of the Book of Ruth* (Leiden: Brill), 1955.

Newmann, L., *Studies in Old Testament Parallelism, I: Parallelism in Amos* (Berkeley: University of California Publications in Semitic Philology), 1918.

O'Connor, M., *Hebrew Verse Structure* (Winona Lake, Ind.: Eisenbrauns), 1980.

———, "Review of T. Collins, *Line-Forms in Hebrew Poetry*," *CBQ* 42 (1980), 91–92.

———, "The Rhetoric of the Kilamuwa Inscription," *BASOR* 226 (1977), 15–29.

———, "The Role of Syntax in Hebrew Verse," Paper read at the Annual Meeting of the American Oriental Society, Boston, 1981.

———, "'Unanswerable the Knack of Tongues': The Linguistic Study of Verse," *Exceptional Language and Linguistics*, ed. L. Obler and L. Menn (New York: Academic Press), 1982, 143–68.

Pardee, D., "The Semantic Parallelism of Psalm 89," *In the Shelter of Elyon. Essays on Ancient Palestinian Life and Literature in Honor of G. W. Ahlstrom*, ed. W. B. Barrick and J. R. Spenser, *JSOT Supplement Series*, 31 (Sheffield: JSOT Press), 1984, 121–37.

———, "Types and Distributions of Parallelism in Ugaritic and Hebrew Poetry," Paper read at the Annual Meeting of the Society of Biblical Literature, New York, 1982.

———, "Ugaritic and Hebrew Metrics," *Ugarit in Retrospect*, ed. G. D. Young, 113–30.

———, "Ugaritic and Hebrew Poetry: Parallelism," Paper read at the First International Symposium on the Antiquities of Palestine, Aleppo, 20–25 September, 1980.

Parker, S., "Parallelism and Prosody in Ugaritic Narrative Verse," *UF* 6 (1974), 283–94.

Pomorska, K., "Roman Jakobson and the New Poetics," *Roman Jakobson. Echoes of His Scholarship*, ed. D. Armstrong and C. van Schooneveld, 363–78.

Pope, M., "Marginalia to M. Dahood's Ugaritic-Hebrew Philology," *JBL* 85 (1966), 455–66.

———, *Job* (Anchor Bible, Garden City: Doubleday), 1973.

Popper, W., *Studies in Biblical Parallelism, Part II: Parallelism in Isaiah* (Berkeley:

University of California Publications in Semitic Philology), 1918–1923.
Porten, B., and Rappaport, U., "Poetic Structure in Genesis IX 7," *VT* 21 (1971), 363–69.
Rauber, D. F., "Literary Values in the Bible: The Book of Ruth," *JBL* 89 (1970), 27–37.
Reckendorf, H., *Über Paronomasie in den semitischen Sprachen* (Giessen: Topelmann), 1909.
Rendsburg, G., "Janus Parallelism in Gen 49:26," *JBL* 99 (1980), 291–93.
Revell, E. J., "Pausal Forms and the Structure of Biblical Poetry," *VT* 31 (1981), 186–99.
Ridderbos, N. H., "The Psalms: Style-Figures and Structure," *Oudtestamentische Studiën* XIII (1963), 43–76.
Riffaterre, M., *The Semiotics of Poetry* (Bloomington: Indiana University Press), 1978.
Ringgren, H., "A Law of Stylistic Balance in Hebrew," *Horae Soederblomianae* 6 (1964), 9–14.
———, "The Omitting of *kol* in Hebrew Parallelism," *VT* 32 (1982), 99–103.
Robertson, D. A., *Linguistic Evidence in Dating Early Hebrew Poetry* (Missoula, Mont.: Scholars Press), 1972.
Robinson, T. H., "Hebrew Poetic Form: The English Tradition," *VT* Supplement 1 (1953), 128–49.
Rummel, S., ed., *Ras Shamra Parallels* III (Rome: Pontifical Biblical Institute), 1981.
Sappan, R., *The Typical Features of the Syntax of Biblical Poetry in its Classical Period* (Ph.D. Dissertation, Hebrew University), 1974.
Sasson, J. M., "Wordplay in the OT," *IDB* Supplement (Nashville, Tenn.: Abingdon), 1976, 968–70.
Sayce, R. A., "The Style of Montaigne: Word-Pairs and Word-Groups," *Literary Style: A Symposium*, ed. S. Chatman, 383–405.
Saydon, P. P., "Assonance in Hebrew as a Means of Expressing Emphasis," *Biblica* 36 (1955), 36–50, 287–304.
Schramm, G. M., "Poetic Patterning in Biblical Hebrew," *Michigan Oriental Studies in Honor of George G. Cameron*, ed. L. Orlin (Ann Arbor: Dept. of Near Eastern Studies, University of Michigan), 1976, 167–91.
Scott, R. B. Y., *Proverbs, Ecclesiastes* (Anchor Bible, Garden City: Doubleday), 1965.
Sebeok, T., *Style in Language* (Cambridge, Mass.: M.I.T. Press), 1960.
Segert, S., "Parallelism in Ugaritic Poetry," *JAOS* 103 (1983), 295–306.
———, "Prague Structuralism in American Biblical Scholarship: Performance and Potential," *The Word of the Lord Shall Go Forth*, ed. C. Meyers and M. O'Connor, 697–708.
———, "Problems of Hebrew Prosody," *VT* Supplement 7 (1960), 283–91.
———, "Ugaritic Poetry and Poetics: Some Preliminary Observations," *UF* 11 (1979), 729–38.
Shapiro, M., *Asymmetry. An Inquiry into the Linguistic Structure of Poetry* (Amsterdam: North Holland), 1976.
Smith, B. H., *Poetic Closure: A Study of How Poems End* (Chicago: University of Chicago Press), 1968.
Soggin, J. A., "Ancient Israelite Poetry and Ancient 'Codes' of Law, and the Sources 'J' and 'E' of the Pentateuch," *VT* Supplement 28 (1974), 185–95.

Stankiewicz, E., "Linguistics and the Study of Poetic Language," *Style in Language*, ed. T. Sebeok, 69–81.

———, "Poetic and Non-Poetic Language in their Interrelation," *Poetics, Poetyka, Poetika*, ed. D. Davie et al., 11–24.

Steiner, G., *After Babel. Aspects of Language and Translation* (New York: Oxford University Press), 1975.

Steinitz, W., *Der Parallelismus in der finnisch-karelischen Volksdichtung* (Folklore Fellows Communication 115, Helsinki: Academia Scientiarum Fennica), 1934.

Stolz, B. A., and Shannon, R. S., ed., *Oral Literature and the Formula* (Ann Arbor: Center for the Coordination of Ancient and Modern Studies, University of Michigan), 1976.

Strus, A., *Nomen-Omen. Stylistique des noms propres dans le Pentateuque* (Rome: Pontifical Biblical Institute), 1978.

———, "La poétique sonore des récits de la Genèse," *Biblica* 60 (1979), 1–22.

Stuart, D. K., *Studies in Early Hebrew Meter* (Missoula, Mont.: Scholars Press), 1976.

Stutterheim, C., "Poetry and Prose, Their Interrelations and Transitional Forms," *Poetics, Poetyka, Poetika*, ed. D. Davie et al., 225–37.

Szalay, L. and Deese, J., *Subjective Meaning and Culture: An Assessment Through Word Associations* (Hillsdale, N.J.: Lawrence Erlbaum), 1978.

Talmon, S., "Synonymous Readings in the Textual Traditions of the O.T.," *Scripta Hierosolymitana* 8 (1961), 335–83.

———, "The Textual Study of the Bible—A New Outlook," *Qumran and the History of the Biblical Text*, ed. F. M. Cross and S. Talmon, 321–400.

Thompson, J., "Linguistic Structure and the Poetic Line," *Linguistics and Literary Style*, ed. D. C. Freeman, 336–46.

Thorne, J. L., "Generative Grammar and Stylistic Analysis," *New Horizons in Linguistics*, ed. J. Lyons, 185–97.

———, "Poetry, stylistics and imaginary grammars," *Journal of Linguistics* 5 (1969), 147–50.

———, "Stylistics and Generative Grammars," *Journal of Linguistics* 2 (1965), 69–78.

Tsevat, M., *A Study of the Language of the Biblical Psalms* (Philadelphia: Society of Biblical Literature), 1955.

T'sou, B. K., "Some Aspects of Linguistic Parallelism and Chinese Versification," *Studies Presented to Professor Roman Jakobson by His Students*, ed. C. Gribble (Cambridge, Mass.: Slavica), 1968, 318–28.

Tur-Sinai, N. H., *Sefer Iyyob* (Tel Aviv: Yavneh), 1954 [Hebrew].

Ullmann, S., "Stylistics and Semantics," *Literary Style: A Symposium*, ed. S. Chatman, 133–55.

Watson, W. G. E., *Classical Hebrew Poetry: A Guide to its Techniques*, *JSOT* Supplement Series 26 (Sheffield: JSOT Press), 1983.

———, "Fixed Pairs in Ugaritic and Isaiah," *VT* 22 (1972), 460–68.

———, "Gender-Matched Synonymous Parallelism in the OT," *JBL* 99 (1980), 321–41.

———, "Gender-Matched Synonymous Parallelism in Ugaritic Poetry," *UF* 13 (1981), 181–87.

———, "Pivot Pattern in Hebrew, Ugaritic, Akkadian," *Zeitschrift für die Alttestamentliche Wissenschaft* 88 (1976), 239–53.

————, "Reversed Word-Pairs in Ugaritic Poetry," *UF* 13 (1981), 189–92.

————, "Review of James L. Kugel, *The Idea of Biblical Poetry. Parallelism and Its History*," *Biblica* 64 (1983), 134–36.

————, "A Review of Kugel's *The Idea of Biblical Poetry*," *JSOT* 28 (1984), 89–98.

————, "Review of M. O'Connor, *Hebrew Verse Structure*," *Biblica* 64 (1983), 131–34.

————, "Review of T. Collins, *Line-Forms in Hebrew Poetry*," *Biblica* 61 (1980), 581–83.

————, "Trends in the Development of Classical Hebrew Poetry: A Comparative Study," *UF* 14 (1982), 265–77.

————, "Verse Patterns in Ugaritic, Akkadian, and Hebrew Poetry," *UF* 7 (1975), 483–92.

Watters, W. R., *Formula Criticism and the Poetry of the Old Testament* (Berlin: Walter de Gruyter), 1976.

Waugh, L., "The Poetic Function and the Nature of Language," *Poetics Today* 2/1a (1980), 57–82.

Weinfeld, M., "Gen. 7:11, 8:1–2 Against the Background of Ancient Near Eastern Tradition," *Die Welt des Orients* 9 (1978), 242–48.

Weingreen, J., *Introduction to the Critical Study of the Text of the Hebrew Bible* (Oxford: Clarendon Press), 1982.

Weiss, M., "Die Methode der 'Total-Interpretation,'" *VT* Supplement 22 (1971), 88–112.

————, *Hamiqra Kidemuto* (Jerusalem: Mosad Bialik), 1962 [Hebrew].

————, "Wege der neuen Dichtungswissenschaft in ihrer Anwendung auf die Psalmenforschung," *Biblica* 42 (1961), 255–302.

Welch, J. W., *Chiasmus in Antiquity: Structures, Analyses, Exegesis* (Hildesheim: Gerstenberg), 1981.

Werth, P., "Roman Jakobson's Verbal Analysis of Poetry," *Journal of Linguistics* 12 (1976), 21–73.

Whallon, W., *Formula, Character, and Context: Studies in Homeric, Old English and Old Testament Poetry* (Cambridge, Mass.: Harvard University Press), 1969.

————, "Formulaic Poetry in the Old Testament," *Comparative Literature* 15 (1963), 1–14.

Whitley, C. F., "Some Aspects of Hebrew Poetic Diction," *UF* 7 (1975), 493–502.

Willis, J. T., "The Juxtaposition of Synonymous and Chiastic Parallelism in Tricola in Old Testament Hebrew Psalm Poetry," *VT* 29 (1979), 465–80.

Wimsatt, W. K., *The Verbal Icon* (Louisville: University of Kentucky Press), 1954.

————, ed., *Versification. Major Language Types* (New York: Modern Language Association and New York University Press), 1972.

Yoder, P., "A-B pairs and oral composition in Hebrew poetry," *VT* 21 (1971), 470–89.

————, *Fixed Word Pairs and the Composition of Hebrew Poetry* (Ph.D. Dissertation, University of Pennsylvania), 1970.

Young, G. D., "Ugaritic Prosody," *Journal of Near Eastern Studies* 9 (1950), 124–33.

————, ed., *Ugarit in Retrospect* (Winona Lake, Ind.: Eisenbrauns), 1981.

Zer-Kavod, M., "Koheleth," *Hamesh Megillot* (Jerusalem: Mosad Harav Kook), 1973 [Hebrew].

The Range of Biblical Metaphors in *Smikhut*

Lida Knorina

Lida Knorina was a Russian linguist who taught biblical Hebrew at Moscow State University. I met her only once, in 1993 in Jerusalem at the Eleventh World Congress of Jewish Studies, where she conversed with me privately in Hebrew. At that conference she reported on her work in progress on metaphors in *smikhut*. In April 1994 I received a brief e-mail message from her saying that she was still at work on that project, which continued to grow. She promised to send it to me when it was completed. The next news I had of her was in August 1994 from her husband, Vladimir Borshchev, informing me of Lida's death on June 4, 1994. He attached her unfinished manuscript, knowing she had wished me to read it, and expressing hope that I could make it known to other scholars. That hope was long deferred. Although I made reference to her work in a published article of mine ("On Reading Biblical Poetry: The Role of Metaphor," in *Congress Volume. Cambridge 1995*, edited by J. A. Emerton [Leiden, New York, and Köln: Brill, 1997], pp. 29-30), this is the first opportunity I have had to bring the entire paper to biblical scholars.

Her paper examines one aspect of biblical metaphor, metaphors that occur in the construct state *(smikhut)*. This is an original way of categorizing metaphors, and it testifies to the linguistic orientation of the author. Knorina's paper is interesting both for the theoretical framework that it suggests for the analysis of this type of metaphor, and for the examples she cites and discusses. For non-linguists, the latter will stimulate more thinking about how metaphors work and how to interpret their meaning.

I am most happy to bring Lida Knorina's work, along with her e-mail message and her husband's letter, to a broader audience. I hope these will commemorate this courageous young woman who had much to contribute to the linguistic study of biblical discourse and who tried to reach out to biblical scholars in Israel and in the English-speaking world at a time when it was still relatively difficult for a Russian scholar to do so.

Adele Berlin
August 2006

To: aberlin
Subject: gratitude
Date: Monday, 4 April 1994
From: Lida Knorina

Dear Adele,

I simply want to tell you that I appreciate your books greatly and use them
all the time. They help me a lot in my studies with the students. Now I
teach Biblical Hebrew at the philosophical department of Moscow State
University. It is very important for me that you in many points base on
Russian linguistic school.

I like very much your simple system of transliteration and use it now myself.

For a long time I postponed writing to you because I wanted to finish and
send to you the article based on my report at the Congress last year. But
this work appears to be endless. And the lost two months I was ill. So I
simply thank you once more for your books.

Yours Lida Knorina.

To Professor Adele Berlin,
Department of Hebrew and East Asian
   Languages and Literatures,
University of Maryland

Moscow, 19 August 1994

Dear Adele!

My wife, Lida Knorina, addressed you by your first name. Maybe you will allow me in her memory to call you in this way. Lida died more than two months ago, on June 4. You know, she was ill since February. Maybe later I will write you about her last months in more details. I know she feels you as a close friend. But now it is not easy for me. I am still in the shock.

Now I write to you about her paper on biblical metaphors that I am sending to you. She was working on it after last year's Jerusalem Congress. For many reasons it was a difficult paper for her. First of all she wrote it in English. But the main difficulties were not in language. She told me that Russian text would be much easier because she knows *Russian* papers on this theme. You know, linguistics is not a global universal science like physics or mathematics. There are the American linguistics, the Russian linguistics etc. And a lot of works well known here are not familiar to American linguists and vice versa.

The paper was founded on her previous works on semantic types. And this was the basic difficulty. It was impossible to retell in this paper the theory of semantic types. And on the other hand it was impossible to formulate her results without this theory.

Besides, Lida feels herself a novice in the field of biblical studies, although I think she found her own niche: the linguistic aspects of the matter. And she hoped that you could understand her work. She liked your book on biblical parallelism very much.

She completed the text in the first days of May (in the second half of April and in the first decade of May she feels herself much better and we thought that her illness is over, but we were wrong). She wanted to ask her friends to brush up her English. They did it after her death. So she did not read the last draft of her paper.

She was going to send her paper to you, to discuss it with you and ask you where it is possible to publish it. And I am doing it.

Very truly yours,

Vladimir Borshchev

My address:
Russia, 123458, Moscow, Tallinskaya str, 2, 156

PS Lida cited me many times the first phrase of your book: *I am not a linguist and not a disciple of linguists.* I can paraphrase farther: *I am not a linguist but I am a husband of a linguist.* I think that Lida was a very good linguist. She has papers on Russian grammar, poetics, semantics, English linguistic school of seventeenth century (she translated and commented the linguistic paper of I. Newton). And her last topic was the linguistics of Biblical Hebrew. And all her works were in close relationship. For example, she read Pasternak (her most beloved poet), tried to grasp the nature of his metaphors, and understood that it was possible only if we will understand the semantic types in nonfigurative text. So she studied these types in Russian genitive construction. And Smikhut is similar to Russian genitive.

By the way, she left a file of biblical *smikhut* metaphors. She went through the *Mandelkern Concordantiae* many times. Of course, it would be better to have an Appendix to her paper with the full list of biblical metaphors classified on semantic types. But she did not prepare the list to publication. She thought she has to work on it farther. I hope I could persuade her graduate student to complete this work.

I will try to publish the collection of her papers, but first of all I would like to publish her last works; in the last two months of her life she completed at any rate four papers. I am sending to you the list of her latest papers.

Excuse me for the long letter and for my English with a heavy Russian accent.

Once more yours,

Vladimir Borshchev

Lida Knorina
Some of her published and unpublished works

1976   Semantic categorization and verbal aspect — in "Semiotics and informatics," N. 7, Moscow

1977   Analysis of uninflected attributes to nouns — in "Scientific and technical information," series 2, N. 8

1978   New words acquisition with respect to analytic tendencies in "Russian-language practice," Moscow

1980   "Hieroglificity" and its influence on word use — in "Scientific and technical information," series 2, N. 10

1981   Case value estimation — in "Problems of structural linguistics — 1979," Moscow

1982   Grammar and norm in poetry — in "Problems of structural linguistics — 1980," Moscow

1986   Isaac Newton: Of a universal language (translation into Russian, notes, afterword) — in "Semiotics and informatics," N. 28, Moscow

1988   Lexicon categories and dictionary definitions — in "National languages and problems of national lexicography," Moscow

1988   Utilitarianism tendency and language theory in "XVIIth-century England — proceedings of the meeting 'Linguistic traditions in oriental countries,'" Moscow

1989   Word usage as component of individual style — in "Language and personality," Moscow

1989   Comparative genitive constructions in Pasternak's poetry — in "Stylistics and poetics," Moscow

1989   Elaboration of Russian-English computerized dictionaries (in co-authorship with N. A. Pastchenko) — in "Problems of information theory and practice," N. 58

1990   Semantic anomaly and metaphor in the genitive construction — in "Logical analysis of language: contradictions and anomalies in discourse," Moscow.

1990   Language theory and language planning — in "Interlinguistical aspects of language reforms and language planning," Tartu

1990   Types of "things" and their perception in language (in coauthorship with V. B. Borschev) — in "Language of logic and logic of language." 1990, Moscow.

1991   Language semantics in medieval Jewish philosophy — in "The East: the past and the future of the peoples." 1991, Moscow

1991   Action perception and generalization in text — proceedings of the conference "Action: linguistical and logical models" (Moscow)

1992   Mikra (review article on "Mikra: text, translation, interpretation. Philadelphia, 1988") — "The world of the Bible"

1992   Language structure representation in language planning in XVIIth-century England (in press)

1992   Grammatical information in Hebrew teaching (in press)

1993   Metadiscourse and situational categorization of actions in text, "Scientific and technical information," series 2, N. 3

1994   Metalexis: An attempt at defining. The report presented to some conference.

1994   Isaac Newton and Jewish tradition (in press)

1994   *Smikhut* in Hebrew teaching (in press)

1994   The range of biblical metaphors in *smikhut.*

1994   The linguistic aspects of Jewish commentary tradition (in press)

Uncompleted works

Measure for Measure in Biblical Word Usage. The report on the Fifth Afro-Asian Congress in Moscow (1993)

The Style of the Hebrew Bible, 25 pp.

The Grammar of the Hebrew Bible, 20 pp.

Linguistic Commentary to *Genesis 1–4,* 20 pp.

Russian Word to Word Translation of *Genesis* (1, 1-14) with a Linguistic Commentary, 13 pp.

The Range of Biblical Metaphors in *Smikhut*

Lida Knorina

Abstract

The mechanism of metaphorical interpretation in *smikhut* (construct state) constructions is studied and compared with the "normal" (non-metaphorical) interpretation of the construction in Biblical Hebrew. We distinguish three models of metaphorical transfer that correspond to three basic types of standard *smikhut* patterns. It is shown that the metaphorical interpretation is limited by the possible identification of the construction members with the semantic types of constituents of the standard construction.

Introduction

The phenomenon of image making is known to occur in different syntactic surroundings; that is why metaphors are usually studied independently of their syntactic realizations.

Nevertheless the mechanism of metaphorical interpretation can't be satisfactorily understood without comparing it with "normal" (non-metaphorical) interpretations of the same constructions.[1]

In the interpretation of biblical metaphors in *smikhut* specific problems arise. Even nonmetaphorical (normal) interpretations of the construction

---

1. Context dependence and its connection to metaphor "predictability" are discussed in Sovran 1993.

This essay originally appeared in L. V. Knorina, *Grammatika, Semantika, Stilistika* [*Grammar, Semantics, Stylistics*] (Moscow: Institut russkogo iazyka, 1996) and in *Moskovskij Lingvisticheskij Jurnal* [*Moscow Journal of Linguistics*] 3 (1996): 80-94. It is published here with the kind permission of Vladimir Borschev.

are extraordinarily varied. As to certain relationships between the constituents of metaphorical combinations — and first of all the "equivalency" relationship (e.g. בגדי נקם — *clothes of revenge* — Isa. 59:17) — it appears that they differ substantially from the normal ones.

Our study is an attempt to find rules that govern the metaphorical interpretation of biblical *smikhut* constructions on the basis of the whole system of ordinary (normal) *smikhut* interpretation in Biblical Hebrew.[2]

We argue that the biblical metaphor models in *smikhut* are based on the standard semantic patterns of *smikhut* and are limited by the possible identifications of the construction constituents with the semantic types represented in normal *smikhut* constructions.

The metaphorical model includes image (vehicle) position, the type of corresponding metaphorizing predicate, and the way it is transferred to the object (tenor) of the metaphor.

The transition to metaphoric interpretation implies the identification of one of the constituents with the predicate[3] (or its indicator), which occupies the same position (HEAD or MODifier) in the standard pattern (almost any denotation of a thing may be identified with different predicates). The identified constituent is recognized as an image with the features of the corresponding predicate strengthened (the latter acting as a metaphorizing predicate).

Identification with a predicate appears evident if one of the constituents (or its synonym) is used in the normal *smikhut* construction, occupying the predicate position in it, but in many cases the "predicativity" of the constituent becomes evident only in its metaphorization.

Predicate features can be actualized in any constituent, and the conflict between possible indications to the metaphorizing predicate, as well as the possible conflict between standard interpretations and metaphorical ones, often makes the construction ambiguous, and sometimes this ambiguity can't be resolved even by widening the context. Nevertheless the identification of an image obeys certain rules which are discussed in the description of the metaphorical models.

2. For a similar description of metaphors in Russian genitive constructions, see Knorina 1990a.

3. It is assumed that the predicate not expressed explicitly is indicated by one of the constituents. The only exception is the non-specific relationship between possession and possessor established by default. A similar analysis based on the material of standard Russian word combinations is given in Knorina 1990b.

The image transfer (recognized in one of the constituents in some way) to the object of the metaphor implies that the other constituent is included in the domain on which the recognized predicate is defined (the metaphorization of the predicate is an extension of its domain).

It is shown that biblical *smikhut* metaphors follow three basic models corresponding to three basic types of standard *smikhut* patterns.

Semantic *smikhut* patterns are labelled according to the roles played by its constituents (HEAD and MOD) in the interpretation. Semantic features of words capable of playing a given role are discussed within the corresponding pattern description.

Metaphor Models

Model (1). The image in the MOD is transferred as a metaphorizing property to the HEAD, which is the object of the metaphor: לב האבן — *heart of stone* (Ez. 11:19)

The underlying standard pattern is thing — property: cf. לחת האבן *tablets of stone* (Ex. 24:12)

Model (2). The image in the HEAD is transferred through a metaphorizing predicate (usually an action or relationship not named explicitly that can be recognized in the HEAD) to the object of the metaphor outlined with the help of MOD or denoted by it: שערי הנהרות — *gates of rivers* (Nah. 2:7).

The underlying pattern is function — argument, usually implying a relationship (indicated by the role played in it by HEAD) between HEAD and MOD: cf. שערי החצר — *gates of the yard* (Ez 44:17 — in this example the relationship "part — whole" is implied).

Model (3). The image in the HEAD is transferred as a metaphorizing property to the MOD, which is the object of the metaphor: גבה רוח — *height* (haughtiness) *of spirit* (Pr. 16:18)

The underlying pattern is property — thing: cf. כגבה ארזים — *as height of cedars* (Am. 2:9)

All metaphors in the examples above are based on words (or their synonyms) recognized as predicates (or their indicators) in normal *smikhut* constructions. In order to perceive these words as images, the corresponding predicates must be extended. Their domains are extended under metaphorical transfer (so that the object of the metaphor could be included in the domain). Denotations of things indicating "hidden" predicates demand additional actualization of predicate features.

The additional recognition of predicate features may also produce images from denotations not indicating specific predicates in normal *smikhut* constructions: e.g., *clothes* — indicating the relationship of functional equivalence in the metaphor *clothes of revenge* — is not normally used in this way.

Additional predicate actualization and especially recognition of predicate features in denotations that do not indicate specific predicates in the normal constructions make metaphor perception more difficult. The identification of a metaphorizing predicate may be rather arbitrary: MOD-thing may be perceived as the embodiment of a property (1); HEAD-thing may be perceived as the indicator of a function (2) or as the embodiment of a property (3).

Denotations of things may combine connotations to different sorts of predicates. Metaphors based on denotations of things may consequently combine various predicate characteristics. Nevertheless no new special models of metaphor interpretation need to be added.

In model (1), the metaphorizing predicate is a property recognized in the MOD. A property recognized in the HEAD is perceived likewise in model (3). In model (2) the predicate is not usually denoted explicitly, but its features are recognized in the HEAD.

A more detailed description is given in the sections dealing with each model (after the corresponding pattern). Before each one of the metaphor models its normal (nonmetaphorical) prototype is described.[4]

Model (1): Thing — Property

Metaphor Possibilities

The pattern is quite widespread in ordinary *smikhut* constructions. The metaphorical effect may be achieved when the property (MOD) is combined with some "extraordinary" thing (HEAD), i.e., a thing which does not characterize this property (a thing beyond this property's domain).

---

4. We include constructions with compatible constituents among normal ones even if they, as a whole, are used as images (like רקב עצמות — *rotting of bones*, a stereotyped expression for the idea of degeneration, used as an image for jealousy in Pr. 14:30).

The effect is based on the transfer of the property to such a thing (the property extends its domain to include the given thing). The thing is in a way compared to (is perceived as being similar to) things that are usually characterized by the property.

Abstract Properties

Identification with a <u>property</u> seems natural for various MODs denoting abstract concepts: אמת — *truth,* רמיה — *deceit,* עני — *suffering,* קדש — *holiness* and the like.

For example, אנשי אמת — *men of truth* (truthful persons — Ex. 18:21).

Unusual bearers of properties denoted by abstract concepts appear rather often, but the corresponding combinations don't produce metaphorical effect.

The domains of such "properties" are usually not clearly limited; i.e., a denotation of abstract character as a rule is not strictly connected with a definite thing. Therefore it can be applied (as MOD) to a seemingly improbable HEAD without real change in the perception of the corresponding thing (the bearer of this property). Some rather extraordinary and very expressive combinations of this kind are thus not genuinely metaphorical: כקשת רמיה *as a bow of deceit,* i.e., a bow that fails to hit the target (Hos. 7:16); לחם עני *bread of suffering,* i.e., bread that recalls the time of suffering (Deut. 16:3).

Assignment denotations, usually names of actions, look like properties: שמן המשחה — *the oil of anointing* (Nu. 4:16). These denotations don't serve as images.

In combinations like *shield of your salvation* (מגן ישעך — Ps. 18:36) the evident image is in HEAD — but *shield* is used as a symbol of *salvation* not only in combination with this word as its MOD (cf. its use in Gen. 15:1: אנכי מגן לך — *I am the shield for you*). The combinations of such symbols with MODs don't evoke metaphorization but just fix the metaphorical identity of the symbols. So the ordinary relationship between a thing and its assignment is used for fixing <u>symbolic equivalence</u>.

On the other hand, many combinations of denotations of things adapted for special functions with abstract concepts in MOD (e.g., *cords of suffering* — Job 36:8) can be analysed otherwise (as considered below within model (2)).

Concrete Properties

Substance denotation in MOD is usually perceived as the <u>material</u> the given thing is made of, and is apparently considered as a kind of property of the thing: לחת האבן — *tablets of stone* (Ex. 24:12).

In combinations with improbable bearers, materials are easily perceived as images, and their connotations are actualized and transferred to unusual HEADS.

For example, in the metaphor *heart of stone* (לב האבן — Ez. 11:19) the property of being a stone is transferred to *heart,* which is compared with things occupying the same (HEAD) position in normal combinations with the name of this property (with things like tablets, i.e., made of stone).

Property Embodiments

Although for other relatively concrete denotations in MOD the role of the property in question is not natural, these denotations can still be perceived as *property embodiments.* The number of combinations with such "properties" is limited, and they are very expressive and apparently fixed, for example: עוֹף כנף — *bird of wing* (Gen. 1:21). Though no actual metaphorical transfer is achieved in them, these "properties" are not given to improbable property bearers.

Thus most denotations in MOD (excluding names of substances) are not likely to be perceived as properties.

In most combinations MOD plays a rather subordinate role determined by the predicate indicated in HEAD or recognized by default — see models (2) and (3).

Model (2): Function — Argument

Metaphor Possibilities

The pattern is widespread because of its variety. The function in HEAD may be indicated by different kinds of words. In normal *smikhut* the function can often be recognized only with the support of MOD, the argument fitting to the governing predicate (which is often not denoted explicitly).

Explicit predicate denotation is not characteristic for construct state metaphors. First of all it should be mentioned that the explicit nominal denotation of the action is not common in Biblical Hebrew.

The explicit denotation of action is also not very suitable for producing an image. The domains of many actions, as well as the domains of abstract properties (see the previous pattern), may not be precisely delimited, and these actions can be applied to seemingly improbable arguments without real extension.

The most fruitful source of metaphors following this pattern involves denotations of things that indicate implied relationships, often generated by the actions that these things connote (the connotation may be supported by word derivational structure).

Each relationship realized in metaphors is realized also in normal combinations, where this relationship is usually indicated in a more standard way and is supported by a MOD suitable for the implied relationship.

The specificity of the model is due to the way the image is transferred: MOD (argument) must naturally be compared with normal arguments of the given (or rather the implied!) predicate, but the real object of the metaphor is not necessarily denoted in MOD, or anywhere else, explicitly.

Actions

In normal *smikhut*, denotations of action in the HEAD combine with the MOD to indicate the most important argument for the given action (its subject or object): צעקת הרעים — *cry of the shepherds* (Jer. 25:36); חנכת המזבח — *dedication of the altar* (Nu. 7:10).

As mentioned above, explicit, nominal denotations of actions are not usually used as images.

Names of processes without real participants (like *burning*) may be replaced by the corresponding "natural powers" (like *fire*).

When the HEAD position is taken by the substitute of the process, the "doubling" of the process and of its argument becomes evident. The expressiveness of such combinations is based on repetition: אש להבה — *fire* (burning) *of the flame* (Hos. 7:6; Lam. 2:3).

Metaphoric interpretation is achieved when the MOD is taken from another semantic field: באש עברתי — *in the fire of my anger* (Ez. 22:31); זלעפות רעב — *storms of famine* (Lam. 5:10).

"Natural" denotations may also be perceived as <u>sources</u> or <u>results</u>

(originally, of natural processes) and indicate relationships generated by actions (considered below).

Participants of Actions

Performers of actions (in the HEAD) are combined with objects of the corresponding action rather often. Participants of actions may be denoted by participles (ישבי הארץ — *inhabitants of the land* — Gen. 36:20), and by nouns derived from action (e.g., the very common noun מלך — *king* can also be translated as *ruler* — derived from *rule;* its arguments are objects of this verb: מלך־מצרים — *king of Egypt*).

Participants of actions (as well as the actions themselves) are often combined with various arguments without real extensions (cf. ישבי חשך — *inhabitants of darkness* — Ps. 107:10).

The metaphorical effect is achieved when the denotation of a thing acts as a performer of a concrete action in combination with an abstract concept as its argument: נפת שוא — *sieve of falseness* (Isa. 30:28). The evident image is *sieve* (performer of separation). *Falseness* is compared with something undesirable that must be removed (as *chaff* is sifted from *wheat*). The context helps to perceive the incompatible combination as a metaphorical description of a device for the removal of falseness: *to sift the nations with the sieve of falseness.*

Relative Words

The most typical indication of a predicate is expressed by so-called <u>relative</u> <u>words</u> — special indicators of roles in implied binary relationships. The MOD naturally denotes the other member of the same relationship, i.e., the member playing the other role in the relationship: בני־נח — *sons of Noah* (Gen. 7:13).

Metaphorization of implied relationships indicated by the <u>relative</u> words gives well-known periphrasis like בני־עני — *sons of suffering*, i.e., sufferers, people in need.

Parts

HEADs denoting "<u>nonautonomous</u>" things tend to indicate the <u>part-</u><u>whole</u> relationship: שערי החצר — *gates of the yard* (Ez 44:17).

The same denotations become typical and easily perceived images in combination with the incompatible "whole." The function of the part is perceived in a more generalized way, and the new whole may be regarded as an argument of the relationship. The argument is compared to the normal "whole." The object of the metaphor is a certain "detail" not denoted explicitly and distinguished in the improbable whole as its part: שערי הנהרות — *gates of rivers* (Nah 2:7).

The metaphor is often strengthened when the action denoted beyond the construction supports a specific image: *gates of rivers opened*. . . .

Typical connotations of HEADS denoting such things as <u>parts</u> of the <u>body</u> to pieces of landscape are not likely to produce creative metaphors. Such usage — conventional or lexicalized — may reflect a mythical vision of the world (see Barr 1967). In any case, such combinations are characteristic of lofty style: ראשי ההרים — *the heads of the mountains* (Ez. 6:13).

Sources and Results

Some denotations (especially action derivatives) may be perceived as sources or results of certain actions and indicate the implied relationships generated by these actions (relationships with the action's <u>product</u> or <u>producer</u>).

Typical indications of this kind are denotations of natural objects (like *source, lightning, fruit*) representing perceived objects as <u>sources</u> or results of the corresponding natural actions or processes (like *flowing, shining, growing*).

The recognition of the implied relationship is supported in normal *smikhut* by a MOD denotation suitable for this relationship. מקור דמיה — *source* (root קוה — *flow*) *of her blood* (Lev. 20:18); פרי־עץ — *fruit* (or *product*, פרה — *produce*) *of the tree* (Gen. 1:29);

In the metaphor the same HEAD denotations (and denotations similar to them) indicate the same functions perceived in a more abstract way and combine with the arguments not relating to the original actions. Many natural denotations of this sort are well-known lexicalized metaphors almost entirely unrelated to their original meanings. Judging by the context, emphasizing their concrete meanings, they are used in the Bible at least as revived (if not living) images: מים עמקים דברי פי־איש נחל נבע מקור חכמה — *deep waters — words of a man's mouth, flowing stream — source of wisdom* (Pr. 18:4); ויאכלו מפרי דרכם — *and they will eat from the fruit of their way* (Pr. 1:31).

In denotations of roads, their function of leading to a certain destination is actualized, and the argument of the implied relationship is therefore the name of the destination: דרך עץ החיים — *path* (i.e., leading to, דרך — *walk*) *of the tree of life* (Gen. 3:24).

In these metaphors, the abstract concept in the MOD is perceived as the destination: בארח צדקה אהלך — *along the road of justice I walk* (Pr. 8:20).

Some denotations are used as indicators of sources only metaphorically — cf. *sun* in וזרחה לכם יראי שמי שמש צדקה — *and shines to you, fearing My Name, the sun of justice* (Mal. 3:20). Since the sun may be perceived not only as a source of light, but also as pouring light itself, the roles of the MOD and HEAD may appear identical; a sort of equivalence is established between them.

Results that outline the limits for the object of the action (quantifiers) are presented separately.

Quantifiers

Actions connected with storage generate specific relationships. Results (or locations) of storing, i.e., <u>collections</u> or <u>containers</u> (they are often not distinguished from each other) actually determine limits for objects of storing, i.e., for <u>contents</u> of these containers. The contents are perceived in "limits" outlined in the HEAD; thus the HEAD is a kind of quantifier.

Names of collections and containers in normal *smikhut* constructions indicate the described relationship only with the MOD's support, when the MOD denotes "elements" (of the collection) or matter (collected or placed in a container) that suit the given quantifier: כעדר העזם — *like a flock of goats;* אצרות השמן — *the storages of* (or *stores of) oil* (1 Chr. 27:28); צרור הכסף — *package of* (i.e. containing) *silver* (or *money* — Pr. 7:20).

Denotations of collections with their "elements" (e.g., עדת בני ישראל — *the community of the sons of Israel* — Lev. 16:5; עדת ישראל — *the community of Israel* — Ex. 12:3) are relatively few. They are quite expressive when "elements" are represented by evaluative denotations, the status of common elements being transferred to them: עדת מרעים — *community of evildoers* (Ps. 22:17).

Collections related to water in combination with MODs not connected with water transfer to these MODs the idea of large amounts: e.g., *rain of voluntary gifts* — גשם נדבות (Ps. 68:10).

Containers are broadly used in metaphor: בצרור החיים — *in the package of life* (1 S. 25:29); כוס חמתו — *the cup of his anger* (Isa. 51:17).

Things of fixed size (including containers) may indicate abstract <u>units</u> of quantified matter: כף קמח — *a hand* (handful) *of flour* (1 K. 17:12). The corresponding meaning is apparently lexicalized, but it is metaphorical in origin (see Sovran 1993). In the combination of units with abstract concepts, the latter are perceived as measurable entities: כף נחת — *a hand of quietness* (Eccl. 4:6).

Quantifiers may also be used to emphasize shape, but visual images are very rare: *canals (riverbeds) of bronze* — אפיקי נחשה (Job 40:18 — a description of the bones of a hippopotamus) *canals of shields* — אפיקי מגנים (Job 41:7, i.e., a row of shields in the description of the scales of a hippopotamus).

Adaptations

Combinations of denotations of things with different abstract concepts including sensations may imply a relationship between an adaptation (indicating a specific function) and a *functioner,* i.e., a concrete object fulfilling the function outlined in the HEAD.

In normal *smikhut* this relationship is indicated only by action derivatives, usually by <u>cover</u> denotations. Their functioners are specific objects fulfilling the function of covering. This relationship in normal *smikhut* is recognized with the MOD's support (MOD denotes something "transformable" into a cover): בסתר ההר — *in the shelter of the mountain* (1 S. 25:20).

Here in a perfectly compatible combination the <u>functional equivalence</u> of constituents is established. More than that: HEAD is in a way perceived as a formation constituted by the functioner.

In the metaphor, covers perceived as symbolic formations adapted for covering combine with abstract concepts which consequently are compared with common covering functioners: מחסה כזב — *refuge of the lie,* i.e., the lie serving as a refuge (Isa. 28:17); מעטה תהלה — *cover of praise* (Isa. 61:3).

MOD, perceived as a functioner, is the object of the metaphor endowed with the function indicated in the HEAD. Compared with its common functioners, it is at the same time compared with the HEAD itself (as if formed by its possible functioner). Here functional equivalence is strengthened in the metaphor by equivalence of form.

Metaphoric functional equivalence and equivalence of form are established only in the juxtaposition of denotations.

In this regard the equivalence differs from "independent" symbolic equivalence (between a thing and its assignment in the framework model of (1)), which is not established by word combinations but only fixed in them. Still there are cases when the difference between these two types of equivalences (between a thing and its MOD) is not so clear.

The furnace, a traditional image for exile (Egypt), is the embodiment of *affliction.* The combination כור עני *(furnace of affliction)* may be perceived as a fixation of traditional identity. Its context in Isa. 48:10 emphasizes in *furnace* the function of purification: *I have purified you not as silver, I have tested you in the furnace of affliction.* In this context *affliction* is viewed as a means of purification.

Most adaptations combine with their functioners only in metaphors.

Action derivatives denoting means of binding (and at the same time formations for binding) and "means of stumbling" combine with abstract concepts, transferring functions of bonds or obstacles to these concepts (as if formed by them). במסרת הברית — *in the bonds of the covenant* (Ez. 20:37); מכשול עונם — *obstacle of* (derived from *stumble*) *their sin* (Ez. 7:19).

Grounds for establishing relationships (and equivalence) with incompatible MODs (as functioners) is usually supported by the context: ילכדון בחבלי־עני — *captured by the cords of suffering* (Job 36:8).

Names of <u>garments</u> — representatives of covers (having close contact with the body) — aside from their evident literal function are often recognized as a symbolic means of expressing sensations. Some special garments (like *sack*) are actually used on special occasions (like *mourning*) or/ and in special social and emotional states.

Garments are actively used as images in similes; cf. עטה אור כשלמה — *covered with light as with a dress* (Ps. 104:2).

In the HEAD position, names of garments combine with the names of emotions, establishing equivalence between constituents. The context may support both their literal function and metaphorization.

For example, the combination בגדי נקם — *clothes of vengeance* — is surrounded in Isa. 59:17 by a context in which many explicit denotations related to clothes appear; several names of garments in the same verse are used as images in similes: *He dressed justice as a breastplate and a helmet of*

salvation on His head, and dressed (i.e., *put on*) *clothes of vengeance as a gar-
ment and covered* [*this*] *with anger as with a robe*.

Tablet is used as an image of adaptation for the fixation of God's will:
. . . *is engraved on the tablet of their heart* (Jer. 17:1), *write them on the tablet
of your heart* (Pr. 3:3; 7:3). In this combination (לוּחַ לֵב — *tablet of heart*)
the word *heart* fulfils the function of tablets, is used like tablets — for writing on it, for the fixation of the will of God.

Names of <u>weapons</u> transfer to the general function of protection or ag-
gression: שֵׁבֶט עֶבְרָתוֹ — *stick of his anger* (Pr. 22:8); שֵׁבֶט מוּסָר — *stick of pun-
ishment* (Pr. 22:15).

The context may indicate more specific functions. For example, the
combination חִצֵּי הָרָעָב — *arrows of famine* (Ez. 5:16) — is used in a context actualizing *arrow* as a missile: *I let loose against you my deadly arrows
of famine.*

<u>Food</u> <u>products</u> (traditionally connected with benevolence) indicate the
function of feeding (supported by context): לֶחֶם דִּמְעָה — *bread of tears* (*you
have fed them with the bread of tears and given them tears to drink* (Ps. 80:6)).

Non-specific Relationships

In default of specific predicate indication, thing denotations (HEADs) are
often perceived as <u>possession</u> (or accessory), implying a non-specific relationship with their <u>possessor</u> (or location). In normal *smikhut*, a MOD denoting a person or location fits in this relationship: בִּגְדֵי עֵשָׂו — *Esau's
clothes* (Gen. 27:15). This relationship is evidently implied also in the case
when HEAD (including predicate derivatives) may indicate a more specific relationship, but MOD (denoting person or location) doesn't fit into
it: אוֹצְרוֹת בֵּית הַמֶּלֶךְ — *stores of the house of the king* (1 K. 14:26).

In combination with an incompatible location, HEAD is perceived as
an image. Sometimes a concrete object — a standard accessory of the
MOD not mentioned explicitly — is used as the object of metaphor. E.g.,
vessels in the combination נִבְלֵי שָׁמַיִם (*vessels [leather receptacles] of the sky* —
Job 37:38) is a visual image for clouds (object with vessel functions situated in the sky).

Since the denotation of a thing in HEAD is usually perceived as an adaptation, the abstract concept accompanying it may be understood both
as the object of the metaphor (fulfilling the function indicated in HEAD)
and as a possessor (the object of the metaphor then has no explicit deno-

tation but is only metaphorically described by the construction as a whole).

E.g., in the combination בחבלי השוא (*cords of vanity* — Isa. 5:18) *vanity* may be understood as something fastening like a cord. But the context supports the interpretation in which *vanity* replaces the word *cart,* the *cord's* standard possessor (or location): *drawing sin along with the cords of vanity* and, *as with ropes of cart,* support a transgression.

Model (3): Property — Thing

Metaphor Possibilities

Within this pattern we consider combinations with HEAD denoting not only evident properties but also states modified by their subject (which must consequently be regarded as the bearer of a property).

This pattern emphasizes the separation of property from its bearer. Usually such separation is characteristic of high, poetical style independently from the metaphorical effect, i.e., even nonmetaphorical realizations of the pattern are marked with expressiveness; cf. שמחת לבו — *joy of his heart* (Song 3:11), כצנת שלג — *as coolness of snow* (Pr. 25:13)

An action designated outside of the construction and formally directed to the separated property (as to its actant) is in fact related to the property bearer: cf. ואכרת קומת ארזיו — *and I cut the height of his cedars,* i.e., high cedars (Isa. 37:24).

The pattern is used relatively seldom (as mentioned above, its realization must yield an expressive effect), and its metaphorical use (i.e., the metaphorical transfer of explicit properties) is not typical either.

In combinations with incompatible property bearers (MODs), a few property denotations occur. It should be mentioned that in fact these denotations are not used with more "natural" bearers. For example, מתק *(sweetness)* is used in construct state twice in the Hebrew Biblical text and both times in relation to "exotic" bearers: ומתק שפתים — *sweetness of lips* (i.e., of words — Pr. 16:21) and ומתק רעהו — *sweetness of his friend* (Pr. 27:9).

In such cases we may suspect the lexicalization of the changed meaning of the property. Lexicalization implies the inclusion of new bearers into the domain on which the property is defined. Consequently, combinations with seemingly improbable bearers result in no actual metaphorical transfer but support the already changed (metaphorically at least from the point of view of its origin) meaning of the property. The other possibility is the complete indifference of the property to its possible bearers, i.e., the meaning of the property from the very beginning is very broad, not implying limitations on the domain where it is defined.

Doubtless cases of metaphorical transfer of this type occur very seldom. Even the use of one and the same property denotation in relation both to its real bearers and to improbable ones (as גבה — *height* combined with *cedars* in Am. 2:9 and with *spirit*, i.e., haughtiness — in Pr. 16:18) may result from lexicalized changes in meaning or from indifference of the property (perceived in the most generalized way) to its bearers. Combinations with the word ערווה *(nakedness)* can be interpreted in a similar way, cf. ערוות הארץ — *bareness of the land* (Gen. 42:9); ערוות אביו — *nakedness of his father* (Gen. 9:22)

Implicit Properties ("Things" Indicating Properties)

Names of substances may rarely be interpreted as property substitutes. Such an interpretation is possible, for example, in the combination of *liquid honey* (נפת) with *nectar* (צופים) as MOD, i.e., honey emphasizes sweetness of nectar: *sweeter than honey and liquid honey of nectar* (Ps. 19:11, about the Lord's laws).

Another possible property substitution is perceived in designations of *death* (and its substitutes, including *holes* and *traps*, which are associated with death in other contexts); these designations combine only with concepts from its own sphere: *grave of nothingness* — שחת בלי (Isa. 38:17); *grave of their net* — שחת רשתם (Ps. 35:7).

Concluding Remarks

The most productive metaphorical model is model (2), which is based on the pattern allowing different relationships between the constituents of the construction.

The most typical images are thing denotations located in HEAD. The most typical ground for comparison with the object is function actualized in perception of a thing used as an image.

Some of the images (called "adaptations" here, such as garments, food products) transfer their function directly to the MOD (as to the object of the metaphor) and establish functional equivalence with the concept denoted in it.

Most of these images are used as images also in other syntactic constructions.

REFERENCES

Barr J. The semantics of biblical language. Oxford, 1967.

Knorina L. V. Semantic anomaly and metaphor in the genitive construction — in "Logical Analysis of Language: Contradictions and Anomalies in Discourse." Moscow, 1990a (in Russian).

Knorina L. V. Types of "things" and their perception in language (in coauthorship with V. B. Borshchev) — in "Language of Logic and Logic of Language." Moscow, 1990b (in Russian).

Sovran T. Metaphor as reconciliation: the logical-semantic basis of metaphorical juxtaposition. — in "Poetics Today." Durham, 1993.

*   *   *

The author died before finishing her work on this text that she wrote directly in English. The editor is grateful to Alexandra Aihenwald, Raisa Rosina and Alexei Sossinski (especially to the latter) for help in English style editing.

[The editor mentioned in the last sentence of the manuscript is Vladimir Borshchev. Adele Berlin corrected several typographical errors in the manuscript.]

INDEX OF BIBLICAL PASSAGES

GENERAL INDEX

aabb patterning, 83–84, 86, 87, 113–114, 132

abab patterning, 84–85, 86, 87, 114–117, 126, 132

abba patterning, 85, 86, 87, 118–121, 126, 146

Accusative case, 51

Active-passive sequence, 36

Adjacent lines, 3

Adjectives
  in different genders, 42–43
  in different numbers, 48

Ambiguity, 96–99

Ambiguous signs, 16

Aspects of linguistics, 27–28

Associated words, reciprocity of, 71–72

Associative processes, 89

Assonance, 103

Avishur, Y., 71

Balanced parallelism in Biblical poetry, 6–7

Basic Sentences, 19

Biblical paronomasia, 153

Biblical poetry
  balanced parallelism in, 6–7
  paratactic style of, 6

Binomial, 149

Binomination, 76–77, 148, 149

Breakup of stereotype phrases, 76

Broken constructs, 149

Browning, Robert, 155

Casanowicz, I. M., 111, 153

Case, contrast in, 51–52

Cassuto, U., 36, 41

Category preservation rule, 74

Ceresko, A., 119

Chiasmus, semantic-sonant, 106

Chiastic order, 116

Chiastic patterning, 41, 85

Clark, H. H., 72, 73, 75

Closure, 87

Collins, Terence, 19–21, 145

Collocation, 29, 30, 145

Combination, 7–8

"Compactness" of poetry, 6

Conative function of language, 9

Conformation of sentences, 1

Conjugation, contrast in, 36–40, 58

Connectedness of poetry, 6, 92

Connectives, 92

Consonance, 103–104

Consonant words, 126

Consonants in sound pairs, 103–105

Constituents of a sentence, 19

Constitutive device, 11
  of sequence, 7

Constructive device, 11

Contextual appropriateness, 96

Contiguity, 7–8, 138, 139
  of elements, 13
  of lines, 6

Continuous sequence of action, 14

Continuum of elevated style, 5

Contrast, 2, 11–13, 27, 140–141
  as important element in poetic structure, 11
  grammatical, 28
  in case, 51–52
  in conjugation, 36–40, 58
  in definiteness, 50–51
  in gender, 41–44
  in grammatical mood, 59–63
  in number, 44–50
  in person, 40–41
  in poetry, 156
  in tense, 35–36
  semantic, 12–13

Conventionalized coordinates, 76, 149, 150

Coordinate relationship, 81

Correspondence, 2, 3; phonologic, 153

Craigie, P. C., 67

Couplet
  as basic poetic entity, 25
  in biblical poetry, 6–7

Culler, J., 135

Dahood, M., 29, 30, 145, 147, 154

Deep structure, 53, 93, 133–134
  level of, 23–24

Deese, J. E., 88–89

Definite nouns, contrast in, 50–51

Definiteness, contrast in, 50–51

Deictic words, 73

Demonstrative pronouns, pairing of, 46

Different word classes, morphologic pairs in, 33–35

Disambiguation, 96–99

Dominance
  of parallelism, 5–6
  of poetic function, 9
  of poetic function in poetry, 9

Dual // plural pairing, 49